Sustainable Finance

Sustainable Finance is a concise and authoritative reference series linking research and practice. It provides reliable concepts and research findings in the ever growing field of sustainable investing and finance, SDG economics and Leadership with the declared commitment to present the theories, methods, tools and investment approaches that can fulfil the United Nations Sustainable Development Goals and the Paris Agreement COP 21/22 alongside with de-risking assets and creating triple purpose solutions that ensure the parity of profit, people and planet through choice architecture passion and performance. The series addresses market failure, systemic risk and reinvents portfolio theory, portfolio engineering as well as behavioural finance, financial mediation, product innovation, shared values, community building, business strategy and innovation, exponential tech and creation of social capital. Sustainable Finance and SDG Economics series helps to understand keynotes on international guidelines, guiding accounting and accountability principles, prototyping new developments in triple bottom line investing, cost benefit analysis, integrated financial first plus impact first concepts and impact measurement. Going beyond adjacent fields (like accounting, marketing, strategy, risk management) it integrates the concept of psychology, innovation, exponential tech, choice architecture, alternative economics, blue economy shared values, professions of the future, leadership, human and community development, team culture, impact, quantitative and qualitative measurement, Harvard Negotiation, mediation and complementary currency design using exponential tech and ledger technology. Books in the series contain latest findings from research, concepts for implementation, as well as best practices and case studies for the finance industry.

Mauro Aliano • Greta Cestari •
Salvatore Madonna

Sustainable Finance for SMEs

The Role of Capital for Sustainable and Inclusive Growth

Springer

Mauro Aliano
Department of Economics and Management
University of Ferrara
Ferrara, Italy

Greta Cestari
Department of Economics and Management
University of Ferrara
Ferrara, Italy

Salvatore Madonna
Department of Economics and Management
University of Ferrara
Ferrara, Italy

ISSN 2522-8285 ISSN 2522-8293 (electronic)
Sustainable Finance
ISBN 978-3-031-74192-0 ISBN 978-3-031-74193-7 (eBook)
https://doi.org/10.1007/978-3-031-74193-7

This Springer imprint is published by the registered company Springer Nature Switzerland AG
The registered company address is: Gewerbestrasse 11, 6330 Cham, Switzerland

To my mentor, Martino, but also: "smoker
and a healthy carrier of temperature".

Foreword

The path towards the array of multiple sustainable transitions—environmental, social, technological, fiscal, financial, demographic—is driven by a complex co-evolution of different transitions occurring at different geographical and impact dimensions. States and the macro regions, socio-economic and innovation systems, industrial districts are the socio-economic and technological frameworks where new business models and social innovations emerge and develop. Through the development of interconnected systems of innovations, through spillovers, trade, and well-designed mix of regulations over innovation, industrial, environmental dimensions, a sound sustainable convergence can be achieved. It is relevant to connect the transition of 'old sectors' and that of new emerging firms, districts, and techno-organisational systems. The overall employment and human capital impact is a composite effect, based on sector integration and convergent innovations, taking into account the diversity of techno-economic specialisations.

Innovation adoption and diffusion by firms are key pillars for the EU strategy on resource efficiency, circular economy, and decarbonisation. The emerging innovative framework is hugely characterised by the emergence of small-scale products and processes (technological, organisational, marketing social innovations), largely developed by SMEs and networks of firms which find new way of cooperation. Environmental policy and demand-side factors are both significant in driving the adoption of innovations that reduce waste and the use of materials.

On the side of policies, SMEs need to incorporate forward looking management of regulations and policies, understanding and anticipating future scenarios (e.g. the evolution of carbon pricing). This is crucial to enhance competitiveness following the seminal works by Michael Porter in the early mid-90s on competitive advantages and environmental policy.

Given that empirical evidence shows that the effectiveness of environmental policies (e.g. carbon pricing, technological standards) is enhanced by the presence of a significant stock of R&D and Human capital, the financial system—banking and non-banking pillars—is necessary to support SMEs in the investment process, which is significant especially in Italy, which witnesses a major gap as far as knowledge-based investments are concerned. Among potential sources of funding for SMEs, crowdfunding schemes may play a role as well.

Against this background, the theoretical and empirical analysis of sustainable finance to accelerate SMEs innovations, enhancing their cooperation and mitigating barriers is crucial. SMEs are a pillar of the Italian and European economy. The complementarity between internal sources and external diversified sources is particularly relevant to increase their role to achieve a just sustainable transition. SMEs are a driver of a just transition for all territories, especially the peripheral ones, as those firms contain and develop a large part of the skills and competences at a very local level. Economic development and convergence highly depends on how the network of SMEs develops through territories and socio-economic systems.

Department of Economics & Management
University of Ferrara
Ferrara, Italy

Massimiliano Mazzanti

Preface

During the writing of this book, we faced two main challenges in discussing topics and issues. The first challenge is related to the concept of sustainability for SMEs, which has evolved over the years. This evolution encompasses changes in laws and regulations worldwide, as well as shifts in practices and case studies. The dynamic nature of sustainability necessitates a continuous update of knowledge and an understanding of how these changes impact SMEs differently across various regions and industries. As sustainability regulations become more stringent and complex, SMEs must adapt their strategies and operations, which can be both an opportunity and a burden, depending on their resources and capabilities.

The second challenge involves the inherent heterogeneity and distinctive features of SMEs. Small and medium-sized enterprises vary widely in terms of size, sector, resources, and market focus. This diversity makes it difficult to apply a one-size-fits-all approach when discussing their challenges and strategies. Each SME has unique characteristics and operates under different conditions, which requires a nuanced understanding and tailored solutions.

These two constraints have influenced the structure and content of our book. On the one hand, they have driven us toward more abstraction and generalization to ensure that the discussions and insights are broadly applicable. Generalization allows us to identify common themes and patterns that can provide valuable guidance to a wide range of SMEs. However, this approach risks oversimplifying the complex realities that individual SMEs face.

On the other hand, we have counterbalanced this abstraction with the inclusion of case studies, examples, and applications. These practical elements are designed to ground our theoretical discussions in real-world contexts, making the book more relevant and useful for practitioners. By showcasing specific examples of how different SMEs have navigated sustainability challenges and leveraged their unique features, we aim to provide actionable insights and inspire readers to apply similar strategies in their own businesses.

Overall, the dual approach of combining general principles with specific case studies aims to strike a balance between theory and practice, ensuring that the book is both informative and applicable. This method acknowledges the complexity of sustainability and the diversity of SMEs while also providing concrete guidance to help practitioners implement effective and sustainable business practices.

The Structure of the Book

The book is structured into three compelling sections, each addressing crucial aspects of sustainability's impact on SMEs. In the first section, "Mechanisms and Institutions," which spans chaps. 1 through 4, we explore how financial and economic theories intersect with sustainability, focusing on short-term activities, innovations, banking practices, and market dynamics. The second section, "Instruments and Methods," covering chaps. 5–8, delves into the tools and techniques used to evaluate sustainability, offering a comprehensive look at the methodologies driving assessment. Finally, the third section, "Companies Crisis," in chaps. 9 and 10, examines how sustainability influences corporate crises, insolvency, and the predictability of bankruptcy. Each part builds upon the previous to provide a thorough understanding of sustainability's multifaceted impact on small and medium-sized enterprises.

Part I—Mechanisms and Institutions

In our book, we begin with an analysis of sustainable finance in the short run, particularly focusing on SMEs within a supply chain context. Chapter 1 evaluates the role of sustainability and the transformative potential of technology in reshaping how companies operate, emphasizing the interconnected nature of businesses rather than viewing them in isolation. In the short run, the adoption of sustainable practices can lead to cost savings, improved risk management, and enhanced reputation. For instance, a small manufacturing company that invests in energy-efficient machinery may see a reduction in operating costs and a smaller carbon footprint, thereby attracting customers who prioritize environmental responsibility. Technological advancements play a crucial role in facilitating these sustainable practices. Digital tools and platforms can streamline supply chain management, making it easier for SMEs to track and reduce their environmental impact. For example, blockchain technology can enhance transparency and traceability in supply chains, ensuring that all parties adhere to sustainable practices. This not only builds trust among stakeholders but also helps companies identify areas for improvement in their sustainability efforts.

Anecdotal evidence further illustrates the practical benefits of these theoretical approaches. Consider a family-owned bakery that sources its ingredients from local, organic farms. By using a blockchain-based supply chain management system, the bakery can verify the sustainability claims of its suppliers, ensuring that their products meet certain environmental standards. This practice not only supports local farmers but also appeals to a growing base of eco-conscious consumers, thereby boosting the bakery's market position. In another example, a textile SME might implement an Internet of Things (IoT) system to monitor and optimize energy usage in its factories. The real-time data collected through IoT devices can help the company identify inefficiencies and make informed decisions to reduce energy consumption. This not only cuts costs but also aligns the company with sustainability goals, such as reducing greenhouse gas emissions.

Combining these theoretical and practical perspectives underscores the importance of sustainability in shaping modern business practices. As companies increasingly recognize the interconnected nature of their operations, the adoption of sustainable finance practices becomes essential for long-term success. This chapter aims to provide a comprehensive understanding of how SMEs can leverage technology to integrate sustainability into their financial strategies, highlighting the significant impact such integration can have on their overall performance.

By examining real-world examples and theoretical frameworks, we illustrate how sustainable finance is not merely a trend but a fundamental shift in how businesses operate. This shift is driven by both the pressing need to address environmental challenges and the opportunity to create value through sustainable practices. In doing so, we offer a nuanced view of sustainability, demonstrating its critical role in shaping the future of SMEs within the broader context of supply chains.

The second chapter then examines, via an analysis of their financial structures and the significance of both internal and external funding, how businesses may financially support their shift toward sustainability. External funds originate from outside sources such as bonds, bank loans, and alternative lending platforms, while internal funds are often defined as equity and self-financing resources. In order to advance green finance and sustainability activities, a company's capital structure—the combination of these funds—must be considered.

The theorem by Modigliani and Miller (1958) proposed that initiatives, not capital structure, define a company's worth. In actuality, though, businesses have difficulties when they lack sufficient loan and equity funding to facilitate green changes. The chapter looks at the difficult decisions that must be made when determining a company's financial structure, including the different kinds of debt and equity, and stresses the significance of taking sustainability factors into account when making financial allocations.

Banks are essential to the financing of sustainable transitions; they help startups with new green technology and assist big fossil fuel companies as they shift to green investments. While multinational firms may be able to obtain loans for carbon offset or renewable energy projects, startups that are having trouble accessing traditional financial markets sometimes turn to venture capital (VC) and business angels (BA) for funding. This emphasizes how crucial it is to have financial inclusion so that businesses of all sizes may obtain financing.

The effect of asymmetric information on funding decisions is covered in this chapter. According to the Modigliani–Miller theorem, financing choices have no impact on a company's value in ideal markets. However, there are flaws in real-world markets, such as asymmetric knowledge, which causes managers to know more about projects than external stakeholders and drives up the cost of external financing. Although they may still require outside funding for significant initiatives, businesses frequently use internal finance to reduce these expenses. Finance is another area where the "hidden action problem" manifests itself, since managers may embark on risky initiatives without fully informing external stakeholders. When compared to internal resources, the cost of external funding is higher due to this unpredictability. Strong governance practices and transparency are necessary to reduce these risks. Including sustainability in business conduct increases the effect of both revealed and hidden activities. In order to fit with sustainability goals, business practices must prioritize openness and accountability. Success should be determined not just by money gain but also by ethical behavior, social responsibility, and environmental care.

The trade-off theory, which weighs the advantages and disadvantages of debt, and the pecking order theory, which gives internal finance precedence over outside funding, are two more capital structure theories that are covered in this chapter. Debt issuance has the potential to mitigate adverse selection issues by communicating business quality to the market, according to signaling models. Empirical research demonstrates how preferences for capital structures vary depending on the situation and how crucial regulatory frameworks are. The chapter concludes by examining banks' sustainability responsibilities and how they balance supporting green ideas even from historically high-emission industries like fossil fuels while also avoiding reputational threats. Selective divestment methods and effective involvement are required to prevent greenwashing initiatives and promote real progress in green innovation and emission reductions.

The third chapter integrating ESG risk into the banking prudential framework in the EU is a crucial topic, particularly regarding its impact on SMEs. Banks play an essential role in financing SMEs, profoundly influencing their growth and sustainability. This complex relationship is shaped by various factors including market power, firm characteristics, and institutional frameworks. Bank market power and firm characteristics can either alleviate or exacerbate credit constraints for SMEs, depending on strategic objectives and regulatory environments. Further research emphasizes the role of banks in enhancing SME sustainability through financial services, technology, and business solutions. Private banks, with their flexible and customized financial solutions, are particularly effective in meeting the unique needs of SMEs. The importance of a strong, trust-based relationship between banks and SMEs in improving financing efficiency and credit terms is also highlighted. The innovative financial solutions provided by Islamic banks and fintech in supporting SMEs, particularly in Indonesia, show the evolving landscape of SME financing.

The chapter explores the limitations banks face due to extensive regulations and oversight designed to ensure financial system stability and fair lending practices. These regulations impact the ability of banks to lend to SMEs, requiring them to maintain specific capital reserves and comply with strict credit underwriting guidelines. Additionally, compliance with anti-money laundering (AML) and counter-terrorism financing (CTF) legislation adds to the complexity, increasing operating expenses and loan processing times.

The lending activities of banks are further influenced by macroeconomic conditions and market demand changes, requiring a balance between preserving financial stability and assisting SMEs. The chapter concludes by addressing potential solutions to improve SME access to funding, enhance credit risk assessment, and streamline compliance procedures. By understanding the intricate relationship between banks and SMEs, policymakers can create a conducive environment for SME growth, contributing to overall economic stability and development.

Part II—Instruments and Methods

Chapter 4 of this book delves into the multifaceted world of financial markets and their profound impact on companies, including SMEs, particularly when they consider going public. For these enterprises, an Initial Public Offering (IPO) can provide significant capital, liquidity, and strategic advantages. It enables the use of shares for mergers and acquisitions and offers flexible employee compensation. However, going public also presents challenges such as loss of control, high compliance costs, and increased scrutiny from investors. Effective signaling through a robust earnings history and strong ESG performance can attract investors and mitigate underpricing, making the IPO process smoother and more beneficial. The chapter begins by examining the critical role of financial markets in enabling companies to gather the resources needed to address sustainability issues and undertake strategic activities. Accessing public capital allows companies to fund projects that enhance their ESG performance, thereby attracting investors focused on sustainable and responsible investments. This integration of sustainability initiatives not only improves a company's market appeal but also secures the necessary funds to drive long-term growth and sustainability efforts. Market efficiency is highlighted as a cornerstone for SMEs, influencing their ability to navigate the competitive business landscape. Unlike larger corporations, SMEs face unique challenges due to constrained resources and distinct decision-making frameworks. These factors shape their strategic marketing initiatives and their ability to leverage available information. Despite these obstacles, SMEs are vital in driving competition and economic progress by influencing market behaviors and regulatory frameworks. Technological advancements are pivotal in boosting SME efficiency, enabling cost reductions and expanding market reach. Effective marketing strategies and digital tools are essential for enhancing competitiveness and operational effectiveness.

The chapter further explores the concept of market efficiency and its relevance to SMEs. It provides a modern perspective on how SMEs can leverage informational, allocative, and operational efficiency to enhance their sustainable practices and overall performance. Additionally, the discussion on financial bubbles examines how these phenomena can hinder SMEs from pursuing public offerings, outlining the mechanics of bubble formation and their impact on financial stability. An empirical analysis of Italian companies, mostly medium-sized enterprises, evaluates whether they are over- or undervalued in the Italian financial market. This section provides detailed insights into the valuation landscape, identifying potential opportunities and threats for these companies within the financial market. Through a combination of theoretical analysis, empirical evidence, and practical case studies, this chapter equips readers with a comprehensive understanding of the intricate interplay between market dynamics and SME performance, fostering a strategic approach to navigating financial markets.

In the face of an urgent need to transition to a sustainable economy, SMEs—which form the backbone of many global economies—find themselves at a crossroads. While SMEs are crucial players in economic development, they are often burdened by the financial challenges of adopting green practices. Chapter 5 addresses these challenges by examining a range of innovative financial instruments designed to support SMEs in their sustainability journey.

SMEs, which account for a significant portion of global greenhouse gas emissions, frequently cite financial constraints as a major barrier to implementing climate-friendly practices. Despite their pivotal role in the economy, many SMEs struggle to secure the necessary funding due to inadequate credit histories and insufficient collateral, which are critical factors for traditional lenders. This situation is exacerbated by the general perception of SMEs as high-risk borrowers, given their smaller scale, limited resources, and higher failure rates compared to larger corporations. The chapter begins by identifying the primary barriers to sustainable finance for SMEs. It explores how traditional financial institutions' stringent requirements—such as substantial collateral and robust credit histories—pose significant hurdles. Many SMEs also face challenges navigating complex loan applications and financial documentation requirements, which can be overwhelming given their limited administrative resources. Additionally, there is often a disconnect between SMEs and financial institutions, with the former being unaware of available funding options and the latter lacking a deep understanding of SMEs' unique needs. The chapter is structured to provide a comprehensive view of the landscape. It starts with an exploration of the main obstacles to sustainable finance, followed by an analysis of public interventions aimed at alleviating these issues. The discussion then shifts to the structure and features of potential sustainable finance operations. Subsequent sections highlight gaps in current sustainability approaches and detail financial instruments and techniques used to bridge these gaps. The chapter concludes with a review of global best practices in sustainable finance, offering insights into successful strategies that can guide SMEs toward a greener future.

In the rapidly evolving world of finance, Chap. 6 offers a deep dive into a transformative development that has reshaped how companies and SMEs approach capital-raising: initial coin offerings (ICOs). This chapter delves into the role of ICOs in financing companies and SME, particularly those focused on addressing sustainability challenges. ICOs, which are often compared to crowdfunding and initial public offerings (IPOs), represent a novel method where businesses generate funds by selling digital tokens to investors. These tokens, unlike conventional financial instruments like shares, are created and traded using blockchain technology and can be purchased with both fiat money and cryptocurrencies such as Bitcoin and Ether.

The origins of ICOs trace back to the aftermath of the 2008 financial crisis, a period marked by a severe credit crunch that restricted the availability of traditional bank loans and venture capital. During this time, financial institutions became increasingly cautious, leading to a contraction in credit flow to startups and growing companies. This tightening of liquidity, coupled with heightened regulatory scrutiny, created a challenging environment for businesses seeking capital. ICOs emerged as a disruptive force in this context, providing an alternative means for companies to raise funds. By leveraging blockchain technology, ICOs enable direct interaction between businesses and investors, bypassing traditional financial intermediaries and their associated complexities. This innovation allows for quicker and more accessible fundraising processes, often at a lower cost. In this chapter, we explore the mechanics of ICOs, their advantages, and their role in supporting businesses, especially those with sustainability-focused projects. We also examine how ICOs have evolved from their origins to become a critical tool in the modern financial ecosystem, offering new opportunities for companies to secure the capital needed for growth and sustainability initiatives. Through this analysis, we aim to highlight the transformative potential of ICOs in the broader context of financial innovation and capital formation.

In Chap. 7, we delve into the pressing issue of greenwashing, an increasingly prevalent problem as global awareness of environmental sustainability intensifies. Over the past decade, the mounting pollution and its environmental impacts have led stakeholders—consumers, investors, and governments—to demand that companies adopt genuinely eco-friendly practices. Sustainable economic development, which aims to balance economic growth, social inclusion, and environmental protection, has become a central focus. This approach emphasizes the need to meet current needs without jeopardizing the ability of future generations to meet their own.

Transitioning to sustainable production is inherently complex and slow. It requires a fundamental shift in how companies operate, involving not just changes in production processes but also a deep integration of sustainability values throughout the organization, including among boards, employees, suppliers, and investors. Such a systemic change affects the entire supply chain and necessitates moving from viewing production merely as a source of surplus value to integrating environmental respect into all facets of business operations. Additionally, the financial commitment required for sustainable investments adds another layer of complexity. However, many companies face the temptation to prioritize market satisfaction over genuine environmental responsibility, leading to the widespread issue of greenwashing. Greenwashing involves creating a misleadingly positive impression of a company's environmental efforts, often through false, exaggerated, or incomplete claims. This deceptive practice not only distorts reality but also undermines progress toward true sustainability. In this chapter, we will explore the various forms and methods of greenwashing, analyzing its impact across different levels of the value chain. We will start by examining greenwashing at the product level, where deceptive practices are employed to boost sales. Next, we will investigate greenwashing at the firm level, focusing on the broader policies and motivations behind such practices. Finally, we will address the implications of greenwashing in financial markets, providing a comprehensive view of how this phenomenon affects the market environment as a whole. Through this analysis, we aim to uncover the internal and external forces driving greenwashing and its pervasive impact on sustainability efforts.

Chapter 8 delves into the increasing emphasis on sustainability and corporate responsibility, particularly within small and medium-sized enterprises (SMEs). This chapter is built upon a detailed survey conducted by the University of Ferrara in 2019 and 2021, which aims to assess the sustainability practices of Italian SMEs through a sophisticated statistical framework. The survey examines critical areas such as circular economy practices, patent innovations, enhancements in products and processes, waste reduction strategies, and labor force conditions. These facets are vital for understanding the extent and effectiveness of sustainability initiatives within SMEs. To provide a more nuanced view, the chapter integrates survey data with financial information from balance sheets, sourced from AIDA Bureau Van Dijk. This integration allows for a thorough analysis that extends beyond qualitative evaluations. While many existing sustainability assessments, such as those from Eikon Refinitiv, include ESG factors, this chapter takes a different approach. Specifically, it excludes the governance dimension from its sustainability scores due to the observation that many Italian SMEs operate with less complex governance structures, making traditional governance metrics less relevant. Despite the omission of governance in the sustainability scores, the Italian regulatory environment underscores its importance. The introduction of the Insolvency and Crisis Code (IC-Code) requires Italian family SMEs to establish robust organizational, management, and accounting systems, reflecting the critical role of governance in ensuring sustainability and regulatory compliance. The chapter also explores the role of strategic leadership and innovation within Italian SMEs, highlighting the need for supportive policies that foster innovation and create a conducive environment for SME growth. The interplay between leadership, innovation, and sustainability is a central theme in this analysis. For the analytical approach, the chapter employs a combination of Correspondence Analysis (CA) for qualitative data and Principal Component Analysis (PCA) for quantitative data. This mixed-method approach allows for a comprehensive exploration of factors influencing sustainability. Additionally, panel regression and quantile regression techniques are used to examine balance sheet determinants, and propensity score analysis assesses the impact of innovations. This comprehensive approach aims to offer valuable insights into the sustainability practices of Italian SMEs and contribute to the broader discussion on corporate sustainability and innovation.

Part—III Companies crisis

The phenomenon of the corporate crisis represents a significant challenge, particularly for SMEs. Chapter 9 examines the crisis phenomenon from both national and international perspectives, highlighting the differences and similarities that exist across various contexts. The corporate crisis has a dynamic nature, manifesting as a process of progressive deterioration in the economic and financial conditions of the company. This deterioration can be slow or rapid, depending on specific circumstances and the company's ability to implement effective recovery interventions. In the absence of such interventions, the company often faces bankruptcy.

Analyzing the dynamism of the crisis requires a dynamic perspective that includes both a punctual diagnosis of the company's current situation and a forward-looking perspective that allows for the prediction of insolvencies. Since the introduction of Altman's model, the scientific literature has made significant strides, developing advanced tools such as neural networks and other technologies based on artificial intelligence and machine learning. Despite the accuracy of these complex models, the simplicity of Altman's model is often preferred, especially for its ease of use and practical application.

This approach not only allows for the timely identification of potential insolvencies of individual companies but can also be applied at a macro level to predict the distress of entire economic sectors. Such analysis is crucial for banks and public policymakers as it enables them to implement effective interventions to support the stability and sustainability of the economic system. The implications of such analyses are particularly relevant in terms of governance, as they contribute to ensuring sustainable resource management and preventing systemic crises that could have devastating impacts on the economy.

Chapter 10 focuses on the economic and organizational sustainability of the tools developed in Chap. 9. It is essential to understand which parameters allow for the appreciation of the economic and organizational sustainability of these insolvency prediction tools. A comparative analysis of existing models helps reconcile academic studies with practical experiences, ensuring that the tools are not only theoretically sound but also practicable and effective in real-world application.

Economic sustainability implies that the tools are cost-effective, meaning their use does not incur excessive costs relative to the benefits obtained. Organizational sustainability, on the other hand, concerns the ability of business structures to integrate and effectively utilize these tools without requiring excessive resources and expertise that might jeopardize their practical implementation. In this context, the adoption of advanced technologies such as artificial intelligence and machine learning must be carefully evaluated, considering both the advantages in terms of accuracy and predictive capability and the organizational and economic challenges they entail.

The sustainability of insolvency prediction tools is thus a crucial element for ensuring the resilience of companies and economic sectors. The implications of accurate and sustainable analysis are significant not only for individual enterprises but also for the economic system, contributing to the prevention of financial crises and the promotion of stable and sustainable economic growth.

Ferrara, Italy — Mauro Aliano
Ferrara, Italy — Greta Cestari
Ferrara, Italy — Salvatore Madonna

Contents

Part I
Mechanisms and Institutions

Chapter 1
Sustainable Supply Chain Finance: Bridging Theory and Practice

1.1 Introduction

Even though the issue of SCF (Supply Chain Finance) has been discussed for over 50 years (Haley & Higgins, 1973), there is no commonly recognized definition of SCF by academics and practitioners. Among the several definitions of Supply chain finance (SCF), one that can fit could be the following: SCF is a collection of products that help improve efficiency and balance working capital within supply chains (SCs) by leveraging relationships between buyers and suppliers. According to financial literature, starting from the subprime financial crisis, SCF plays a key role for companies, because the credit crunch and the bank crises in most countries push firms to rethink working capital, debt and expenditure on interest rate. But SCF has become important also for sustainability issues, through activities that allow companies to be more sustainable, it can be defined as Sustainable Supply Chain Finance (SSCF). Especially for short term needs, SMEs can use SFC for financing their activities also because they can often be excluded by traditional financing channels. Because this strategy has the potential to add value to the supply chain, a supplier default could have a detrimental effect on the chain as a whole, and a customer default could result in additional defaults or financial difficulties for supply chain members' organizations. This consideration must be measured in a holistic vision of the production dimension, as well as the evaluation of the probability of default of each element in the supply chain. This chapter is organized as follows.

In the second section, we establish a comprehensive framework to define and position SCF, elucidating its fundamental principles and significance in modern supply chain management. This section aims to provide a clear understanding of SCF, outlining its mechanisms, benefits, and the various stakeholders involved. We will explore how SCF can enhance liquidity and efficiency within supply chains, benefiting both suppliers and buyers.

M. Aliano et al., *Sustainable Finance for SMEs*, Sustainable Finance,
https://doi.org/10.1007/978-3-031-74193-7_1

The third section delves into the intersection of SCF and sustainability, highlighting how innovative approaches such as blockchain technology can be leveraged to promote sustainable practices within supply chains. We will discuss the potential of blockchain to enhance transparency, traceability, and accountability, thereby fostering more sustainable and ethical supply chain operations. This section will illustrate how SCF, when integrated with blockchain, can drive environmental and social benefits while also improving financial performance.

In the fourth section, we examine the concept of the domino effect and the risk of contagion within supply chains. This analysis will cover how financial distress in one part of the supply chain can propagate through the network, causing widespread disruption. We will review existing literature and real-world examples to understand the mechanisms behind contagion and the strategies that can be employed to mitigate these risks. This section aims to provide a thorough understanding of the systemic risks associated with SCF and how they can be managed effectively.

To enrich our discussion, we will combine anecdotal evidence from industry practitioners with insights from academic research. This approach will ensure a holistic perspective, blending practical experiences with theoretical frameworks. By integrating real-world case studies and scholarly analysis, we aim to offer a balanced view that is both informative and applicable to practitioners and researchers alike.

1.2 Classification of Supply-Chain: A Financial Perspective

SCF can be broadly categorized into two primary types based on its principal functions: finance-oriented and supply chain-oriented, as delineated by Gelsomino et al. (2016).

The finance-oriented SCF focuses on providing financial solutions and services to SMEs by transforming illiquid assets into cash, which includes assets such as raw materials, inventories, and accounts receivable. This approach to SCF leverages the liquidity of these assets to facilitate the turnover of working capital, thereby improving the cash flow across all transaction activities and processes among all participants involved in the SCF. By doing so, it aids SMEs in overcoming liquidity constraints and ensuring smoother operational flows. The central premise of this type of SCF is to create a seamless flow of cash that mirrors the flow of goods and services within the supply chain, enhancing overall financial stability and operational efficiency. This form of SCF serves as a collaborative tool, enabling all stakeholders to benefit from improved cash flow dynamics, reduced financial risk, and enhanced access to financing.

In contrast, the supply chain-oriented SCF integrates financial resources with the physical aspects of supply chain management (SCM). Stemmler (2002) highlights that this function of SCF is integral to SCM, with its primary goal being the amalgamation of financial resource flows into the physical supply chain. This integration is crucial for synchronizing financial activities with the logistical and managerial aspects of the supply chain, thereby creating a more cohesive and efficient system. Hofmann (2005) further elucidates that this type of SCF is a method that merges financing, logistics management, and SCM to offer flexible financial services to supply chain stakeholders. This collaborative approach generates value throughout the SC process by ensuring that financial considerations are interwoven with logistical operations, thus fostering a more resilient and responsive supply chain. The supply chain-oriented SCF helps in aligning the interests of various stakeholders, promoting transparency, and enhancing the overall performance and competitiveness of the supply chain. By integrating financial and physical flows, this type of SCF supports the development of a more agile and adaptive supply chain capable of responding to dynamic market conditions and mitigating risks effectively.

1.3 The SSCF and a Blockchain Perspective: Sustainable Financial Application Development

From a classical financial perspective, in the SCF there are multiple subjects involved that could increase asymmetric information between players. The lack of information coupled with its asymmetric information has an impact on the efficiency of transactions and could lead to a domino effect in the case of default, under a pathologic perspective. From a physiological perspective, in SCF there can be imperfect credit mechanisms, and a non-standard credit scenario, and it is a logical fit for blockchain technology. People's attention has been drawn to the application of blockchain technology to alleviate suffering in the supply chain finance business as described above.

Contract orders and accounts receivable, among other things, characterize the upstream supply chain, where the supplier relies on the transaction connection with the core businesses to acquire credit support. Logistics financing in the core enterprise interval is mostly based on the credit of the material itself. The material's credit is related to standardization, fluidity, pledge and salvage value, and so on. As a result, the commitment consists of warehouse storage and futures created by the movement of bulk commodities. Financial products such as credit loans, receivables pledges, and so on are included in the downstream segment of the supply chain. The majority of financial product design in the supply chain requires documentation, transaction records, credit status, and other information from the chain's firms.

Once the transaction is formed, the relevant data can be traced and verified using blockchain technology, thereby alleviating the core enterprise's difficult self-certification innocence, small and medium-sized enterprises financing difficult financing problems (Ma et al., 2020).

Consider order financing in the supply chain's early stages. Manufacturing firms buy raw materials from upstream raw material suppliers through contracts with downstream core companies. Manufacturing businesses borrow money from banks to pay for raw materials, and their finished and semi-finished goods are tracked by third-party logistics. Sales money will be used to repay the bank's principal and interest. However, in real production and operation activities, upstream manufacturing businesses are far removed from the core enterprises in the production process, and obtaining commercial documents directly connected to the core enterprises is difficult. A business document that has not been endorsed by a core firm may have funding challenges, which the blockchain can alleviate. Non-tamper able and traceable data characteristics lower invoicing and financing expenses. Order financing of financial institutions necessitates the provision of transaction data by manufacturing firms; nevertheless, due to the competitive interaction between manufacturing companies, transaction privacy protection is required. On the one hand, the transaction price between rivals must be kept secret; on the other hand, the trading behavior of specific enterprises, such as military units, requires privacy protection. This aspect of privacy protection could be enlarged for companies at the worldwide level, especially for those sectors where data and privacy protection are important.

Example of Agriculture Farms
One of the biggest benefits of blockchain technology is that it removes the need for middlemen in transactions, which is important for industries like agriculture as well as cryptocurrencies. Blockchain technology eliminates the need for a central authority in the world of cryptocurrencies, transferring confidence from an authority to encryption and peer-to-peer architecture. This change could reduce transaction costs in the agri-food industry by restoring trust between farmers and consumers. Blockchain offers a trustworthy way to track transactions between unidentified parties, making it possible to quickly spot flaws and fraud. Real-time fault notifications are made possible by smart contract usage, which addresses the challenge of item tracing in the extensive agri-food supply chain.

Concerns about food safety and quality are major concerns for governments, businesses, and consumers alike, and this technology offers answers.

Blockchain guarantees openness among all stakeholders and makes it easier to gather trustworthy data at every stage of a product's lifecycle, from production to disposal. In order to create data-driven facilities and insurance solutions, which will make farming more intelligent and less vulnerable, trustworthy data from the farming process is essential. Blockchain technology, thus, increases transparency and makes it possible to obtain reliable data, thereby addressing the concerns of governments, consumers, and other stakeholders regarding food quality and safety.

1.3.1 The Case of Agricultural Insurance

Weather extremes threaten agricultural production, putting food security at risk. Both crop and livestock production are affected, and climate change is expected to further exacerbate weather extremes in the future. Agricultural insurance schemes are traditionally a well-recognized tool to manage weather-related risks. Here, farmers pay an insurance premium before the cropping cycle begins and receive an insurance payout whenever they experience a loss on their farm. Thus, the insurer bears all the insured risk and farmers are able to manage their financial exposure to weather extremes, i.e., financial losses caused by weather extremes.

Furthermore, in the event of weather hazards that impact all insured farmers on a systemic level, the insurer can further hedge the systemic portion of the risk through a reinsurance business. Agricultural insurance policies differ in terms of how losses are assessed and, as a result, how payouts are triggered. Indemnity-based insurances are those that compensate farmers based on a damage estimate done by an expert on the farm. Indemnity-based insurances can accurately pay losses, but they are vulnerable to asymmetric knowledge concerns. In particular, information on the riskiness of agricultural output and production techniques is transferred asymmetrically between farmer and insurer. Farmers are expected to be better informed about both, which incentivizes adverse selection and moral hazard.

Farmers with higher ex ante risk exposure are more inclined to obtain insurance than farmers with lesser risk, according to adverse selection. When farmers are insured, they are more likely to engage in riskier agricultural techniques. If the insurer lacks sufficient knowledge on the two scenarios, these circumstances result in market failure of the insurance plan. As a result, indemnity-based insurances are prone to costly damage assessment and must include safeguards such as deductibles to minimize difficulties caused by asymmetric knowledge. Furthermore, products that cannot be quantified, such as grazed meadows, cannot be covered, although causing financial loss. Motivated by the shortcomings of indemnity-based insurance, the concept of index-based insurance arose as an alternative or supplement to traditional products.

In this case, the compensation is triggered by a quantifiable index, such as rainfall at a local weather station, rather than by the loss itself. If this weather station has long enough historical weather data, both the farmer and the insurer will have identical knowledge of the insured value, and agricultural methods will have no effect on the insurance payout. As a result, adverse selection and moral hazard are no longer factors, and the technical method for triggering a payout has been significantly simplified. Furthermore, full insurance coverage with no deductibles is feasible, and payments may be sent on time and automatically immediately after a bad weather event is measured. However, differences in payment and on-farm loss might arise, which is referred to as basis risk.

There are three potential sources of basis risk. Geographical basis risk denotes any discrepancies in observed and on-farm weather, such as geographical distance. Temporal basis risk suggests that an imprecise time window was used to calculate the index, such as whole-year rainfall vs. growth season rainfall. All remaining causes, such as missing meteorological data or biased technological implementation, are summarized in the design foundation risk. To summarize, index insurance is becoming a more essential risk management instrument for farmers, whereas basis risk reduction is of primary importance. In two ways, blockchain can help to improve index insurance. First, payments may be issued on time and automatically depending on meteorological data that triggers a smart contract payout.

Second, weather data and other data sources, such as plant growth data or data gathered by farm machinery, may be automatically incorporated via a smart oracle, reducing basis risk and enhancing the index calculation and payment process.

Smart contracts that employ smart oracles to integrate external data have previously proved beneficial in various crypto-economic applications. The first smart index insurance contract prototypes are already in the works or have been released. Etherisc1, a Swiss-based firm, for example, provides decentralized crop insurance based on blockchain technology, with payouts in DIP as local currency (DIP—Decentralized Insurance Protocol tokens).

Furthermore, WorldCover2, a New York City-based insurance company that sells index insurance contracts to smallholder farmers in Ghana, simulated the use of an Ethereum blockchain-based smart contract. As a result, payouts would be made in the cryptocurrency Ether. Arbol3 is yet another clever crop insurance supplier. A farmer can submit a contract with Arbol that comprises the premium payment, a payout, and a weather event that triggers the payout. Following that, an investor acting as a counterparty might consent to the proposed contract. Ether is used for both the initial and final payments.

Aside from the benefits of decentralized insurances based on smart contracts that make automatic payouts, the applicability of bitcoin payouts to compensate farmers must be shown in the field. Furthermore, farmers, particularly in underdeveloped countries, may lack access to the necessary infrastructure to participate in a decentralized blockchain-based insurance scheme.

Blockchain can be used in a wide range of productive sectors, for example the blockchain technology can monitor the provenance of food, assisting in the creation of trustworthy food supply chains and the development of trust between producers and consumers. This application needs a different approach in the use of the supply chain, that could be led by data information and that can allow the relationship between customers and producers.

It promotes the adoption of data-driven technology to make farming smarter since it is a reliable method of storing data. Furthermore, when combined with smart contracts, it enables timely payments between stakeholders that may be triggered by data changes in the blockchain. In this sense, the use of blockchain technology in food supply chains, agricultural insurance, smart farming, and agricultural product transactions from both theoretical and practical viewpoints could be useful.

We also talk about the difficulties of tracking transactions done by smallholder farmers and developing an ecosystem for using blockchain technology in the food and agricultural sectors. When SC crosses the border of the country, if SCF encourages sustainability (so called SSCF), it must consider the difference for each regional system, not only under the economic perspective, but also in light of different cultural, religious and behavioral backgrounds (see Tseng et al., 2021).

1.3.2 Sustainable Supply Chain Finance

SSCF is a pivotal component of contemporary supply chain management, seamlessly integrating financial mechanisms with sustainable practices to foster environmental and social responsibility across supply chains (Liu et al., 2022). SSCF's primary goal is to synchronize financial flows with sustainable development objectives, ensuring that economic progress aligns with environmental conservation and social well-being (Liang et al., 2018). By embedding sustainability criteria into financial decision-making, SSCF motivates businesses to embrace eco-friendly practices, support local communities, and maintain ethical standards throughout their supply chains (Wu et al., 2022).

The implementation of SSCF involves utilizing financial tools and strategies that prioritize sustainability, such as green financing, impact investing, and social responsibility bonds (Liu, 2024). These instruments not only provide capital for sustainable projects but also incentivize companies to enhance their environmental and social performance to attract investment (Dong, 2024). For instance, green financing facilitates funding for projects aimed at reducing carbon footprints or conserving natural resources, while impact investing focuses on generating measurable social and environmental benefits alongside financial returns. Social responsibility bonds, meanwhile, raise funds specifically for initiatives that promote social good, such as improving labor conditions or community development.

The role of SSCF in advancing a sustainable economy is multifaceted. It drives businesses to adopt circular economy principles, reduce carbon emissions, and promote fair labor practices within their supply chains (Liu, 2021). By doing so, SSCF not only contributes to mitigating climate change and preserving ecosystems but also supports social equity and economic stability. Companies that integrate SSCF can leverage these practices to differentiate themselves in the marketplace, appealing to increasingly conscientious consumers and investors who prioritize sustainability.

One of the critical arguments for SSCF is its potential to transform traditional supply chain finance into a driver for sustainability. Traditionally, supply chain finance has focused on optimizing cash flow and reducing costs. While these goals remain important, SSCF expands the focus to include environmental and social dimensions, thereby aligning financial practices with broader societal goals. This shift is crucial in the context of global challenges such as climate change, resource depletion, and social inequality.

Moreover, SSCF can enhance the resilience and adaptability of supply chains. Sustainable practices often lead to more efficient resource use, waste reduction, and improved risk management. For example, companies that invest in renewable energy sources or sustainable raw materials can reduce their exposure to volatile fossil fuel prices or supply disruptions. Similarly, businesses that promote fair labor practices can mitigate risks associated with workforce unrest or reputational damage. Thus, SSCF not only supports long-term sustainability but also strengthens the overall stability and competitiveness of supply chains.

In addition to these benefits, SSCF fosters innovation by encouraging the development and adoption of new technologies and practices. Financial incentives for sustainability can spur investments in research and development, leading to breakthroughs in areas such as renewable energy, waste management, and sustainable agriculture. These innovations can, in turn, create new business opportunities and drive economic growth.

SSCF also plays a vital role in fostering collaboration among stakeholders. Sustainable supply chain finance requires the cooperation of various actors, including suppliers, manufacturers, financial institutions, and governments. This collaborative approach can lead to more comprehensive and effective sustainability strategies, as stakeholders share knowledge, resources, and best practices. Furthermore, it can enhance transparency and accountability within supply chains, ensuring that sustainability commitments are upheld.

In conclusion, Sustainable Supply Chain Finance (SSCF) is an essential strategy for integrating sustainability into supply chain management. By aligning financial flows with sustainable development goals, SSCF promotes environmental conservation, social well-being, and economic resilience. The adoption of SSCF encourages businesses to implement sustainable practices, supports innovation, and fosters collaboration among stakeholders. As the global economy increasingly prioritizes sustainability, SSCF will play a crucial role in driving the transition towards a more sustainable and equitable future.

1.3.3 The Case of Walmart

The concept of Sustainable Supply Chain Finance (SSCF) is a novel strategy that combines sustainable practices with financial mechanisms to promote social and environmental responsibility in supply chains. Walmart's effort, which makes use of its extensive supply chain to encourage sustainability through financial incentives, is a noteworthy example of SSCF. A Sustainable Supply Chain Finance program has been created by Walmart and HSBC to assist suppliers in lowering their greenhouse gas (GHG) emissions. This initiative is a component of Walmart's larger Project Gigaton, which intends to reduce greenhouse gas emissions from its global supply chain by one billion metric tons by 2030. Suppliers who show improvement in lowering their environmental effect through science-based targets and enhanced sustainability practices are eligible for attractive financing terms under the program.[1]

SMEs are the focus of Walmart's program because it is acknowledged that these companies frequently lack the means and know-how to carry out meaningful environmental changes on their own. Walmart provides incentives to its suppliers to embrace environmentally sustainable practices by offering higher financing rates

[1] https://www.walmartsustainabilityhub.com/project-gigaton

that are tied to sustainability performance. This strategy supports Walmart's objectives to lower Scope 3 emissions, or indirect emissions from its value chain, while also assisting suppliers in becoming more sustainable.[2]

As part of the SSCF program, participants must either meet predetermined CDP climate change report scores or set science-based targets that have been verified by the Science Based Targets Initiative (SBTi). Suppliers who fulfill these requirements are eligible for early invoice payment at a rate that is based on their sustainability performance. With the help of this financial assistance, suppliers can lower their carbon footprint by making the necessary investments in sustainable practices, including the use of sustainable materials and energy-efficient technologies.[3]

Walmart's initiative is a perfect example of how SSCF may promote economic growth and yield major environmental advantages. Walmart promotes a more robust and sustainable supply chain ecosystem in addition to achieving its own corporate sustainability goals by including sustainability into its supply chain finance.

This model demonstrates the potential of SSCF to transform supply chain practices across industries, encouraging other corporations to adopt similar strategies to achieve broader environmental and social impacts.[4]

1.4 Contagion Effects in SCF

After a default incident, supply chains can experience contagion effects that affect linked businesses all the way up the supply chain network, well beyond the initial defaulter. According to Jorion and Zhang (2009), the failure of a company sets off a series of events that cause financial distress and propagate throughout the supply chain ecosystem. These contagion dynamics, which impact companies with common links and dependencies throughout the supply chain, are frequently triggered by cash flow shocks particularly to a given industry (Huaqiao, 2023). Supply chain default risk contagion is a mechanism that amplifies hazards throughout the entire network by operating through a particular network topology, akin to a "domino" effect (Shen, 2023). This spread has the potential to cause major losses for various businesses, nations, and the world economy. It can also inhibit the development of supply chains and economic progress (Shen, 2023). Depleting enterprises' capital buffers due to macroeconomic shocks that lower asset values make networks less resilient to defaults, which in turn exacerbates contagion effects (Cont et al., 2013).

[2] https://corporate.walmart.com/news/2023/04/04/walmart-outlines-growth-strategy-unveils-next-generation-supply-chain-at-2023-investment-community-meeting?_x_tr_sl=en&_x_tr_tl=it&_x_tr_hl=it&_x_tr_pto=sc

[3] https://corporate.walmart.com/content/dam/corporate/documents/esgreport/our-esg-priorities/2023%20CDP%20Climate%20Submission.pdf

[4] https://corporate.walmart.com/news/2021/12/08/walmart-creates-industry-first-by-introducing-science-based-targets-for-supply-chain-finance-program

Research demonstrates that there is default contagion throughout supply networks, with different firms in financing portfolios experiencing different levels of contagion (Zhang et al., 2019). Credit risk can spread throughout the supply chain network when one party defaults, resulting in losses for other participants (Chen et al., 2021). This spreads beyond individual companies to include related credit risks in the supply chain, directly endangering banks that lend money to network members (Xie et al., 2023).

Due to the interconnectedness of supply chains and company interconnections, contagion can spread quickly after default. Contagion models examine the direct relationships that occur in networks, whereby the default of one item can raise the probability of other entities to default as well, resulting in "infectious defaults" and systemic hazards (Zheng, 2011; Haworth & Reisinger, 2007).

Furthermore, industry-wide failures and credit stress that impact the whole economy might result from credit risk contagion inside supply chains (Ellis, 2020). According to Berloco et al. (2021), supply chain spillover effects have a considerable impact on individual firms' default probabilities, underscoring the interdependence and interconnection within networks. In order to manage contagion risks and avoid systemic breakdowns and financial crises inside supply chains, it is imperative to comprehend these processes.

In conclusion, post-default supply chain contagion effects are intricate and multidimensional, with the potential to upset financial stability in linked businesses as well as the whole economy. Developing a thorough understanding of contagion dynamics, building strong models to evaluate related credit risks, and implementing efficient risk mitigation techniques are essential to improving supply chain resilience and reducing the negative effects of network defaults.

Investigating the various factors that contribute to the spread of contagion effects is crucial in order to go further. Because companies in a supply chain are interconnected, a financial shock to one might have an impact on others.

For instance, all the businesses that depend on a major supplier for components or supplies will be impacted if that supplier suddenly experiences cash flow difficulties and defaults. These dependent enterprises may experience production delays, cost increases, and eventually financial difficulties as a result of this disruption.

Several factors can increase the severity of these contagion effects. The degree of inter-firm reliance within the network is a crucial element. A high degree of reliance indicates that the downfall of one company directly and significantly affects the others. The state of a company's finances before the default occurrence also matters. Weaker financial circumstances make a company less resilient to shocks and more inclined to spread the pain.

It is impossible to ignore the significance of financial institutions in this network. When a default happens, banks and other lenders who finance supply chain players take on more credit risk. The lender may incur losses in the event of a borrower's default, which may limit their capacity to provide credit to other businesses. This decrease in credit availability may make the supply chain's financial problems worse.

The features unique to a certain industry that may affect the dynamics of contagion should also be taken into account. The automobile and electronics industries, which have highly linked supply chains, are especially susceptible to the spread of infectious diseases. Production lines in these sectors are heavily dependent on one another, so when one supplier fails, it can affect the entire supply chain.

Businesses and legislators need to concentrate on a number of tactics in order to reduce these risks. First and foremost, it is imperative to strengthen each firm's resilience and financial health. Better risk management techniques, like supplier diversification and obtaining stronger financial buffers, can help achieve this. Secondly, companies can gain a better understanding of their dependence and potential vulnerabilities by improving supply chain transparency. Blockchain technology, which offers an unchangeable and transparent record of interactions and transactions along the supply chain, can be quite helpful in this area.

Lawmakers can also make a difference by establishing legislative frameworks that support supply chains' resiliency and financial stability. This could entail taking steps to guarantee the financial stability of important suppliers or offering assistance to businesses experiencing brief financial difficulties in order to stop them from spiraling into more significant systemic risks.

To anticipate and control contagion hazards, advanced models must be developed and used in addition to these precautions. These models can assist businesses and decision-makers in comprehending the possible effects of a default event and creating plans to lessen such effects. Stress testing supply chains, for example, can help businesses identify weak points and create backup plans by putting them through various situations.

The ultimate objective is to design supply networks that are shock-resistant and efficient. This necessitates a comprehensive strategy that considers advanced risk management tools, regulatory assistance, financial health, and openness. By doing this, businesses may better manage the intricate dynamics of supply chain contagion and safeguard against the negative consequences of default events for both the larger economy and them.

In conclusion, supply chain default events can have far-reaching consequences that raise serious concerns about the development of financial instability. Because supply chains are interrelated, a failure in one area of the network can spread swiftly to affect other businesses and possibly have wider economic repercussions. Businesses and legislators can improve supply chain resilience and lessen the negative effects of such occurrences by comprehending these dynamics and putting strong risk management techniques into practice.

1.4.1 The Case of Americanas SA

In January 2023, Americanas SA, a prominent Brazilian retail giant, filed for bankruptcy protection after uncovering a significant financial discrepancy amounting to around 20 billion reais (approximately $3.9 billion USD). The discovery of this substantial accounting inconsistency, which had been ongoing for years, led to a dramatic financial crisis for the company, shaking investor confidence and prompting legal and regulatory scrutiny.[5] Americanas SA, one of Brazil's largest and most popular retailers, operates a vast network of stores and an extensive online presence. The company, known for its diversified portfolio including electronics, clothing, and household goods, was considered a staple in the Brazilian retail market. However, in early January 2023, the company revealed that it had identified accounting irregularities that inflated its financial health and masked its true debt levels.[6]

The announcement of the financial discrepancies led to a sharp decline in the company's stock price, wiping out billions in market value within days. Investors reacted strongly to the news, causing a significant loss of confidence in the company's governance and financial practices. The CEO and other top executives faced intense scrutiny, leading to leadership changes and a broader investigation into the company's financial management.[7] Facing mounting pressure and a liquidity crisis, Americanas SA filed for bankruptcy protection on January 19, 2023, under Brazilian bankruptcy laws. This move aimed to provide the company with a structured environment to reorganize its debts and attempt to stabilize its operations while seeking to safeguard its assets and continue business activities.[8] The bankruptcy filing triggered a series of legal and regulatory actions. Creditors, including major banks and suppliers, sought to recover their investments and mitigate losses. The Brazilian Securities and Exchange Commission (CVM) launched an investigation into the company's accounting practices and the potential involvement of auditors and executives in the financial misreporting.[9]

The bankruptcy had a profound impact on Americanas SA's supply chain, causing widespread disruption and uncertainty. Suppliers, many of whom are small and medium-sized enterprises, faced delayed payments and uncertain future orders. This disruption in the supply chain affected not only Americanas but also its extensive network of suppliers who relied on the retailer for significant portions of their business.[10] With Americanas unable to meet its financial obligations, suppliers experienced severe cash flow issues, leading to operational challenges and, in some cases, jeopardizing their own financial stability. The ripple effect of Americanas' financial crisis permeated through the entire supply chain, highlighting the

[5] https://www.reuters.com/business/brazils-americanas-ceo-rial-cfo-covre-resign-amid-38-bln-accounting-2023-01-12/

[6] (https://www.ft.com): "Brazilian retailer Americanas files for bankruptcy."

[7] https://www.ft.com/content/0aeb718a-f274-4b82-8ac0-34c81a4c73d2

[8] (https://www.reuters.com): "Brazil's Americanas faces extended bankruptcy battle with creditors - sources."

[9] https://www.economist.com/business/2023/02/09/alleged-fraud-at-a-brazilian-retailer-sparks-a-corporate-reckoning

[10] (https://finance.yahoo.com): "Bankrupt Brazilian retailer Americanas owes about $8 billion, court finds"

interconnectedness of modern retail operations and the critical importance of financial health at each link in the chain.[11]

The collapse of Americanas SA had broader implications for the Brazilian retail market and the country's financial sector. It highlighted the importance of robust financial oversight and transparency, prompting other companies to reassess their accounting practices and governance structures. The incident also led to increased scrutiny of the role of auditors and regulatory bodies in preventing and detecting financial fraud.[12]

References

Berloco, C., Morales, G., Frassineti, D., Greco, G., Kumarasinghe, H., Lamieri, M., et al. (2021). Predicting corporate credit risk: Network contagion via trade credit. *PLoS One, 16*(4), e0250115. https://doi.org/10.1371/journal.pone.0250115

Chen, W., Li, Z., & Xiao, Z. (2021). On credit risk contagion of supply chain finance under covid-19. *Journal of Mathematics, 2021*, 1–13. https://doi.org/10.1155/2021/1281825

Cont, R., Moussa, A., & Santos, E. (2013). *Network structure and systemic risk in banking systems*. 327-368. https://doi.org/10.1017/cbo9781139151184.018.

Dong, J. (2024). Sustainable development of the real economy: Supply chain finance and enterprise financialization. *Sustainability, 16*(9), 3574. https://doi.org/10.3390/su16093574

Ellis, C. (2020). Are corporate bond defaults contagious across sectors? *International Journal of Financial Studies, 8*(1), 1. https://doi.org/10.3390/ijfs8010001

Gelsomino, L. M., Mangiaracina, R., Perego, A., & Tumino, A. (2016). Supply chain finance: A literature review. *International Journal of Physical Distribution and Logistics Management, 46*, 1–19. https://doi.org/10.1108/IJPDLM-08-2014-0173

Haley, C. W., & Higgins, R. C. (1973). Inventory policy and trade credit financing. *Management Science, 20*(4-part-i), 464–471. https://doi.org/10.1287/mnsc.20.4.464

Haworth, H., & Reisinger, C. (2007). Modeling basket credit default swaps with default contagion. *The Journal of Credit Risk, 3*(4), 31–67. https://doi.org/10.21314/jcr.2007.055

Hofmann, E. (2005). Supply chain finance—Some conceptual insights. *Logistik Management.*, 203–214. https://doi.org/10.1007/978-3-322-82165-2_16

Huaqiao, S. (2023). *Research on the mechanism of supply chain default risk contagion*. https://doi.org/10.21203/rs.3.rs-3361236/v1

Jorion, P., & Zhang, G. (2009). Credit contagion from counterparty risk. *The Journal of Finance, 64*(5), 2053–2087. https://doi.org/10.1111/j.1540-6261.2009.01494.x

Liang, X., Zhao, X., Wang, M., & Li, Z. (2018). Small and medium-sized enterprises sustainable supply chain financing decision based on triple bottom line theory. *Sustainability, 10*(11), 4242. https://doi.org/10.3390/su10114242

Liu, J. (2021). Research on the prevention and control of supply chain financial risks from the perspective of enterprise financing. *Finance and Market, 6*(1), 49. https://doi.org/10.18686/fm.v6i1.3263

Liu, J., Li, J., Wang, J., Uddin, M., & Zhang, B. (2022). Research on the application of blockchain technology in coal supply chain finance. *Sustainability, 14*(16), 10099. https://doi.org/10.3390/su141610099

[11] https://ca.finance.yahoo.com/news/billionaire-backed-americanas-files-bankruptcy-115822845.html

[12] https://brazilian.report/business/2024/07/27/americanas-recovery-boosted/

Liu, Y. (2024). Redefining supply chain financing: The role of long-term investors and intangible assets from a resource-based view perspective. *Advances in Economics Management and Political Sciences, 72*(1), 313–318. https://doi.org/10.54254/2754-1169/72/20240685

Ma, H. L., Wang, Z. X., & Chan, F. T. (2020). How important are supply chain collaborative factors in supply chain finance? A view of financial service providers in China. *International Journal of Production Economics, 219*, 341–346.

Shen, H. (2023). Research on u-shaped relationship between short-term debt for long-term use and supply chain enterprise default risk: Evidence from chinese listed firms. *PLoS One, 18*(10), e0293284. https://doi.org/10.1371/journal.pone.0293284

Stemmler, L. (2002). The role of finance in supply chain management. *Cost Management in Supply Chains*, 165–176.

Tseng, M. L., Bui, T. D., Lim, M. K., Tsai, F. M., & Tan, R. R. (2021). Comparing world regional sustainable supply chain finance using big data analytics: A bibliometric analysis. *Industrial Management & Data Systems, 121*(3), 657–700. https://doi.org/10.1108/IMDS-09-2020-0521

Wu, C., Liu, J., & Zhang, H. (2022). Data ecology and accurate portrait: Optimization of credit risk system for smes in supply chain finance based on big data technology. *Journal of Risk Analysis and Crisis Response, 11*(4). https://doi.org/10.54560/jracr.v11i4.310

Xie, X., Zhang, F., Liu, L., Li, Y., & Hu, X. (2023). Assessment of associated credit risk in the supply chain based on trade credit risk contagion. *PLoS One, 18*(2), e0281616. https://doi.org/10.1371/journal.pone.0281616

Zhang, M., Zhang, J., Ma, R., & Chen, X. (2019). Quantifying credit risk of supply chain finance: A chinese automobile supply chain perspective. *IEEE Access, 7*, 144264–144279. https://doi.org/10.1109/access.2019.2939287

Zheng, H. (2011). *A copula contagion mixture model and its pricing impact on portfolio credit derivatives*. https://doi.org/10.2316/p.2011.704-044.

Chapter 2
How Can Companies Financially Sustain their Transition?

2.1 Introduction

When companies embark on financing their operations, they make crucial decisions about sourcing funds internally or externally. Essentially, the amalgamation of these internal and external funds constitutes the financial structure of a company. In financial literature, internal funds typically refer to equity and self-financing resources, whereas external funds originate from sources outside the company. Various financial instruments contribute to both internal and external funds. For instance, internal funds include common stocks, preferred stocks, and other equity-hybrid instruments, while external funds comprise bank loans, diverse types of bonds, and alternative forms of lending such as peer-to-peer platforms. The capital structure of companies plays a pivotal role in facilitating sustainable transitions and driving green innovations.

Originating from Modigliani and Miller's Theorem (1958), which posits that a company's value is determined solely by the value of its projects irrespective of its capital structure, theories in financial intermediation underscore the relevance of capital structure. From an operational standpoint, a dearth of debt and equity capital may pose constraints to promoting green finance and sustainability initiatives. Furthermore, within the realm of internal and external financial resource choices lie a plethora of instruments.

To simplify this discussion, there exists a primary level of choice in a company's financial structure and at least a secondary level. Why "at least"? Because within the domain of debt, there exist various sources such as bonds or loans, each with distinct typologies and features, often subordinate to differing degrees of seniority. This complexity persists even for small companies in rural areas around the globe. If the aforementioned considerations hold true for all projects and companies, then incorporating green and sustainability features into the financial allocation process becomes imperative. This chapter aims to elucidate the fundamental reasons behind

M. Aliano et al., *Sustainable Finance for SMEs*, Sustainable Finance,
https://doi.org/10.1007/978-3-031-74193-7_2

the significance of corporate finance and capital structure theory in bolstering sustainability efforts and facilitating the transition toward a green economy.

2.2 Does Size Really Matter?

The financing of sustainable transitions involves various mechanisms and actors, with banks playing a crucial role as financial intermediaries. Let's explore how banks can facilitate financing for companies pursuing sustainability initiatives, ranging from multinational corporations in the fossil fuel sector transitioning to green investments to startups focusing on CO2 emission reduction patents.

For multinational corporations transitioning to green investments, banks can provide financing to support their shift towards sustainable practices. This may involve loans for investments in renewable energy projects, energy-efficient technologies, or carbon offset initiatives.

Despite the differing financial needs of such corporations compared to startups, access to financial resources remains paramount. Banks can offer tailored financial solutions that align with the specific sustainability goals and investment strategies of these corporations.

On the other hand, startups and small companies often face challenges accessing traditional financial markets and bank loans due to their size and lack of collateral. This is where alternative sources of financing, such as venture capital (VC) and business angels (BA), become crucial. VC and BA investors specialize in supporting early-stage innovations, including those focused on green technologies and sustainability. By providing capital and expertise, they enable startups to develop and scale their environmentally friendly solutions.

However, the size of companies does matter when it comes to accessing financial markets and obtaining resources. Larger corporations may have easier access to financing due to their established track record and asset base. In contrast, startups and small companies often struggle to attract investment and secure loans, particularly if they lack tangible assets or a proven market presence.

Financial inclusion is also a key consideration in sustainable financing, as it ensures that companies of all sizes have equal opportunities to access capital. Banks and other financial intermediaries need to adopt inclusive lending practices and consider sustainability criteria when evaluating potential borrowers. This may involve assessing the environmental and social impact of projects alongside traditional financial metrics.

As we transition into a sustainable era, investors are increasingly incorporating sustainability criteria into their decision-making processes. This shift reflects a growing recognition of the importance of environmental, social, and governance (ESG) factors in assessing investment risks and opportunities. By integrating sustainability considerations into their lending and investment strategies, financial intermediaries can drive positive change and support the transition to a more sustainable economy.

Internal or External Funds?

Indeed, the Modigliani-Miller theorem, a fundamental theory in corporate finance, posits that in the absence of taxes, bankruptcy costs, and asymmetric information, the financing decisions of a firm do not affect its value. Under this theorem, a firm's value is determined solely by its investment decisions and the cash flows generated by those investments. Therefore, in a perfect market where information is freely available and there are no imperfections, companies can choose between internal or external financing without facing any constraints, and their decisions are solely driven by the profitability of projects. However, as you rightly pointed out, real-world financial markets are not perfect, and imperfections such as asymmetric information exist.

The "hidden information problem" is a significant imperfection in financial markets, wherein there is a disparity in information between the company's management (who possess more information about the project) and external stakeholders, such as lenders or investors. For instance, consider a project's cash flow, which represents the ability of a company's activities to repay the initial investment. Managers often have more information about the expected values and risks associated with a project compared to external lenders or investors. This information asymmetry creates uncertainty and risk for external stakeholders, as they may not have a complete understanding of the project's potential outcomes or the likelihood of success. As a result, lenders and investors may demand higher returns or impose stricter terms on financing arrangements to compensate for the perceived risks associated with asymmetric information. This can lead to financing constraints for companies, particularly startups or those with limited track records, as external stakeholders may be hesitant to provide funding without adequate information or assurances regarding the project's viability.

In practice, companies often employ various strategies to mitigate the impact of asymmetric information, such as providing detailed financial disclosures, engaging in transparent communication with stakeholders, and obtaining third-party certifications or evaluations to validate the quality of their projects. Additionally, financial intermediaries, such as banks or investment firms, play a crucial role in evaluating and mitigating risks associated with asymmetric information through due diligence processes and risk management techniques.

When lenders perceive projects as riskier due to their lack of complete information, they often demand higher interest rates or impose stricter terms to compensate for the perceived risk. This effectively increases the cost of external financing compared to using internal resources, where the company's management and insiders have more comprehensive knowledge about the projects.

Given this scenario, companies facing the choice between internal and external financing would likely consider the cost of capital as a critical factor in their decision-making process. Internal financing, such as retained earnings or funds generated from operations, typically comes at a lower cost since there are no associated interest payments or external demands for compensation due to risk. Therefore, if the cost of external financing is perceived to be significantly higher due to asymmetric information, companies may prefer to utilize internal resources whenever possible to fund their projects. By doing so, they can minimize financing costs and retain greater control over their operations and decision-making processes. However, it's important to note that there are limitations to relying solely on internal financing. Not all projects may be fully funded through internal resources, especially for large-scale investments or expansion initiatives. In such cases, companies may still need to seek external financing despite the higher associated costs. Additionally, using internal resources for financing may limit the company's ability to pursue other growth opportunities or retain sufficient liquidity for operational needs. Overall, while the impact of asymmetric information may make external financing more expensive compared to internal financing, companies must carefully evaluate the trade-offs and consider a balanced approach to financing that aligns with their long-term strategic objectives and financial capabilities.

An important aspect of imperfect information in financial markets known as the "hidden action problem," which pertains to the behavior of managers after a project is financed. This problem arises because external providers of financial resources, such as lenders or investors, lack complete visibility into managers' actions and how they utilize the funds allocated for the project. In this scenario, managers may have asymmetric information regarding the risks and potential returns associated with different projects, and they may choose to pursue riskier but potentially more profitable ventures without fully disclosing this information to external stakeholders. For instance, if a company has two projects, A and B, and both require a $1 million initial investment, with A being riskier but potentially more profitable than B, managers might allocate the funds to project A after securing financing from a bank.

The hidden action problem creates uncertainty for lenders, as they cannot accurately assess the risk associated with the projects and the likelihood of repayment. As a result, lenders may demand higher interest rates or impose stricter terms to compensate for this uncertainty and mitigate the risk of moral hazard, where managers may act in their own self-interest rather than in the best interests of the company and its creditors.

If lenders had perfect knowledge of managers' behavior and the risks associated with each project, they could differentiate interest rates, accordingly, charging higher rates for riskier projects to reflect the increased likelihood of default. However, due to the hidden action problem, lenders often apply a uniform interest rate or adopt conservative lending practices to account for the uncertainty surrounding managers' actions.

As a result, the cost of external financing tends to be higher than internal financing, where managers are more accountable to internal stakeholders, such as shareholders or the board of directors. Internal financing may also provide greater control and flexibility over the allocation of funds, as managers are subject to internal governance mechanisms and oversight. Overall, the hidden action problem contributes to the perceived riskiness of external financing and underscores the importance of transparency, monitoring, and governance mechanisms in mitigating moral hazard and ensuring the efficient allocation of financial resources.

In the context of sustainability, the impact of both disclosed information and undisclosed actions is significantly amplified, especially when companies prioritize non-financial objectives. This observation underscores the interconnectedness between sustainability issues and corporate behavior.

This perspective leads to the consideration of profound implications. It suggests that in today's business landscape, where sustainability concerns are increasingly central, the consequences of corporate actions extend well beyond financial metrics. Instead, they reverberate through various dimensions of society, affecting stakeholders, ecosystems, and future generations.

Recognizing this amplification effect emphasizes the importance of transparency and accountability in corporate practices. It's not sufficient for businesses to merely disclose their sustainability initiatives; they must ensure that their actions align with their stated goals. Failure to do so not only risks reputational damage but also exacerbates the negative impacts of unsustainable practices.

Moreover, this perspective encourages a reassessment of how corporate performance is evaluated. Success can no longer be solely measured in financial terms; instead, it must encompass broader considerations such as environmental stewardship, social responsibility, and ethical conduct. In essence, sustainability becomes not just a checkbox but a fundamental aspect of corporate strategy and identity.

In summary, this perspective highlights the intertwined nature of sustainability, corporate behavior, and stakeholder trust. It serves as a reminder that in the pursuit of non-financial goals, the consequences of actions are amplified, making transparency, integrity, and sustainability essential pillars of modern business practices.

2.3 Capital Structure: Theoretical Foundations and Empirical Insights

2.3.1 Trade-off Theory

The trade-off theory of capital structure, evolving from Modigliani and Miller's foundational work, emerged in the 1970s to integrate practical factors like tax advantages and bankruptcy risks. According to this theory, companies aim to strike a balance between the benefits of debt—such as tax shields—and the associated costs, which encompass personal tax implications, bankruptcy risks, and agency costs (Berens & Cuny, 1995). This strategic approach allows firms to determine their optimal mix of debt and equity in order to maximize their overall value (Qin, 2024).

In real-world applications, the trade-off theory involves analyzing how changes in capital structure, influenced by factors like interest tax shields and the probability of insolvency, impact a company's financing decisions (Reinhard & Li, 2010). By carefully evaluating these elements, firms can assess the trade-offs inherent in debt financing and strive to achieve a capital structure that balances the advantages and disadvantages effectively (Chemosit & Atheru, 2021). This approach recognizes that companies typically utilize a combination of debt and equity financing to fulfill their financial requirements, underscoring the importance of maintaining a balanced approach to optimize long-term strategic objectives (Buvanendra, 2017).

Moreover, the trade-off theory emphasizes the critical task of identifying an optimal capital structure that maximizes company value by meticulously weighing the costs and benefits associated with assuming additional debt (Ahadiya, 2021). Furthermore, the dynamic trade-off theory expands on these principles by acknowledging that firms may not always operate at their target capital structure but engage in adaptive behavior over time to approach this ideal level (Ford, 2020).

Empirical studies have explored various facets of the trade-off theory, including its application in the context of corporate tax policies and capital structure decisions. While corporate taxes exert an influence on debt financing choices, empirical evidence regarding the precise application of the trade-off theory remains mixed ("Effect of Corporate Tax Cuts on Capital Structure in the US: A Short Run Analysis", 2019). This nuanced analysis underscores the complexity of balancing debt and equity considerations in corporate finance.

In contrast to the pecking order theory, which posits that firms prioritize internal financing sources before external debt issuance (Serrasqueiro & Caetano, 2014), the trade-off theory emphasizes a deliberate evaluation process to optimize firm value through the strategic use of debt and equity. Comparative studies between these theories have sought to elucidate whether small and medium-sized enterprises (SMEs) align more closely with the assumptions of the trade-off theory or the pecking order theory in their capital structure decisions (Martínez et al., 2019).

In summary, the trade-off theory of capital structure remains a cornerstone concept in corporate finance, providing firms with a framework to navigate the intricacies of financing decisions. By carefully assessing the trade-offs associated with debt financing, companies can aim to establish an optimal capital structure that enhances their overall value and resilience in competitive markets.

2.3.2 Pecking-Order Theory

Myers (1984) proposed the pecking-order theory as an alternative view, suggesting that firms have a preference for internal financing (retained earnings) over external financing (debt or equity issuance). This preference stems from asymmetric information between managers and investors: managers believe that external financing signals undervaluation, potentially leading to adverse market reactions. Thus, firms prefer internal funds first, followed by debt, and equity as a last resort.

The most cited papers on the Pecking Order Theory provide valuable insights into the dynamics of capital structure decisions in corporate finance. One of the seminal works in this area is by (Frank & Goyal, 2003), which delves into testing the pecking order theory of capital structure. This study contributes significantly to understanding how firms prioritize internal financing over external sources like debt and equity issuance. Another notable paper is by (Sofat & Singh, 2017), which explores the determinants of capital structure through an empirical study of manufacturing firms in India. By analyzing the relationship between various theories of capital structure and empirical data, Sofat and Singh shed light on the factors influencing firms' financing choices, particularly emphasizing the pecking order theory. These papers underscore the importance of the pecking order theory in guiding firms' capital structure decisions and offer valuable insights into the practical implications of this theory in the realm of corporate finance.

2.4 Signalling Theory and Agency Costs

Signalling models in corporate finance, introduced by Ross (1977) and expanded by Leland and Pyle (1977), provide a framework to address the issue of asymmetric information between insiders, typically management, and outsiders, such as investors. The fundamental premise of signalling models is that firms can use their capital structure decisions, particularly the issuance of debt, as a means to convey valuable information about their quality and future prospects to the market.

In a market plagued by information asymmetry, where insiders possess more detailed knowledge about the firm's operations and financial health than external investors, the issuance of debt can serve as a credible signal. By choosing to take on debt, firms signal to the market that they are confident about their future profitability and cash flow prospects. This confidence is inferred because debt holders have a priority claim on the firm's cash flows, implying that the firm expects to generate sufficient cash to meet its debt obligations. This signal helps mitigate adverse selection problems, where potential investors may be wary of investing due to incomplete or asymmetric information.

Moreover, signalling through capital structure decisions aligns the interests of shareholders and management. Managers, acting as stewards of shareholder wealth, have an incentive to maximize firm value. By strategically choosing the level and type of debt, managers can signal their commitment to safeguarding shareholder interests and pursuing value-enhancing projects. This alignment is crucial in large corporations where the separation of ownership (shareholders) and control (management) can lead to agency costs.

Agency costs, as highlighted by La Porta et al. (1998, 2000), arise due to conflicts of interest between shareholders and managers. These conflicts are exacerbated by the delegation of decision-making authority to managers who may prioritize their own interests over those of shareholders. One-way managers can mitigate agency costs is by retaining cash rather than distributing it as dividends or using it for debt repayment. This conservative approach signals to shareholders that management is committed to maintaining financial flexibility and safeguarding against potential future adverse conditions.

Furthermore, the signalling effect of debt issuance can influence capital structure decisions beyond just conveying information. For instance, firms may choose to issue equity rather than debt if they believe their prospects are uncertain or if they want to avoid sending misleading signals of financial distress. This strategic decision-making process underscores the complexity of capital structure decisions in balancing financial risk and signalling clarity.

Empirical studies have supported the validity of signalling models in various contexts. For example, firms with stronger financial health and growth prospects are more likely to issue debt at lower costs, reflecting market confidence in their future performance. Conversely, firms facing financial difficulties or with uncertain prospects may find it more challenging or expensive to raise debt capital, as investors interpret such actions as signals of heightened risk.

In conclusion, signalling models offer a valuable perspective on capital structure decisions by emphasizing the role of debt issuance in communicating firm quality and prospects to the market. By signalling their financial health and commitment to shareholder value, firms can mitigate adverse selection problems, align shareholder-manager interests, and manage agency costs effectively. As such, understanding the dynamics of signalling in capital structure decisions remains essential for corporate finance theory and practice alike.

Some evidence

Empirical studies have provided insights into how capital structure varies across different countries and economic environments. Rajan and Zingales (1995) conducted a pioneering study across G7 countries, identifying significant differences in capital structure preferences influenced by legal, institutional, and cultural factors. Their findings underscored the importance of regulatory environments and financial market development in shaping corporate financing decisions.

Graham and Harvey's (2001) survey of Chief Financial Officers (CFOs) corroborated the pecking-order theory, indicating that firms tend to prioritize internal financing over external sources due to perceived adverse market reactions to equity issuance. This survey highlighted industry-specific variations in capital structure preferences, influenced by sector-specific risks and opportunities.

Cheng et al. (2010) explored non-linear relationships between financial leverage and firm performance among Chinese firms, revealing an inverted-U relationship known as the trade-off theory. This empirical finding suggests that while moderate levels of debt may enhance firm value through tax shields and increased financial flexibility, excessive leverage can lead to financial distress and reduced profitability.

Pre-2009 studies by Sarni (2008) illustrated the challenges faced by small and medium-sized enterprises (SMEs) in southern Italy, where firms relied heavily on internal resources due to limited access to external financing. Recent research by Cipollini and Parla (2018) further highlighted asymmetries in credit supply between northern and southern regions of Italy, underscoring the regional dimensions of capital structure decisions.

2.5 Introduction to Banks' Commitments and Sustainable Innovations

From the banks' perspective, if management considers reputational risk related to not being seriously involved in sustainability and climate change, they may prefer to cut financial resources provided to certain sectors, such as fossil fuels. This cautious approach stems from growing scrutiny by stakeholders, including investors, customers, and regulatory bodies, who increasingly expect financial institutions to contribute positively to environmental goals. However, there is evidence suggesting that the fossil fuel sector contributes significantly to innovations that drive a decarbonized economy.

The reputational risk associated with funding high-emission industries has become a pressing concern for banks. As public awareness and regulatory pressures regarding climate change intensify, banks are motivated to align their portfolios with sustainable practices. This alignment not only helps mitigate reputational risks but also appeals to a growing segment of environmentally conscious investors and clients. Consequently, many banks have set ambitious climate targets, pledging to reduce or eliminate financing for fossil fuel projects to showcase their commitment to sustainability.

Fossil fuel companies significantly contribute to green innovation, as highlighted by Cohen et al. (2020), suggesting that divestment might inadvertently impede the progress of essential climate solutions. Fossil fuel companies, with their substantial resources and expertise, are well-positioned to develop and implement green technologies. Their investment in research and development can lead to breakthroughs in reducing emissions and improving energy efficiency, thus playing a crucial role in the transition to a sustainable economy. Therefore, a blanket divestment from these companies might not only hinder the development of green technologies but also slow down the overall pace of achieving climate goals.

Similarly, Ye (2022) finds that banks setting climate targets reduce lending to high-emission firms, which leads to a decrease in green patent filings by these firms. This indicates that high-emission firms rely heavily on financial support to invest in green innovations. When banks withdraw funding, these firms' ability to pursue and develop green technologies diminishes, resulting in fewer green patents. However, Ye also observes that this reduction in green patent filings by high-emission firms is offset by an increase in green patent filings by other firms. This suggests a redistribution of innovation efforts, where firms that are already more aligned with green practices or have better access to funding continue to push forward with green innovations.

Measuring engagement in low-emission strategies, rather than divestment, is challenging because engagement requires more time and valuable measures in terms of emission reductions. Engagement involves working closely with high-emission firms to help them transition to greener practices, which can be a long and complex process. It involves setting targets, providing technical assistance, and monitoring progress, which are all resource-intensive activities. Moreover, the results of such engagement, in terms of emission reductions, may not be immediately visible, making it difficult to measure and assess the effectiveness of these strategies.

Consequently, it is easier to measure divestment rather than the engagement efforts of banks, which may also lead to potential greenwashing or green window dressing. Divestment is a straightforward action that can be easily quantified and communicated to stakeholders. However, it does not necessarily lead to real-world emission reductions or improvements in green innovation. In contrast, engagement, though harder to measure, can lead to significant and sustainable changes in corporate behavior and emissions. The risk of greenwashing arises when banks and other financial institutions highlight their divestment efforts to appear environmentally responsible without making substantial contributions to actual emission reductions or supporting green innovations. This superficial approach can mislead stakeholders and undermine the broader efforts to combat climate change.

In conclusion, while divestment from high-emission firms might seem like a direct way to address climate change, it is essential to consider the potential drawbacks, such as impeding green innovation by fossil fuel companies. A more effective strategy might involve a balanced approach that includes both engagement and selective divestment. By working with high-emission firms to support their transition to greener practices, banks and other financial institutions can foster meaningful progress in green innovation and emission reductions. However, this requires robust mechanisms to measure and communicate the impact of engagement efforts to avoid greenwashing and ensure that real progress is being made.

References

Ahadiya, A. (2021). Assesing the financial performance: In perspective environmental performance, csr, gcg, and leverage. *Iptek Journal of Proceedings Series, 0*(1), 266. https://doi.org/10.12962/j23546026.y2020i1.7856

Berens, J., & Cuny, C. (1995). The capital structure puzzle revisited. *Review of Financial Studies, 8*(4), 1185–1208. https://doi.org/10.1093/rfs/8.4.1185

Buvanendra, S. (2017). Capital structure dynamics: Near vs. off target firms in Sri Lanka. *Colombo Business Journal International Journal of Theory and Practice, 8*(1), 62–81. https://doi.org/10.4038/cbj.v8i1.13

Chemosit, J., & Atheru, G. (2021). Financial leverage and performance of the energy and petroleum sector companies listed in the Nairobi securities exchange. *International Journal of Current Aspects in Finance Banking and Accounting, 3*(2), 113–128. https://doi.org/10.35942/ijcfa.v3i2.208

Chen, C., Huang, H., & Lee, C. H. (2022). Supply chain, product pricing, and dynamic capital structure. *International Review of Economics & Finance, 80*, 938–952.

Cheng, M., Lin, J., Hsiao, T., & Lin, T.W. (2010). Invested resource, competitive intellectual capital, and corporate performance, *Journal of Intellectual Capital, 11*(4), pp. 433–450. https://doi.org/10.1108/14691931011085623

Cipollini, A., & Parla, F. (2018). Credit demand and supply shocks in Italy during the great recession. *Applied Economics, 50*(53), 5795–5813. https://doi.org/10.1080/00036846.2018.1488066

Cohen, L., Gurun, U. G., & Nguyen, Q. (2020). *The ESG-innovation disconnect: Evidence from green patenting*. European Corporate Governance Institute–Finance Working Paper No. 744/2021. Revised February 2024

Ford, J. (2020). An empirical investigation of dynamic trade-off theory: Evidence from sri lankan non-financial firms. *Peradeniya Management Review, 2*(2), 65. https://doi.org/10.4038/pmr.v2i2.40

Frank, M., & Goyal, V. (2003). Testing the pecking order theory of capital structure. *Journal of Financial Economics, 67*(2), 217–248. https://doi.org/10.1016/s0304-405x(02)00252-0

Graham, J. R., & Harvey, C. R. (2001). The theory and practice of corporate finance: Evidence from the field. *Journal of Financial Economics, 61*, 187–243.

La Porta, R., Lopez-de-Silanes, F., Shleifer, A., & Vishny, R. W. (2000). Agency problems around the world. *Journal of Finance, 55*, 1–33.

La Porta, R., Lopez-de-SIlanes, F., Shleifer, A., & Vishny, R. W. (1998). Law and finance. *Journal of Political Economy, 1998*(106), 1113–1155.

Leland, H. E., & Pyle, D. H., (1977). Informational asymmetries, financial structure, and financial intermediation. *Journal of Finance, 32*, 371–387. https://doi.org/10.2307/2326770

Martínez, L., Scherger, V., & Guercio, M. (2019). Smes capital structure: Trade-off or pecking order theory: A systematic review. *Journal of Small Business and Enterprise Development, 26*(1), 105–132. https://doi.org/10.1108/jsbed-12-2017-0387

Modigliani, F., & Miller, M. H. (1958). The cost of capital, corporation finance and the theory of investment. *The American Economic Review, 48*(3), 261–297. (37 pages).

Myers, S. C. (1984). The capital structure puzzle. *J. Finance, 39*, 575–592. https://doi.org/10.1111/j.1540-6261.1984.tb03646.x

Qin, J. (2024). Application of trade-off theory in real-life corporate capital structure adjustments. *Advances in Economics Management and Political Sciences, 76*(1), 88–93. https://doi.org/10.54254/2754-1169/76/20241901

Rajan, R. G., & Zingales, L. (1995). What do we know about capital structure? Some evidence from international data. *The Journal of Finance, 50*(5), 1421–1460.

Reinhard, L., & Li, S. (2010). A note on capital structure target adjustment—Indonesian evidence. *International Journal of Managerial Finance, 6*(3), 245–259. https://doi.org/10.1108/17439131011056242

Ross, S. A. (1977). The determination of financial structure: The incentive signaling approach. *The Bell Journal of Economics, 8*, 1–32.

Sarni., D., 2008. Capital structure and growth of the firms in the backward regions of the south Italy, Applied Financial Economics 18(10):821-833 https://doi.org/10.1080/09603100701222309

Serrasqueiro, Z., & Caetano, A. (2014). Trade-off theory versus pecking order theory: Capital structure decisions in a peripheral region of Portugal. *Journal of Business Economics and Management, 16*(2), 445–466. https://doi.org/10.3846/16111699.2012.744344

Sofat, R., & Singh, S. (2017). Determinants of capital structure: An empirical study of manufacturing firms in India. *International Journal of Law and Management, 59*(6), 1029–1045. https://doi.org/10.1108/ijlma-05-2016-0051

Ye, Z. (2022, October 16). *Bank divestment and green innovation*. Available at SSRN: https://ssrn.com/abstract=4324996 or https://doi.org/10.2139/ssrn.4324996.

Chapter 3
Integrating ESG Risk into the Banking Prudential Framework in EU: The Impact on SMEs

3.1 Banks and SMEs: What Are Connections?

Banks play a crucial role in financing SMEs, profoundly impacting their growth and sustainability. The dynamic relationship between banks and SMEs is complex, influenced by various factors including market power, firm characteristics, and institutional frameworks. This intricate interplay is well-documented in various research studies, each shedding light on different aspects of SME financing.

Ryan et al. (2014) delve into how bank market power can either alleviate or exacerbate credit constraints faced by SMEs. Their study, focusing on 20 European countries, reveals that significant bank influence can both support and hinder financial accessibility for SMEs, depending on the strategic objectives and regulatory environments of these banks. This study sets the stage for understanding how market power can shape the SME financing landscape.

Building on this foundation, Dong and Men (2014) explore the dynamics of SME financing in emerging markets. They emphasize the interplay between firm characteristics, banking structures, and institutional frameworks, highlighting the diverse factors that influence SME financing. For instance, an SME's size, age, and industry sector significantly impact its ability to secure financing, as does the regulatory and economic context of its operating country. This analysis underscores the multifaceted nature of SME financing, presenting a broader view of the challenges and opportunities within emerging markets.

Shihadeh et al. (2019) further emphasize the critical role banks play in enhancing SME sustainability by providing essential financial services, technology, and business solutions. Banks act as enablers for SMEs, contributing to their long-term viability through tailored financial products, advisory services, and digital banking solutions. This study highlights the importance of technology, noting how digital banking platforms can streamline access to financial services and improve transaction efficiency. Wu and Wang (2021) offer insights into the role of private banks in

M. Aliano et al., *Sustainable Finance for SMEs*, Sustainable Finance,
https://doi.org/10.1007/978-3-031-74193-7_3

alleviating financing challenges for SMEs. Their work underscores the importance of diverse banking institutions in addressing the financial needs of SMEs. Private banks, with their flexibility and ability to offer customized financial solutions, can be particularly effective in meeting the unique needs of SMEs. This perspective broadens the understanding of the financial ecosystem, emphasizing the need for a variety of banking options. Zhang (2021) shifts the focus to the factors influencing the financing efficiency of SMEs, particularly the bank-enterprise relationship. This study highlights the interconnectedness between banks and SMEs, emphasizing the symbiotic nature of their relationship. A strong, trust-based relationship can enhance financing efficiency, reduce borrowing costs, and improve credit terms for SMEs. This research underscores the importance of building robust relationships to facilitate better financial outcomes for SMEs. Adding a unique dimension to the discussion, Trimulato (2021) examines the synergy between Islamic Banks and Fintech in supporting SMEs, particularly in Indonesia. This highlights the evolving landscape of SME financing, where innovative financial solutions are being leveraged to empower small businesses and drive economic growth. Islamic banking principles, combined with fintech innovations, offer new financing avenues compliant with Sharia law and accessible to a broader segment of the SME population. Love and Pería (2014) delve into how bank competition impacts firms' access to finance, shedding light on the implications of competitive dynamics on SME lending. Increased competition among banks can lead to better terms and conditions for SME loans, although it can also result in tighter credit standards and more stringent risk assessments. This study is crucial for understanding the nuances of bank competition and its effect on the availability of financing options for SMEs. Effendi and Yasmin (2017) focus on Islamic Rural Banks (BPRS) in Indonesia and their role in providing financing for SME development. These banks operate under Islamic banking principles and play a vital role in supporting SMEs in rural areas by offering interest-free loans and profit-sharing arrangements. This research showcases the diverse range of banking institutions that contribute to SME financing in different regions. Maiti (2018) provides insights into the financing landscape for Micro, Small, and Medium Enterprises (MSMEs) in India, highlighting the dominance of domestic banks in catering to the financing needs of these enterprises. Domestic banks, with their deep understanding of the local market and regulatory environment, are well-positioned to offer financial products and services tailored to the needs of MSMEs. This study underscores the importance of local banking institutions in supporting MSME growth. Gololo (2017) evaluates the role of commercial banks in financing SMEs in Nigeria, emphasizing the pivotal role these banks play in addressing the financing requirements of small and medium-scale enterprises. Despite challenges such as high default rates and limited credit information, commercial banks in Nigeria remain crucial in providing the necessary financial support for SME growth. This research highlights the regional variations in SME financing and the essential role of commercial banks in different economic contexts.

In conclusion, the role of banks in financing SMEs is multifaceted, encompassing aspects of market power, sustainability, competition, and institutional diversity. By understanding the intricate relationship between banks and SMEs, policymakers and stakeholders can work towards creating a conducive environment for SME growth and development through tailored financial solutions and supportive banking practices. This comprehensive approach can lead to a more vibrant and resilient SME sector, contributing to overall economic growth and stability.

Banks are not free in their lending activities due to the extensive regulations and oversight imposed by various authorities. These rules and regulations are designed to ensure the stability and integrity of the financial system, protect consumers, and promote fair lending practices. However, they also create a complex operating environment for banks, which must navigate these constraints while striving to meet the financial needs of their clients, particularly SMEs.

SMEs are critical to economic growth, innovation, and employment, making access to financing vital for their development and sustainability. Banks play a crucial role in providing this financing, offering a range of financial products and services that support SME growth. These include loans, lines of credit, and financial advisory services tailored to the unique needs of smaller enterprises. The relationship between banks and SMEs is symbiotic: SMEs rely on banks for capital, while banks benefit from the business and growth of these enterprises.

In this chapter, we summarize the importance of banks for SMEs by exploring how banks facilitate their growth and the broader economic impact of this support. We highlight the crucial role that banks play in offering not just financing, but also the expertise and resources necessary for SMEs to thrive in a competitive market. This includes helping SMEs manage their cash flows, investing in new projects, and navigating periods of financial uncertainty. After this synopsis, we go into the limitations that banks have when it comes to lending money to SMEs. These limitations result from a plethora of legislative mandates and the supervision of financial authorities. Regulations that control banks' capital requirements, lending policies, and risk management procedures are enforced by regulatory agencies, including central banks, financial supervisory authorities, and international organizations like the Basel Committee on Banking Supervision. Banks are required, for example, to maintain a specific level of capital reserves in relation to their risk-weighted assets under capital adequacy standards. This restricts the amount of capital that can be lent, but it also guarantees that banks can absorb losses and safeguard depositors. Furthermore, SMEs may find it more challenging to get approved for loans because of strict credit underwriting guidelines and risk assessment processes that are intended to reduce default risk, particularly for those with little collateral or credit history. The lending procedure is made even more difficult by the need to comply with anti-money laundering (AML) and counter-terrorism financing (CTF) legislation. In order to make sure they are not supporting illegal activity, banks need to perform extensive due diligence on all of their clients, including SMEs. This may result in higher operating expenses and longer loan processing times, adding to the obstacles faced by SMEs looking for funding in a timely manner.

Furthermore, banks are subject to onerous administrative obligations due to a variety of reporting and transparency requirements, including those imposed by the Dodd-Frank Act in the US and the Capital Requirements Directive (CRD) in the European Union. Resources may be diverted from customer-facing activities and towards regulatory compliance in order to comply with these laws, which call for extensive reporting on lending activity, risk exposures, and financial health.

The lending activities of banks are influenced not just by regulatory limitations but also by macroeconomic considerations and market conditions. The availability and cost of loans can be impacted by market demand changes, interest rate swings, and economic downturns. Banks must strike a compromise between the requirement to preserve financial stability and profitability and the need to assist SMEs.

The need for banks to strike a careful balance between lending money to SMEs and adhering to regulations is highlighted in this chapter. We can comprehend the difficulties banks encounter and look at potential solutions to improve SME access to funding by knowing the regulatory environment and how it affects lending practices. This could involve efforts to enhance credit risk assessment for SMEs, regulatory changes that expedite compliance procedures, and creative financial products catered to the requirements of smaller enterprises.

This chapter is organized as follows. Section 3.2 delves into the complexities of transition and reputational risks that banks face in managing a decarbonized economy. It explores how these risks arise from the shift towards sustainable practices and the implications for banks' reputations if they fail to adapt effectively. The discussion encompasses the various dimensions of transition risk, including policy changes, technological advancements, and market shifts, and examines how these factors can influence a bank's operational and strategic decisions.

Section 3.3 provides an in-depth analysis of how transition risk is regulated within the European Union. This section highlights the legislative frameworks and regulatory guidelines that govern the management of transition risk. It discusses the integration of these regulations into a strategic view, emphasizing the importance of aligning bank strategies with EU policies to mitigate risks and capitalize on opportunities in the green transition. The section also examines case studies of EU banks that have successfully integrated transition risk management into their strategic planning.

Section 3.4 shifts focus to the regulatory constraints that impact lending activities, particularly for SMEs. It outlines the roles of various regulatory bodies and the specific rules that banks must adhere to when lending. This section discusses how these constraints can limit lending activities and the potential repercussions for SMEs that rely heavily on bank financing. It also explores the balance banks must strike between complying with regulations and meeting the financing needs of SMEs, which are crucial for economic growth and innovation.

In Sect. 3.5, the chapter describes various models for assessing the impact of ESG factors on credit portfolios, as recommended by the European Banking Authority (EBA). This section introduces different methodologies for integrating ESG considerations into credit risk assessment, providing a detailed overview of best practices and innovative approaches. It covers the technical aspects of these models, including data requirements, analytical techniques, and the interpretation of results, and highlights the benefits and challenges of incorporating ESG factors into credit risk management.

Finally, Section 3.6 concludes the chapter by addressing the challenges banks face in managing transition risks. This section synthesizes the insights from the previous sections and presents a comprehensive view of the obstacles and opportunities in the transition to a decarbonized economy. It discusses the strategic, operational, and regulatory challenges that banks encounter and suggests potential solutions and strategies for overcoming these hurdles. The conclusion emphasizes the critical importance of proactive risk management and the need for banks to continuously adapt to the evolving landscape of sustainability and regulatory requirements.

Throughout the chapter, a combination of theoretical analysis, empirical evidence, and practical case studies is used to illustrate the key points and provide a robust understanding of the issues at hand. The goal is to equip readers with the knowledge and tools needed to navigate the complex interplay of risks and regulations in the context of a transitioning economy and to foster a strategic approach to managing these challenges.

3.2 Bank and Sustainability: Between Transition and Reputational Risks

The challenge of transitioning to a decarbonized world is huge, impacting not only humanity but also the global banking system in profound ways. Recognizing the urgency of combating climate change while sustaining financial performance, banks play a pivotal role in addressing climate challenges. They support countries' efforts to adapt to environmental pressures and enhance financial resilience against climate risks (Park & Kim, 2020). Moreover, the banking sector serves as a cornerstone in driving the transition towards a sustainable green economy (Kılıç & Kuzey, 2019; Cerrone, 2022), shifting its focus from mere profit maximization to addressing reputational risks associated with insufficient action on climate change.

From a financial standpoint, transitioning to a decarbonized economy poses potential risks to bank loan portfolios. Banks may need to reduce exposures to carbon-intensive sectors, thereby impacting revenues from lending activities. A disorderly transition could jeopardize financial stability, extending risks beyond loans to bonds and equities where banks allocate resources (European Central Bank, 2024). Despite generating significant interest income, these sectors' high exposure may expose banks to reputational risks due to perceived lack of commitment to economic transition goals (Basel Committee, 2021). Shifting consumer sentiments and heightened scrutiny could exacerbate these risks, leading to liability issues related to controversial environmental financing (European Central Bank, 2020). Moreover, companies in carbon-intensive sectors may face increased default risks as they adjust production to align with sustainability requirements, potentially impacting credit risks. Loss Given Default (LGD) could rise if collateral values decline amid the sustainability shift, necessitating robust risk management strategies.

In contrast, media reports highlight that banks' efforts to combat climate change and facilitate economic decarbonization have been inadequate. Despite global advocacy for climate mitigation, major banks continued substantial financial support for fossil fuel industries, with $705 billion directed towards them in 2023 alone (Banking on Climate Chaos report, 2024). Since the Paris Agreement, these banks have collectively channeled approximately $6.9 trillion into fossil fuel enterprises, indicating a persistent reliance on fossil fuels despite evolving market conditions and regulatory pressures (The New York Times, The Banker). This trend underscores ongoing challenges in aligning financial strategies with environmental goals, influenced by diverse energy policies and global banking decisions.

In summary, while transitioning to a low-carbon economy is crucial for global sustainability, it presents multifaceted challenges and risks for the banking sector. Effective management, strategic planning, and enhanced transparency are essential to navigate these challenges while maintaining financial stability and making meaningful contributions to climate action.

3.3 Introduction to ESG Risk in Banking: Evidence from EU

In recent years, Environmental, Social, and Governance (ESG) risks have become a pivotal focus for the banking sector, driven by increasing regulatory pressures and the growing awareness of the impact of these risks on financial stability. To ensure resilience and sustainability, it is imperative to integrate ESG risks into the banking prudential framework. This chapter explores how banks are currently exposed to ESG risks, the projected impacts over various time horizons, and the comprehensive approaches recommended by the European Banking Authority (EBA) to manage these risks effectively. This surge in interest is driven by the increasing recognition of the critical role that banks play in promoting sustainable finance and the broader impact of their operations on environmental and social outcomes. Various studies have delved into the realm of ESG evaluation in banks, shedding light on sustainable finance and its impact on bank performance.

Menicucci and Paolucci (2022) provided valuable insights into the Italian banking sector, revealing that ESG policies can have a negative impact on operational and market performance. This finding highlights the complexities involved in balancing sustainability practices with financial outcomes within the banking industry. It suggests that while ESG initiatives are essential for long-term sustainability, they may pose short-term challenges that banks need to manage carefully.

Kosasih et al. (2021) highlighted the need to assess the impact of sustainable banking disclosure on bank efficiency. Their study indicated the relevance of evaluating the performance of banks implementing sustainable practices. By assessing how sustainable banking disclosures influence operational efficiency, banks can identify best practices and areas for improvement in their ESG strategies. Buallay (2019) investigated the association between sustainability reporting (ESG) and performance in the European banking sector. The study emphasized the relationship between ESG factors and operational, financial, and market performance metrics. Buallay's findings suggest that robust sustainability reporting practices are linked to better performance outcomes, reinforcing the importance of transparent ESG disclosures.

The literature also delves into the regulatory aspects of sustainable finance within the banking sector. Abubakar and Handayani (2019) discussed the juridical implications of implementing sustainable finance principles, emphasizing the importance of sustainable reporting for bank accountability and governance transparency. Pyka and Nocoń (2021) focused on banks' capital requirements in the context of sustainable finance, highlighting the integration of green finance principles into risk management strategies. They argued that incorporating ESG considerations into capital requirements is essential for promoting sustainable banking practices and ensuring long-term financial stability.

Azad et al. (2022) provided policy insights on green finance and sustainable finance disbursement, emphasizing the need for banks to align with SDGs goals through increased green and sustainable finance initiatives. Their study highlighted the importance of policy frameworks in promoting sustainable finance practices and achieving global sustainability targets.

Overall, these studies collectively underscore the importance of evaluating ESG practices, integrating sustainable finance principles, and aligning banking operations with environmental, social, and governance considerations to drive long-term value and sustainability within the banking sector. The comprehensive evaluation of ESG practices not only enhances the sustainability and resilience of banks but also contributes to broader societal and environmental goals, reinforcing the critical role of the banking sector in promoting sustainable development.

3.3.1 The Role of Green Asset Ratio (GAR)

The European Union's Sustainable Finance Action Plan, which was created to direct money toward sustainable investments and manage financial risks associated with climate change and environmental degradation, gave rise to the Green Asset Ratio (GAR) for European banks. The EU Taxonomy Regulation, which established a categorization system for sustainable economic activities and was implemented in June 2020, formally required the GAR. Financial institutions, including banks, are required to reveal the percentage of their lending and investment activities that are in line with the taxonomy,[1] with the goal of establishing a common language for investors, businesses, and policymakers.

According to the EU Taxonomy, the GAR calculates the percentage of a bank's assets that are ecologically sustainable. This includes loans, investments, and other financial exposures that provide a substantial contribution to environmental goals,

[1] https://ec.europa.eu/info/publications/sustainable-finance-taxonomy_en

including biodiversity, water and marine resource conservation, pollution avoidance, the circular economy, and climate change adaptation and mitigation. The ratio of green assets to total assets—which includes all the bank's assets—is the formula for GAR. Green assets are those that satisfy the EU Taxonomy requirements.

It is anticipated that GAR would improve accountability and transparency about banks' contributions to environmental sustainability, enabling stakeholders and investors to make more informed decisions. By encouraging banks to move their holdings toward more environmentally friendly assets, it supports green investments. It also assists regulators and banks in recognizing and controlling environmental hazards in the financial system. The GAR can help banks gain more credibility and attract investors if they show a strong commitment to sustainability.[2]

The GAR has, nonetheless, raised a number of issues. Because of the EU Taxonomy's complexity, banks have a difficult time evaluating and classifying their assets in accordance with its precise requirements. Due to its intricacy, extensive data collection and analysis are necessary, which increases the administrative workload. Since smaller banks might not have the resources to comply, opponents contend that the uniform approach of the taxonomy may not be appropriate for all banks.[3] There have also been concerns expressed about banks seeming more environmentally friendly by inflating the sustainability of their assets, a practice known as "greenwashing." Furthermore, by focusing too much on some industries and ignoring others, the concentration on assets that are in line with taxonomy may cause market distortion and have unforeseen economic repercussions. Banks may have to continuously modify their GAR computations as the taxonomy changes, which might lead to ambiguity and compliance issues.

To summarize, the Green Asset Ratio is a noteworthy advancement in the integration of sustainability into the financial system. Nevertheless, in order to guarantee that it successfully propels the shift to a greener economy without unanticipated negative effects, implementation issues must be solved.

3.3.2 Exposure to ESG Risks: Present and Future Perspectives

There are a number of ways that banks might become exposed to ESG risks in the near future. The short-term operational and financial health of a bank might be immediately impacted by new environmental legislation, societal upheavals, or governance scandals. Changes in stakeholder expectations, market dynamics, and transitional hazards related to the transformation to a low-carbon economy might provide major obstacles in the medium run. Long-term environmental shifts,

---

[2] https://www.ecb.europa.eu/pub/pdf/other/ssm.202101_finalguideontheclimaterelatedandenvironmentalrisks~58213f6564.en.pdf

[3] www.afme.eu/portals/0/globalassets/downloads/consultation-responses/afme-eu-taxonomy-position-paper.pdf

enduring societal problems, and changes in governance can significantly affect the risk environment, calling for proactive and flexible risk management techniques.

ESG risks can have profound implications for different types of financial risks within a bank. Environmental degradation or social instability can impair the ability of borrowers to repay loans, leading to higher default rates and impacting credit risk. Fluctuations in market values due to ESG-related events can affect trading portfolios and investment valuations, influencing market risk. ESG events can also trigger sudden cash outflows or reduce the marketability of certain assets, thereby impacting liquidity. Furthermore, failures in managing ESG issues can lead to operational disruptions and damage the bank's reputation, affecting customer trust and business continuity. Investors and depositors increasingly consider ESG factors influencing a bank's access to capital and funding costs, thereby affecting funding risk.

The European Banking Authority (2021) has identified three primary approaches to integrating ESG risks into the banking prudential framework: the portfolio alignment method, the risk framework method (including scenario analysis), and the exposure method. These approaches provide a structured pathway for banks to align their portfolios with ESG objectives, integrate ESG risks into their risk management frameworks, and assess their exposure to ESG-related factors.

3.4 Strategic Integration of ESG Risks

At the strategic level, banks need to plan for at least a 10-year horizon, testing different scenarios, including qualitative assessments. This involves setting strategic objectives and key performance indicators (KPIs) to define clear ESG-related goals and metrics to track progress. Engaging with borrowers, investee companies, and other stakeholders is crucial to aligning efforts and achieving strategic ESG objectives. Additionally, banks must assess the need for new sustainable products or adjust existing ones to support ESG goals.

Effective governance is crucial for managing ESG risks. Banks should develop clear working procedures for integrating ESG considerations into business operations and define specific ESG-related responsibilities across business lines. Establishing dedicated committees to oversee ESG risk management and revising remuneration policies to align compensation structures with ESG performance and objectives are also essential steps.

To manage ESG risks effectively, banks must establish robust policies that incorporate ESG risks into the assessment of counterparties' financial robustness. Implementing risk monitoring metrics at various levels, including exposure, counterparty, and portfolio, ensures comprehensive oversight. ESG risks should be integrated into the Internal Capital Adequacy Assessment Process (ICAAP) and Internal Liquidity Adequacy Assessment Process (ILAAP). Identifying data and methodology gaps and taking corrective actions are vital for continuous improvement. Developing methodologies to test the resilience of business models and investment strategies against ESG risks is also crucial for understanding and enhancing their robustness.

The EBA emphasizes the importance of integrating ESG risks into the supervisory evaluation of institutions under the CRR/CRD framework. ESG risks need to be proportionately incorporated into various aspects of the business model analysis, including the assessment of the business environment, current business model, strategy, viability, and sustainability. The existing Supervisory Review and Evaluation Process (SREP) may not adequately capture the longer-term impact of ESG risks, necessitating the introduction of a new aspect of analysis focusing on the long-term resilience of business models against relevant public policies or transition trends, with at least a 10-year horizon. ESG risks should be integrated into the assessment of internal governance and controls, as well as drivers of financial risks such as capital, liquidity, and funding risks. Initially, institutions and supervisors should prioritize managing climate-related and broader environmental risks while gradually incorporating social and governance factors into their risk management and supervision processes.

Integrating ESG risks into the banking prudential framework is not just a regulatory necessity but a strategic imperative. By adopting comprehensive approaches and enhancing governance, risk management, and supervisory practices, banks can better navigate the complexities of ESG risks, ensuring long-term resilience and sustainability.

3.4.1 EBA Mandate and Motivations

Article 98(8) of the CRD5 (Capital Requirements Directive and Regulation 5) mandates the development of a uniform definition of ESG risks, encompassing both physical risks and transition risks, with the latter including risks associated with asset depreciation due to regulatory changes. This provision calls for the creation of appropriate qualitative and quantitative criteria to assess the impact of ESG risks on the financial stability of institutions over short, medium, and long-term horizons. These criteria must incorporate stress testing processes and scenario analyses to evaluate the impact of ESG risks under various severity scenarios. Furthermore, it requires institutions to implement specific arrangements, processes, mechanisms, and strategies to identify, assess, and manage ESG risks. This includes the development of analytical methods and tools to determine the impact of ESG risks on lending and financial intermediation activities. Additionally, under Article 434a and Article 449a19 of the CRR2, the EBA is tasked with developing a technical standard for incorporating ESG risks into the Pillar 3 disclosure requirements outlined in Part Eight of the CRR2. This second mandate emphasizes enhancing transparency and accountability in how institutions disclose ESG risks, thereby strengthening the overall resilience and sustainability of the financial sector.

In the financial sector, there is currently a notable lack of a common definition of ESG factors. This absence of uniformity presents significant challenges for banks and financial institutions striving to align with sustainable practices and meet regulatory requirements. Despite this, various global initiatives and frameworks aim to provide guidance and establish standards for integrating ESG considerations into financial operations. Collectively, these initiatives form a complex and evolving landscape that banks must navigate to enhance their sustainability practices.

3.5 A Sea of Rules and Authorities

The United Nations Sustainable Development Goals (SDGs) are a set of 17 interlinked global objectives designed to achieve a better and more sustainable future for all by 2030. These goals encompass a broad range of social, environmental, and economic objectives, providing a comprehensive framework for institutions to align their strategies with global sustainability targets. Banks are encouraged to incorporate these goals into their business models to contribute to overarching sustainability efforts.

Asset owners, institutional investors, investment managers, and service providers may integrate environmental, social, and governance (ESG) considerations into their ownership and investment choices with the help of the Principles for Responsible Investment (PRI). Financial institutions may create long-term profit and manage risk by following these guidelines to make sure that their investing plans represent ethical and sustainable practices.

The Principles for Responsible Banking of the United Nations Environment Programme Finance Initiative (UNEP FI) seek to harmonize bank business strategies with the goals of the SDGs and the Paris Agreement. These guidelines give banks a framework for integrating sustainability into the heart of their business operations, ensuring that their actions support social progress, environmental preservation, and economic expansion.

An improved understanding, management, and communication of an organization's influence on sustainability-related issues is made possible by the Global Sustainability Standards Board Global Reporting Initiative (GRI). Banks may improve their openness and accountability by adhering to GRI standards, giving stakeholders a thorough understanding of their ESG performance and promises.

The Equator Principles offer a common baseline and framework for identifying, assessing, and managing environmental and social risks in project financing. By adopting these principles, banks can ensure that their project financing activities adhere to rigorous environmental and social standards, minimizing risks and promoting sustainable development.

The World Economic Forum (WEF) report on 'Measuring Stakeholder Capitalism' introduces a core set of common metrics and disclosures on non-financial factors. These metrics enable companies to align their mainstream reporting on performance against ESG indicators and track their contributions to the SDGs, enhancing transparency and comparability across the financial sector.

The International Integrated Reporting Council (IIRC) Integrated Reporting Framework provides a comprehensive approach for integrated reporting along six capitals: financial, manufactured, intellectual, human, social and relationship, and natural. This framework aims to offer a more complete picture of how companies create value, integrating ESG factors into their overall business strategy and reporting.

The International Finance Corporation (IFC) Environmental and Social Performance Standards define IFC clients' responsibilities for managing environmental and social risks. These standards offer detailed guidelines for banks to assess and manage ESG risks in their operations and investments, ensuring compliance with international best practices.

The OECD Due Diligence Guidance for Responsible Business Conduct provides practical support to enterprises, offering recommendations on implementing the OECD Guidelines for Multinational Enterprises. These guidelines cover non-binding principles and standards for responsible business conduct in a global context, helping banks navigate ESG-related challenges in international operations.

The Committee of Sponsoring Organizations of the Treadway Commission (COSO) and the World Business Council for Sustainable Development (WBCSD) Guidance for Applying Enterprise Risk Management (ERM) to ESG-related risks proposes approaches to overcome ESG-related risk challenges across the ERM process. This guidance provides methods for managing both upside and downside ESG-related risks, integrating ESG considerations into the overall risk management framework of financial institutions.

The Sustainability Accounting Standards Board (SASB) Standards identify the subset of ESG issues most relevant to financial performance in each of 77 industries. Designed to help companies disclose financially-material sustainability information to investors, these standards enable banks to communicate their ESG performance effectively, aligning sustainability practices with financial objectives.

The multitude of frameworks and initiatives underscores the importance of establishing a common definition of ESG within the banking sector. By leveraging these guidelines, banks can enhance their ESG practices, contributing to global sustainability efforts and ensuring alignment with regulatory expectations. As the landscape of ESG definitions continues to evolve, banks must remain agile and committed to integrating sustainable practices into their core operations, driving long-term value and resilience. Also, for each pillar of ESG, there are a lot of rules.

3.5.1 Environmental Pillar

The Natural Capital Protocol and its Supplement for the Finance sector provide a standardized framework for organizations to identify, measure, and value their impacts and dependencies on natural capital. This protocol helps banks assess the environmental implications of their activities and investments, promoting more sustainable decision-making processes.

The recommendations of the Financial Stability Board Taskforce on Climate-related Financial Disclosures (TCFD) offer a framework to help public companies and other organizations more effectively disclose climate-related risks and opportunities. By integrating TCFD recommendations into their reporting processes, banks can enhance transparency and provide stakeholders with a clearer understanding of how climate risks and opportunities are managed.

The Climate Bond Initiative's Climate Bonds Standard provides sector-specific eligibility criteria for assets and projects that can be labeled as green investments. This standard ensures that investments labeled as green truly contribute to environmental sustainability, helping banks and investors make informed decisions about green finance.

The International Capital Market Association's Green Bond Principles serve as process guidelines that clarify the approach for issuing green bonds. These principles ensure that the proceeds from green bonds are used for environmentally beneficial projects, enhancing the credibility and impact of green finance initiatives.

The Partnership for Carbon Accounting Financials (PCAF) Global GHG Accounting and Reporting Standard for the Financial Industry offers methodological guidance to measure and disclose greenhouse gas emissions associated with various asset classes, including listed equity, corporate bonds, business loans, project finance, commercial real estate, mortgages, and motor vehicle loans. By adopting this standard, banks can systematically account for and disclose their carbon footprint, contributing to global efforts to reduce greenhouse gas emissions.

The Science-Based Targets initiative (SBTi), supported by the Climate Disclosure Project (CDP), UN Global Compact (UNGC), World Resources Institute (WRI), and World Wildlife Fund (WWF), provides targets aligned with the latest climate science necessary to meet the goals of the Paris Agreement. Through SBTi, companies, including banks, can define their paths to reduce greenhouse gas emissions in line with global climate goals, demonstrating a commitment to sustainable development.

These frameworks and standards represent a sea of rules that guide banks in integrating ESG considerations into their operations. By adhering to these guidelines, banks can enhance their sustainability practices, mitigate risks, and contribute to the global agenda of achieving a more sustainable and equitable future. The continuous evolution of these frameworks underscores the dynamic nature of ESG integration in the financial sector, requiring banks to stay informed and adaptive in their approach to sustainability.

3.5.2 Social Pillar: Human Rights and Labor Standards in ESG Frameworks

Incorporating ESG principles into banking practices is not only about environmental sustainability and corporate governance but also about ensuring respect for human rights and labor standards. Several international guidelines and conventions provide a robust framework for banks to follow, ensuring that their operations and business relationships uphold fundamental human rights and labor principles.

The UN Guiding Principles on Business and Human Rights offer a comprehensive set of guidelines for states and companies to prevent, address, and remedy human rights abuses within business operations. These principles emphasize the responsibility of businesses to respect human rights and the role of governments in enforcing these standards. For banks, integrating these principles means conducting due diligence to identify, prevent, mitigate, and account for how they address their impacts on human rights throughout their operations and supply chains.

The "eight fundamental Conventions of the International Labour Organization (ILO)" cover essential subjects considered to be fundamental principles and rights at work. These include the freedom of association and the effective recognition of the right to collective bargaining, the elimination of all forms of forced or compulsory labor, the effective abolition of child labor, and the elimination of discrimination in employment and occupation. For financial institutions, adherence to these conventions is crucial in ensuring that their operations, as well as those of their clients and partners, do not infringe on these fundamental labor rights.

The "United Nations Global Compact" is a non-binding pact designed to encourage businesses worldwide to adopt sustainable and socially responsible policies and to report on their implementation. This initiative provides a principle-based framework for businesses, outlining ten principles in the areas of human rights, labor, the environment, and anti-corruption. By committing to the Global Compact, banks can publicly demonstrate their dedication to responsible business practices and sustainable development. The principles cover a broad spectrum, from supporting and respecting the protection of internationally proclaimed human rights to working against corruption in all its forms, including extortion and bribery.

These frameworks and guidelines underscore the importance of integrating human rights and labor standards into the broader ESG strategy of banks. By adhering to these international standards, banks not only fulfill their ethical and legal responsibilities but also enhance their reputational capital, foster trust among stakeholders, and contribute to a more sustainable and equitable global economy. The evolving landscape of ESG criteria necessitates a proactive approach from banks, ensuring that their policies and practices are aligned with these critical human rights and labor standards, thus promoting a holistic approach to sustainability.

3.5.3 Common Features

In the realm of ESG factors, there exists a distinction between traditional financial considerations and those deemed non-financial. Traditionally, financial factors encompass metrics such as profits, capital, and costs, which directly influence financial statements. In contrast, non-financial factors reflect characteristics like greenhouse gas emissions, environmental footprint, social welfare, poverty alleviation, equal rights, and ethical practices. These non-financial factors are critical as they encompass broader societal impacts that may not be fully captured within financial reporting frameworks.

One significant challenge in integrating ESG factors into financial analysis is the uncertainty about their impacts. These impacts can manifest over varying timeframes—short, medium, or long term—and may trigger effects that extend over even longer periods. It's crucial to recognize that ESG factors aren't solely relevant in the medium to long term; they can also pose immediate risks, such as acute environmental hazards or sudden shifts in environmental policies, which can affect operational continuity and financial stability in the short term.

A notable concern surrounding ESG factors is the existence of negative economic externalities. These externalities, such as greenhouse gas emissions and pollution, often represent costs borne by society at large rather than by the entities responsible for their generation. Despite their significant societal impact, these costs are typically not fully captured by market mechanisms or reflected in financial statements. For instance, the collective cost of greenhouse gas emissions from various sources remains inadequately priced within current market frameworks, thereby obscuring the true financial risks associated with climate-related externalities.

Patterns emerging from an entity's value chain also warrant attention in ESG assessments. An entity's activities and interactions with stakeholders across its value chain—both upstream and downstream—can indirectly expose it to diverse ESG factors through debtors, creditors, suppliers, and customers. Understanding and managing these indirect impacts is crucial for comprehensive ESG risk management and sustainable business practices.

Furthermore, the sensitivity of businesses to changes in public policies underscores the dynamic nature of ESG considerations. Commitments such as those outlined in the Paris Agreement and the Sustainable Development Goals (SDGs) necessitate significant shifts in public policies and regulatory frameworks. Efforts to mitigate climate change and address other environmental challenges may lead to regulatory changes that affect industries profoundly, potentially prompting broader structural shifts that can be challenging to predict and navigate.

In conclusion, integrating ESG factors into financial analysis requires recognizing their dual nature—both as immediate risks and as long-term strategic imperatives. Addressing these factors comprehensively involves enhancing transparency, improving risk management frameworks, and fostering accountability across the financial sector to promote sustainable economic development and resilience in the face of evolving global challenges.

3.6 Impact's Dimensions of ESG Risk

Understanding the impact of climate change on a company involves examining both an "outside-in" and "inside-out" perspective. The "outside-in" perspective assesses how climate change and related environmental factors affect the company externally. This includes the physical risks posed by climate change, such as extreme weather events, sea-level rise, and changes in temperature patterns. These external impacts can disrupt operations, damage infrastructure, increase insurance costs, and affect supply chains and customer demand.

Conversely, the "inside-out" perspective focuses on how the company's activities contribute to climate change, particularly through its Scope 1 and Scope 2 greenhouse gas emissions. Scope 1 emissions refer to direct emissions from owned or controlled sources, such as emissions from company-owned vehicles and facilities. Scope 2 emissions are indirect emissions from the generation of purchased electricity consumed by the company. Understanding and mitigating these emissions are critical to reducing the company's carbon footprint and managing its contribution to climate change.

Both perspectives highlight that the impacts can be either positive or negative. Positive impacts may include opportunities to innovate and develop new products or services that address climate challenges, enhance operational efficiency through sustainable practices, or gain competitive advantage in a low-carbon economy. Conversely, negative impacts may involve regulatory risks, reputational damage, increased operational costs due to carbon taxes or emission trading schemes, and potential disruptions from physical climate risks.

ESG risks encompass any negative financial impact on an institution resulting from the current or prospective effects of ESG factors on its counterparties or invested assets. These risks can arise from various sources, such as regulatory changes affecting emissions standards, shifts in consumer preferences towards sustainable products, or supply chain disruptions due to climate-related events. Managing ESG risks requires proactive measures to assess, monitor, and mitigate these impacts, thereby safeguarding financial performance and ensuring resilience in the face of evolving environmental challenges.

3.6.1 Environmental Risk Impacts

Environmental risks can significantly impact the financial performance or solvency of entities, sovereigns, or individuals in multiple ways, reflecting a dual materiality approach. From a financial materiality perspective (outside-in), these risks can affect the profitability and competitiveness of businesses. For instance, the imposition of a carbon tax can reduce the profitability of carbon-intensive industries or make their products less competitive in the market. Conversely, from an environmental materiality perspective (inside-out), the activities of these entities, such as high emissions of CO_2, can negatively impact the environment, leading to financial repercussions through regulations or shifts in consumer preferences.

Physical risks associated with environmental factors pose immediate threats. Acute risks include sudden environmental disasters like storms, floods, or wildfires, which can damage infrastructure, disrupt supply chains, and incur significant financial losses. Chronic risks, on the other hand, involve gradual changes in climate and weather patterns, such as rising sea levels or shifts in temperature, which can diminish ecosystem services over time and affect long-term financial stability.

Uncertainty surrounding the transition to an environmentally sustainable economy adds another layer of complexity. This uncertainty is driven by three primary factors: policy changes aimed at mitigating climate impacts (e.g., carbon pricing mechanisms), technological advancements that render existing practices obsolete or uncompetitive, and evolving consumer preferences towards sustainable products and services. These factors can trigger asset repricing, impact investment decisions, and lead to reputational risks for institutions not adapting swiftly to sustainability trends.

The interaction between physical and transition risks is intricate. Persistent greenhouse gas emissions and unsustainable economic practices exacerbate physical risks, increasing environmental hazards and socio-economic impacts. In response, policymakers may introduce mitigation policies that influence consumer behavior and market dynamics. Institutions, in turn, face exposure to counterparties vulnerable to bankruptcy from regulatory changes, while assets held as collateral may be at risk during environmental incidents.

Overall, the scale and distribution of physical and transition risks have significant implications for the real economy and financial system. Industries such as agriculture, energy, tourism, and construction are particularly vulnerable, affecting overall output levels, growth rates, and labor conditions. Moreover, the uneven distribution of these risks across populations can exacerbate social unrest and uncertainty, potentially challenging the solvency of sovereigns heavily reliant on vulnerable sectors. Managing these interconnected risks requires robust risk assessment frameworks and proactive measures to navigate the evolving landscape of environmental sustainability and regulatory frameworks.

3.6.2 *Social Risks*

The integration of social factors such as equality, health, inclusiveness, and workplace safety into business strategies is becoming increasingly important. Businesses are recognizing that these factors not only contribute to societal well-being but also have significant implications for financial performance and solvency. For instance, the COVID-19 pandemic highlighted the criticality of health and safety measures in maintaining business continuity and employee welfare. Changes in policies and market sentiment towards a more inclusive society, including advancements in labor rights and social equality, are also shaping business environments.

Considering social factors help businesses manage risks effectively and enhances their reputation among stakeholders. By adopting socially responsible practices, such as ensuring fair labor practices and promoting diversity and inclusion, businesses contribute to sustainable development and position themselves for long-term success. Stakeholders, including investors, customers, and employees, increasingly value businesses that prioritize social responsibility, viewing them as more resilient and aligned with broader societal goals.

In navigating environmental risks like those posed by COVID-19 and responding to shifts in policies and societal expectations, businesses that proactively integrate social factors into their strategies are better positioned to adapt, thrive, and build trust in an evolving global landscape.

3.6.3 Governance Risks

Governance factors encompass a wide spectrum of practices that play crucial roles in shaping the financial performance and solvency of entities, sovereigns, or individuals. These factors include executive leadership, executive compensation, audit practices, internal controls, tax strategies, board independence, protection of shareholder rights, and efforts to combat corruption and bribery. Moreover, the integration of environmental and social considerations into corporate policies is increasingly recognized as a fundamental aspect of effective governance in the context of ESG (Environmental, Social, and Governance) criteria.

Unlike governance arrangements specific to supervised financial institutions, governance factors in ESG contexts focus on their impact on or interaction with counterparties or invested assets. Robust governance frameworks for environmental and social factors are integral to establishing comprehensive policies and procedures within organizations. For instance, governance practices that promote transparency and ethical conduct regarding environmental impacts or social issues are vital for maintaining stakeholder trust and compliance with regulatory standards.

Inadequate governance practices among counterparties can pose significant risks to institutions. For example, if a counterparty is involved in bribery scandals or lacks transparency in its governance practices, it may face severe market repercussions, including financial penalties, legal sanctions, and reputational damage. Institutions that fail to assess and mitigate such risks effectively may find themselves exposed to operational disruptions, financial losses, and diminished investor confidence.

Therefore, integrating strong governance practices that encompass environmental, social, and ethical considerations is essential for mitigating risks, enhancing operational resilience, and safeguarding long-term financial sustainability. By prioritizing effective governance frameworks, organizations can foster a culture of accountability, transparency, and responsible business conduct, thereby bolstering their resilience amid evolving regulatory landscapes and societal expectations.

3.6.4 Challenges in Integration ESG Risks

Integrating ESG risks into financial risk management presents significant challenges for institutions across various dimensions.

Firstly, there is a high level of uncertainty surrounding ESG risks, particularly in predicting when and how policies and regulatory interventions will impact financial markets, especially in relation to physical risks such as those associated with climate change. This uncertainty complicates risk assessment and strategic planning, making it difficult for institutions to accurately gauge the potential financial impacts of ESG-related developments.

Secondly, the availability and quality of ESG data pose substantial hurdles. Data on ESG factors is often scarce, particularly for SMEs, local governments, and entities in developing or emerging markets. This scarcity limits the ability to assess how ESG risks affect financial assets and hampers efforts to translate available data into reliable forecasts of financial performance. Moreover, the annual availability of ESG data further complicates ongoing risk monitoring and assessment.

Methodologically, integrating ESG risks into existing risk management frameworks is challenging. Traditional risk models typically rely on historical financial data that may not encompass comprehensive ESG considerations. This limitation makes it difficult to incorporate ESG risks into standard risk parameters such as probability of default or loss given default. Additionally, the lack of harmonized definitions for sustainability-oriented activities complicates the development of standardized approaches to assess and mitigate ESG risks effectively.

Furthermore, there is a significant time-horizon mismatch between the gradual development of environmental impacts over decades and the shorter-term strategic planning horizons of financial institutions. This disparity makes it challenging for institutions to align their risk management strategies with the long-term nature of ESG risks.

ESG risks also exhibit multi-point impacts across various financial risk categories. Changes driven by the transition to a sustainable economy, for example, can disrupt existing business models and necessitate costly adaptations, affecting overall financial positions.

Finally, the non-linear nature of ESG risks adds another layer of complexity. Environmental risks, in particular, can trigger chain reactions and cascade effects that amplify their financial consequences over time. Events like significant temperature increases or extreme weather events can have disproportionately large impacts relative to their immediate scale, complicating risk assessments and mitigation strategies.

Addressing these challenges requires institutions to enhance data collection capabilities, develop more sophisticated risk management frameworks that integrate ESG factors, and adopt flexible approaches to adapt to the dynamic nature of ESG risks. By doing so, institutions can better navigate the complexities of sustainability-related risks and enhance their resilience in an evolving global financial landscape.

Asses ESG Risks

Assessing ESG risks is a critical process that involves several key steps to effectively manage these complex factors within institutional frameworks.

Identification

The first step in ESG risk assessment is identifying and classifying assets based on their ESG characteristics. This classification helps institutions pinpoint potential risks associated with environmental, social, and governance factors. Assets are categorized across various dimensions, such as asset classes, sectors, counterparties, geographic locations, or maturity levels. For instance, geographic classification aids in identifying assets vulnerable to physical risks like climate-related hazards in specific regions, while sector classification highlights exposures susceptible to transition risks such as regulatory changes or technological advancements. This initial categorization lays the groundwork for a focused analysis on areas posing significant ESG risks.

Evaluation

Once assets are classified, the evaluation phase involves applying methodological tools to assess how ESG risks could impact the institution's exposures. Methodologies for quantifying these risks are continually evolving, requiring a flexible approach that can adapt to new data and insights. The evaluation provides a deeper understanding of the institution's financial vulnerability to ESG risks, enabling informed decision-making and strategic planning. It helps prioritize areas for risk mitigation and informs the development of robust risk management strategies tailored to specific ESG exposures.

Action

Following the evaluation phase, institutions take action to integrate ESG risks into their overall risk management framework. This involves adopting business strategies and risk management approaches that effectively monitor and control ESG risks across the organization. Actions may include setting specific targets and limits for ESG exposures, adjusting investment or lending practices to align with sustainability goals, and implementing changes to organizational structures or governance frameworks to enhance ESG risk oversight and management.

By systematically identifying, evaluating, and taking action on ESG risks, institutions can strengthen their resilience to environmental, social, and governance-related challenges, thereby safeguarding their financial stability and sustainability in the long term.

References

Abubakar, L., & Handayani, T. (2019). Juridical implications of the sustainable finance principles implementation in the banking sector on the obligations of sustainable reporting. *Jurnal Dinamika Hukum, 19*(1), 52. https://doi.org/10.20884/1.jdh.2019.19.1.2189

Azad, M., Islam, M., Sobhani, F., Hassan, M., & Masukujjaman, M. (2022). Revisiting the current status of green finance and sustainable finance disbursement: A policy insight. *Sustainability, 14*(14), 8911. https://doi.org/10.3390/su14148911

Basel Committee on Banking Supervision. (2021, April). *Climate-related risk drivers and their transmission channels.*

Buallay, A. (2019). Is sustainability reporting (esg) associated with performance? Evidence from the european banking sector. *Management of Environmental Quality an International Journal, 30*(1), 98–115. https://doi.org/10.1108/meq-12-2017-0149

Cerrone, R. (2022). *Banking regulation for esg principles and climate risk.* https://doi.org/10.5772/intechopen.104110.

Dong, Y., & Men, C. (2014). Sme financing in emerging markets: Firm characteristics, banking structure and institutions. *Emerging Markets Finance and Trade, 50*(1), 120–149. https://doi.org/10.2753/ree1540-496x500107

Effendi, J., & Yasmin, N. (2017). The effect of internal and external factors of banking to the smes financing for bprs in Indonesia. *Jurnal Keuangan Dan Perbankan, 21*(3). https://doi.org/10.26905/jkdp.v21i3.1221

European Central Bank. (2020). *Guide on climate-related and environmental risks.*

European Central Bank. (2024). *Risks from misalignment of banks' financing with the EU climate objectives.*

Gololo, I. (2017). An evaluation of the role of commercial banks in financing small and medium scale enterprises (smes): Evidence from Nigeria. *Indian Journal of Finance and Banking, 1*(1), 16–32. https://doi.org/10.46281/ijfb.v1i1.82

Kılıç, M., & Kuzey, C. (2019). Determinants of climate change disclosures in the turkish banking industry. *The International Journal of Bank Marketing, 37*(3), 901–926. https://doi.org/10.1108/ijbm-08-2018-0206

Kosasih, W., Rahman, A., & Prastiwi, A. (2021). Does sustainable banking disclosure affect bank efficiency? Evidence from Indonesia. *Journal of Accounting and Investment, 22*(2), 375–391. https://doi.org/10.18196/jai.v22i2.11349

Love, I., & Pería, M. (2014). How bank competition affects firms' access to finance. *The World Bank Economic Review, 29*(3), 413–448. https://doi.org/10.1093/wber/lhu003

Maiti, M. (2018). Scope for alternative avenues to promote financial access to msmes in developing nation evidence from India. *International Journal of Law and Management, 60*(5), 1210–1222. https://doi.org/10.1108/ijlma-06-2017-0141

Menicucci, E., & Paolucci, G. (2022). Esg dimensions and bank performance: An empirical investigation in Italy. *Corporate Governance, 23*(3), 563–586. https://doi.org/10.1108/cg-03-2022-0094

Park, H., & Kim, J. (2020). Transition towards green banking: Role of financial regulators and financial institutions. *Asian Journal of Sustainability and Social Responsibility, 5*(1). https://doi.org/10.1186/s41180-020-00034-3

Pyka, I., & Nocoń, A. (2021). Banks' capital requirements in terms of implementation of the concept of sustainable finance. *Sustainability, 13*(6), 3499. https://doi.org/10.3390/su13063499

Ryan, R., O'Toole, C., & McCann, F. (2014). Does bank market power affect sme financing constraints? *Journal of Banking & Finance, 49*, 495–505. https://doi.org/10.1016/j.jbankfin.2013.12.024

Shihadeh, F., Gamage, S., & Hannoon, A. (2019). The causal relationship between sme sustainability and banks' risk. *Economic Research-Ekonomska Istraživanja, 32*(1), 2743–2760. https://doi.org/10.1080/1331677x.2019.1655465

Trimulato, T. (2021). Linkage sharia banking and sharia fintech to support halal industry in Indonesia. *Annual International Conference on Islamic Economics and Business (Aicieb), 1*, 138–151. https://doi.org/10.18326/aicieb.v1i0.15

Wu, B., & Wang, T. (2021). The small and medium-sized enterprises financing: A perspective of the private bank. *E3s Web of Conferences, 275*, 01038. https://doi.org/10.1051/e3sconf/202127501038

Zhang, Y. (2021). *Analysis of the factors influencing the financing efficiency of smes.* https://doi.org/10.2991/assehr.k.211209.231.

Chapter 4
Sustainability and Market Efficiency for SMEs: Bubble or Opportunity?

4.1 Introduction

For companies, including SMEs, going public provides significant capital, liquidity, and strategic advantages, such as using shares for mergers and acquisitions and offering flexible employee compensation. However, it comes with challenges like loss of control, high compliance costs, and increased scrutiny from investors. Effective signaling, particularly through strong earnings history and ESG performance, can attract investors and reduce underpricing. Despite the benefits, the long-term underperformance of IPOs is linked to market inefficiencies and information asymmetries, requiring careful consideration of timing and market conditions.

Financial markets play a crucial role in enabling companies to gather the financial resources needed to address sustainability issues and undertake other strategic activities. By accessing public capital through financial markets, companies can secure funding for projects aimed at improving their ESG performance. This, in turn, can attract a growing segment of investors who are increasingly focused on sustainable and responsible investment opportunities. Thus, the integration of sustainability initiatives can enhance a company's market appeal and facilitate the acquisition of the necessary funds to drive long-term growth and sustainability efforts.

In this sense, market efficiency stands as a cornerstone in the realm of SMEs, profoundly influencing their capacity to navigate and excel within the competitive business landscape. Unlike their larger counterparts, SMEs encounter distinctive challenges rooted in constrained resources and unique decision-making frameworks. These factors significantly shape how SMEs strategize their marketing initiatives and leverage available information. Despite these inherent obstacles, SMEs play an important role in driving competition and shaping economic progress by influencing market behaviors and regulatory frameworks. Technological advancements play a pivotal role in bolstering SME efficiency, enabling cost efficiencies

M. Aliano et al., *Sustainable Finance for SMEs*, Sustainable Finance,
https://doi.org/10.1007/978-3-031-74193-7_4

and expanding market reach. Essential to enhancing competitiveness and operational effectiveness are robust marketing strategies and digital tools. Nevertheless, SMEs encounter barriers when striving to innovate environmentally sustainable products, navigating resource limitations and evolving market expectations. Nevertheless, SMEs can harness the power of digital marketing and CRM technologies to stimulate growth and foster innovation. The overarching impact of market efficiency on SME sustainability and performance underscores the imperative for strategic adaptation and digital transformation. Through the adoption of innovative marketing approaches, the integration of technological advancements, and the cultivation of dynamic capabilities, SMEs can reinforce their competitive standing, drive expansion, and adeptly respond to shifting market dynamics. Understanding the intricate interplay between market efficiency and SME dynamics is essential for cultivating an environment where small businesses thrive and contribute significantly to economic development.

In Sect. 4.2, we explored the advantages and challenges of going public. Through an Initial Public Offering (IPO), companies can secure fresh financial resources that are crucial for growth and expansion. Additionally, sustainability practices play a pivotal role in attracting capital and financial resources. Demonstrating strong ESG (Environmental, Social, and Governance) performance can enhance a company's appeal to investors, who are increasingly prioritizing sustainable and responsible investments. As a result, companies that integrate sustainability into their business strategies may find it easier to attract the necessary capital when going public.

In Sect. 4.3, we explore the meaning of market efficiency and how this concept can assist SMEs (Small and Medium-sized Enterprises) in their sustainable activities. This section revisits the classical definition of market efficiency, providing a modern perspective on how it applies to today's business environment, particularly for SMEs striving for sustainability. The discussion will cover various aspects of market efficiency, including informational, allocative, and operational efficiency, and how these dimensions can be leveraged by SMEs to enhance their sustainable practices and overall performance.

In Sect. 4.4, we delve into the possibility of bubbles in financial markets, examining how these bubbles can hinder SMEs from pursuing public offerings. We will discuss the mechanics of bubble formation, the conditions under which they arise, and their potential impacts on financial stability. By understanding these dynamics, we aim to highlight the risks that bubbles pose to SMEs, particularly in terms of accessing capital markets and the broader implications for their growth and sustainability. This section will also explore historical examples of financial bubbles and their repercussions on small and medium-sized enterprises.

In Sect. 4.5, we conduct an exercise to determine whether Italian companies, most of which are medium enterprises, are over or undervalued in the Italian financial market. This empirical analysis involves a detailed examination of financial metrics, market trends, and valuation models. The goal is to provide insights into the current state of the Italian market, offering a clearer picture of the valuation landscape for medium-sized enterprises. This analysis will help identify potential opportunities and threats for these companies within the financial market, contributing to a better understanding of their economic positioning and strategic options.

4.2 Advantages and Challenges of Going Public

A firm that goes public can benefit from a number of things, but one of the main ones is that it can obtain substantial capital proceeds that are not available to private markets. This infusion of funds can be used to finance a range of expansion plans, including business expansion and project investment. Brau and Fawcett (2006) found that a primary driver of companies' decision to go public is the "need for capital to support growth" in a managerial poll. Additional advantages of public capital markets include higher liquidity, which makes it easier to buy and sell shares (Bodnaruk et al., 2008; Pagano et al., 1998). Due to the ease of exit for investors, this liquidity can increase a company's appeal to them.

A crucial currency for mergers and acquisitions is also provided by becoming public. Publicly traded shares can be paid for in purchases, eliminating the need for capital and enabling growth through targeted acquisitions. Celikyurt et al. (2010) emphasize this as a noteworthy benefit. Moreover, transparency increases the flexibility of employee compensation. Offering stock options and other equity-based remuneration can assist public companies attract and retain talent by bringing employee incentives into line with shareholder interests.

Founders must, however, balance these advantages against any potential disadvantages. The possible loss of control is one major worry. The original owners of a company typically dilute their ownership position when it goes public, which might limit their influence over company choices (Brau & Fawcett, 2006). If the company's new shareholders have conflicting goals or strategic ambitions, this dilution of control may be very troubling.

Going public comes with a number of costs in addition to the possible loss of control. These comprise one-time listing expenditures including investment bank fees, legal fees, and other IPO-related costs. Moreover, continuous compliance expenses may be high. Strict legal obligations, such as the need for regular financial reporting, which demands a large investment of resources, apply to public firms (Aghamolla & Thakor, 2022; Farre-Mensa, 2017). For smaller businesses in particular, the price of staying in compliance with these requirements can be prohibitive.

The higher chance of a takeover is another possible disadvantage. Public businesses are more vulnerable to hostile takeovers, in which outside parties get a majority stake in the business without the incumbent management's approval. Founders and current management teams may find this danger disturbing (Zingales, 1995).

Additionally, investors and market analysts put short-term pressure on publicly traded corporations. These demands may cause one to prioritize short-term results above long-term strategic objectives. The misalignment of managers' and shareholders' interests can also give rise to agency difficulties and possible conflicts (Asker et al., 2015; Bernstein, 2015).

The advantages of going public can be significant, notwithstanding these difficulties. But it's crucial to remember that since 1996, when it peaked, IPO activity has been decreasing (Doidge et al., 2013; Ewens & Farre-Mensa, 2020; Gao et al., 2013). Although this decline has attracted a lot of attention from academics and policymakers, study and discussion on its fundamental origins and effects are still ongoing.

The theory of signaling is essential to IPOs. According to the signaling theory, businesses communicate their quality and prospects for the future to the market through signals. Good indicators, including a track record of profitable operations, can predict future performance and draw in investors (Barry et al., 1990; Hong Teoh et al., 1998). Certification is also seen as a strong positive indicator since it comes from a credible third party endorsing the company's worth. One indication of a company's potential is when a reputable investment bank underwrites its initial public offering (IPO).

Enhanced transparency of data pertaining to sustainability might also be seen favorably. Investors now place a greater emphasis on sustainability and ESG (environmental, social, and governance) considerations. Successful businesses can lessen knowledge asymmetries, make better investment choices, and incur less in underpricing and IPO expenses (Al-Shaer & Zaman, 2018; Harasheh & Provasi, 2022). Using an Italian sample, Harasheh (2023) demonstrated the importance of ESG performance in the early phases of an IPO.

A phenomenon known as "post-IPO financial underperformance" occurs when the stock price drops after the IPO. Inadequate information flow and market inefficiencies are the causes of this underperformance. Behavioral theories, methodological issues, and short-term underperformance theories are some of the hypotheses used in the literature to explain long-term underperformance (Perera & Kulendran, 2016).

According to Miller's (1977) divergence of opinions hypothesis, price and yield decrease with time as new information becomes accessible, bringing investors' optimistic and pessimistic viewpoints closer together. Prices gradually change to reflect a more realistic assessment of the company's prospects as the initial euphoria wanes. According to the impresario theory (Aggarwal & Rivoli, 1990), fads in the IPO market can cause momentary spikes in demand. Investment bankers may take advantage of these trends by lowering IPO pricing in order to create excitement and provide large initial profits that subsequently decline.

According to the "hot" windows opportunity theory (Ritter, 1991), companies go public when the market is doing well and conditions are favorable. But as these times pass, prices frequently go down. According to this hypothesis, businesses and their underwriters time their initial public offerings (IPOs) to take advantage of advantageous market conditions.

Long-term underperformance is explained by agency cost theory as a result of higher agency costs brought on by the division of ownership and control. This division is quantified by the ownership retention rate, which shows how much ownership of the business stays with the original owners after the initial public offering. Increased separation may cause disputes between shareholders and managers, which could harm the company's long-term success.

Perera & Kulendran (2016) examine how uncertainty theory controls long-term returns with variables including firm age, issue size, company size, offer price, and market value to explain underperformance. Larger concerns, smaller organizations, and younger firms frequently carry higher levels of uncertainty, which might affect how well they perform after an IPO.

The majority of underpricing research is devoted to ideas of asymmetric information. Underpricing, in which the IPO is priced below the first day trading price, is indicative of information flow problems and market inefficiencies. These asymmetries are a result of the recent interest in non-financial information, particularly that which is connected to ESG. Enhancing investment decisions, lowering underpricing, and reducing these asymmetries are all possible with improved disclosure of sustainability-related information.

A significant component of IPOs is signaling theory. Positive indicators can point to future potential and draw in investors, such as a solid track record of earnings or outstanding ESG performance. Reputable third-party certification can likewise be interpreted favorably. An endorsement of an IPO, for instance, by an investment bank, may be a sign of the bank's confidence in the company's future.

Early on in an IPO, ESG performance is particularly crucial. Harasheh (2023) demonstrated that ESG factors are critical for reducing information asymmetries and improving investment decisions using an Italian sample. Good ESG performance can attract more investors and possibly cut the cost of going public by lowering underpricing.

In conclusion, becoming public has several advantages, such as easier access to money, more liquidity, and advantageous positioning for mergers and acquisitions, but it also comes with a lot of difficulties. The possible loss of control, significant expenses, and heightened scrutiny from authorities and investors are challenges that founders must overcome. These trade-offs must be carefully considered before going public, with signaling theory and ESG performance being key factors in reducing some of the risks involved. Post-IPO performance is still a complicated topic that is impacted by a number of variables, such as behavioral dynamics, information asymmetries, and market conditions. Even with the decrease in initial public offerings (IPOs), many businesses looking to develop and expand find going public to be a compelling option due to its inherent benefits.

4.3 Efficiency Meanings

Sustainability is increasingly communicated and represented externally by businesses to their stakeholders through information dissemination. The behaviors of these businesses regarding sustainability also provide information for investors and other stakeholders. In classical economic theory and microeconomics, market information plays a crucial role in investment decisions and determines the price of shares or other financial instruments traded in the market. Conversely, the price of a share or financial instrument reflects (or technically "discounts") all available information. The ability of share prices or other financial instruments to represent all available information is defined as a form of market efficiency. When discussing sustainability, one wonders whether prices encapsulate sustainability-related information among other factors.

However, there are caveats. Firstly, as mentioned earlier, information can be processed by market operators who consider both what is communicated to the market (e.g., through sustainability reports, available ESG scores, etc.) and what the company actually does in terms of sustainability. Focusing solely on green aspects, the gap between words and actions represents a potential definition of greenwashing (for further insights, refer to Greenwashing chapter). Thus, the processing of information by operators who subsequently determine prices can occur in various ways. As discussed further in this chapter, this issue presents a constraint on the hypothesis of market efficiency in sustainability matters.

Secondly, assuming that all available information, in its various forms, is the same for all operators, does not imply that availability occurs simultaneously for everyone. These issues have already been debated and extensively covered in the economic literature addressing market efficiency. Although, in fairness, classical theoretical models underlying market efficiency research often used the rationality of economic operators who acted based on expected dividend utility from various companies. It is useful to contextualize this period when the stakeholder theory had not yet fully developed.

In the case of sustainability, assessments related to investment decisions likely complicate efficiency evaluation because investor utility depends not only on expected dividends but also on other sustainability dimensions. Alongside the concept of market efficiency linked to information dissemination, microeconomic aspects, and rational investor choices, there are also considerations about market operational efficiency.

For SMEs entering the market for the first time, understanding the price at which instruments such as shares or bonds will be listed is crucial. The primary market facilitates resource exchanges between surplus and deficit entities, presenting one of the highest forms of information asymmetry, albeit partly mitigated by disclosure obligations. Moreover, technical market functioning components can determine, through placement prices, the extent of financial resource inflows. Techniques like flipping by initial placers or subscribers can represent a form of market technical efficiency.

Lastly, but not less importantly, another element to evaluate is allocative efficiency, referring to the financial system's ability to allocate resources. All three levels of efficiency are interrelated and together would lead to greater overall efficiency. From this perspective, in line with Tobin (1984 and other contributions), there are different definitions of efficiency.

4.3.1 *Market Efficiency: Diverse Meanings*

Following Tobin's approach, a market is efficient to the extent that, given publicly available information, it does not allow above-average profits on average. The basic idea is straightforward and intuitive, aligning with the theory and functioning of the non-arbitrage mechanism; markets adjust quickly to changes in informational bases and "discount" information swiftly. In other words, if there were an opportunity somewhere to earn more than others, markets would have already discounted this information, allowing for arbitrage activities to level prices and correct these imperfections. Hence, the common expression: "the market discounts everything." Following Tobin's approach, there are four levels of market efficiency.

This first level of efficiency is termed information-arbitrage efficiency, focusing on the dissemination and utilization of information.

A second level of efficiency in Tobin's interpretation is that current prices reflect all future payments (fundamental valuation efficiency). This second level aligns with the hypothesis of rational expectations of operators. In terms of sustainability, it has been observed that investor sensitivities in evaluating stocks encompass not only the ability to discount future payment flows but extend beyond, in another dimension of rationality where multiple dimensions are present.

Tobin's third level refers to Arrow-Debreu economy states and defines a market efficient to the extent that operators can ensure the transfer of financial resources or risks under any future circumstances (full insurance efficiency).

Connected to this third efficiency level is functional efficiency, evaluating efficiency in terms of correctly allocating risks from Arrow-Debreu economies. Improvements in functional terms, facilitated by technological advancements and institutional innovations, will likely enhance the thorough and better allocation of financial resources.

Consider, for instance, the improved performance of payment systems concerning better allocation of risks associated with different counterparties.

4.3.2 *Informational Efficiency*

The assessment of informational efficiency is the most debated and studied in the literature. Early contributions, akin to archaeological findings concerning more recent publications, are credited to financial consultant Alfred Cowles, who later founded the Cowles Commission. Essentially, Cowles and other authors argued that randomly choosing stocks in financial markets or choosing through a consultant would not yield different profits. Over the years, technical analysts have attempted to refute this theory, and the findings presented by Cowles and other authors. In the modern reinterpretation of Cowles' results, the random walk model has been introduced to describe stock returns and prices. Essentially, since the market discounts everything, the distribution of prices and returns follows a random pattern that cannot be predicted better by anyone over the medium to long term.

Certainly, the most substantial contribution came from economist Eugene Fama and the subsequent debate surrounding different levels of market efficiency, although during that particular historical period, between the late 1960s and the 1970s, many other interventions were made by equally authoritative economists (Fama et al., 1969). The debate also involved economic thought in a dispute between empiricists and those who sought to "micro-found" the results obtained. In the first and subsequent formulations, based, as previously mentioned, on the empiricism of results up to that point, it is asserted that markets discount all available information at a given time. Analogous to a competitive market, since the marginal cost of this information is zero, so should be the marginal revenue. This observation, reported in an extremely concise manner, encapsulates the intuition of Fama et al. (1969). This reconstruction, framing the spirit of the initial market efficiency research, is credited to Ray Ball. The assumptions leading to a form of efficiency are highly restrictive: (1) there are no transaction costs; (b) all information is available to everyone; (c) everyone agrees on the implications of future incomes.

Alongside the approach suggested by Fama, defined as empiricist (of the so-called Chicago School), there are others more aligned with information economics, which rather than seeking to explain price evolution, analyze operator behaviors (Berkley School, including Rubinstein, Sharpe, among others). Grossman, Stiglitz, Jordan work on a different definition of market efficiency, micro-economically founded. In summary, according to them, there would be no utility in publicly disseminating information.

Following Fama's approach, there are three levels of efficiency that can be tested, referring to the type of information present and disseminated in the market.

A first form of efficiency is defined as weak, referring to the information contained in the historical series of stock prices. There is weak-form efficiency when, based on past price series, no above-average profits can be realized. Thus, this first level of efficiency refers to information contained in historical series. Hypotheses of the so-called Random Walk are tested, rather than the utility of technical analysis using investment strategies that yield higher returns than average.

A second level of efficiency refers to publicly available information concerning the company. Within this realm are studies involving stock price reactions to corporate events or general events that may involve the company.

Finally, there is strong efficiency, which refers to the information set of groups of investors operating under a monopoly regime.

In this regard, for example, Jensen tests the hypothesis that mutual funds can achieve above-average profits compared to other operators. Whether information alone influences stock prices is a hypothesis also tested by Shiller (1981), who finds that price volatility is too high to be justified by a change in information sets. Among the hypotheses put forward is one that takes into account "fashion," in the sense of following some form or vehicle of investment considered at that time. Considering this hypothesis explains the volatility formations that occur in the market. In this case, reference is often made to the beauty contest used by Keynes in the "General

Theory of Employment Interest and Money." Another explanation, with a microeconomically founded formalization, is provided by Grossman and Shiller (1981). In summary, the authors state that behind the variance not explained by available information, there could be an instantaneous adjustment of discount rates, calculated through the study of consumption as the marginal rate of substitution between present and future consumption. The conditions underlying informational efficiency, according to Fama, are nevertheless sufficient conditions, but not necessary ones.

4.3.3 Fundamental Valuation

In a classic sense, the fact that prices discount fundamentals mainly refer to the consideration that the current price represents the discounting of future cash flows from a specific company, primarily dividends. Therefore, there is an evaluative efficiency to the extent that a company's prices reflect future dividends. If we add to this classic consideration, in line with the theory of rational expectations, the issue of sustainability, evaluations of expected returns will also consider sustainability as fundamental.

The theme that fundamentals are reflected in prices clashes with the presence of bubbles in markets. Indeed, a bubble (or speculative bubble) could be defined as a timeframe outside of which prices do not follow fundamental trends.

On this topic, there is a vast literature, among which the most interesting branch may be represented by the so-called increasing rational bubbles. Among various authors (see for example, Blanchard & Watson, 1982), a modeling spread using explanations related to the rational creation of bubbles is perfectly rational. From an analytical perspective, they were constants in the price.

4.3.4 Full Insurance Efficiency

Contracts for every state of nature, as theorized by Arrow and Debreu, represent an ideal where there are specific contracts for every possible future situation, allowing individuals to cover any risk. Applying this concept to the financial market, one can envision a system capable of meeting all participants' needs, covering a wide range of eventualities. In the past, the costs associated with creating and managing such contracts were a significant obstacle to their widespread adoption. However, with the advancement of technologies and institutional infrastructures, this scenario is becoming increasingly realistic. Technological innovations like blockchain and smart contracts drastically reduce transaction and management costs, making it more feasible to create markets and contracts for every state of nature. These emerging new markets respond to increasingly specific needs, similar to how new products are developed to meet new demands. Consequently, the ability to "insure" in the Arrow-Debreu sense increases, as technology enables the coverage of risks that were previously impossible to efficiently insure. Thus, modern technological evolution not only expands the number of states of nature that can be contractualized but also enhances the effectiveness with which the market can offer tailored coverages and solutions.

4.4 Speculative Bubbles and Explanations: Is Sustainability a Bubble?

There is a branch of economic theory that admits the possibility of rational, increasing bubbles, meaning that even though the theory of rational expectations is accepted, it does not exclude the possibility of bubbles forming. Technically, in economists' jargon, rational bubbles represent explosive solutions to price equations (Blanchard & Watson, 1982; Diba & Grossman, 1982; Tirole, 1982). In other words, operators are aware that prices are much higher than the market fundamentals, but they still purchase the underlying asset because they expect further price increases. According to Garber (1990), even the tulip bubble can be considered a rational bubble, where all operators were aware that the price was much higher than the fundamentals and simply bought because they expected (rationally) a further rise in tulip bulb prices. In these cases, operators rationally purchase the underlying asset, expecting everyone to believe that prices will rise in the future.

4.4.1 The Minsky Moment

Hyman Minsky's worldwide fame, as often happens with important figures, came after his life as a researcher and scholar of financial markets. His recognition is due to financial crises, or rather, to the theory he developed to explain their occurrence. Paradoxically, his theory, which made the origins of financial crises endogenous, kept him on the margins of the academic world for many years. In fact, his career took place during a period when markets were considered efficient, following the work of Fama and other authors. Unlike Fama and Lucas, Minsky believed that the structure of the financial system played a crucial role in resource allocation and could not be ignored. Even in the reformulation of Keynesian theory by Hicks and Hansen, there was no room for the structure of the financial system, which for Minsky was fundamental. The endogeneity of crises in Minsky's theory starts from a clear concept of investment: using money today to gain future benefits. According to Minsky, also known for his "Financial Instability Hypothesis" (FIH), the seeds of what will determine the next crisis can be analyzed from this simple statement. Investment involves exchanging money now for the future, and to finance an investment, a company has two options: use its own cash flow or borrow from banks. It is important to remember that Minsky's theory assumes that the financial system is complex: "the characterization of the economy as a capitalist economy with expensive assets and a complex, sophisticated financial system" (Minsky, 1992). At the heart of the discussion is the indebtedness of companies, necessary to anticipate the liquidity needed to realize the investment. Evaluations on expected economic return and sustainability are functions of the expected profitability of the investment. According to Minsky, the "institutional complexity" of the financial system complicates the relationships between borrowers and lenders. Simplifying, there are three main relationships that economic units can undertake regarding borrowing, in relation to the expected profits necessary to repay capital and interest. The first relationship, called "hedge", allows borrowers to repay both capital and interest with generated profits. This relationship is sustainable in both the short and long term, as the cash flow generated from the investment compensates for the outflows. The second relationship, called "speculative finance", involves the company taking on new debt to meet liquidity needs, unable to repay the initial debt. This category also includes governments, which often take on new public debt to repay maturing debts. Finally, there are "Ponzi schemes", where the cash flow is insufficient to repay loans, forcing additional borrowing of resources or assets to pay interest. In a world characterized by "hedge" finance, it is unlikely that a crisis will develop, whereas in the other cases, it is more likely to occur in the long term. Therefore, financial stability will prevail if "hedge" behaviors predominate; in the other two cases, "seeds" for future crises are sown. These conditions represent Minsky's "first theorem". The second theorem of a dynamic nature refers to what happens to the financial system during prolonged periods of prosperity: it moves from a "hedge" condition to one characterized by speculative or "Ponzi" attitudes.

This theory has implications for policymakers' ability to manage economic processes, such as government interventions concerned with inflationary phenomena. By reducing the amount of money in circulation, authorities (or central banks) encourage the shift from speculative finance to Ponzi finance. The proactive role of authorities and institutions can accelerate or decelerate the occurrence of endogenous financial crises.

Briefly reviewing this approach, one can theorize a genesis of internally originated financial crises, defined as endogenous. The definition of the Minsky moment is attributed to Paul McCulley (PIMCO manager) who sought to explain the Russian crisis of 1998 through Minsky's theory. Minsky's theory has been further explored by several authors and is often cited in specialized publications.

4.4.2 Capital Market Inflation

In the arguments proposed by Minsky to explain an endogenous crisis, there is little room for another source of funding for companies: equity. More generally, the role of the capital markets, especially the stock market, is not fully considered in explaining the endogeneity of financial crises. Toporowski himself, in relation to Minsky's theory, states that "... the banking system does not cover the whole financial system, as it might in the countries of continental Europe where the universal banking tradition is stronger" (Toporowski, 1999). Like Minsky, the approach to the endogenous explanation of crises is Keynesian in nature and starts from a preference for liquidity. The price of a stock, and more generally a financial instrument, is determined by the interaction between supply and demand.

An excess demand for a financial instrument, such as a stock, understood as the desire to buy a particular financial asset, defines a liquidity supply for those who might have the willingness to sell it. Indeed, in the event of selling shares, the willingness to buy them at a certain price can represent the physiological liquidity of the instrument. By the same mechanism, the stock market collapses when the selling price finds no demand, and if the seller needs to get rid of the instrument, they are willing to sell it at a lower price. Reversing this process, high demand leads to higher prices of financial assets, outlining what can be defined as an "accumulation phase," triggering a mechanism that causes financial asset prices to rise recursively. Told in this way, a market disequilibrium condition seems almost physiological.

Therefore, a continuous period of rising financial asset prices will determine investor behavior aimed at realizing a "capital gain," that is, making a profit from the difference between the purchase price and a potentially positive selling price. Among these operators are mainly those who do not have deadlines in terms of returning invested capital, such as pension funds. For the latter, outgoing investor flows, net of extraordinary needs, are planned (and programmable) over time and do not require particularly complex short-term liquidity management. Under equal other conditions, a higher stock price produces effects on corporate financing choices.

Instead of turning to the banking market, companies can obtain financial resources from the market because they are less onerous. Indeed, for a company, the return on equity capital (which can be understood as a cost of capital) is represented by dividends, which can be kept low in a context characterized by rising prices, as the expected gain for the investor is almost all in terms of capital gain, placing dividends in the background. Between the interest rate and the dividend, net of other considerations in terms of proprietary assets, the company will prefer the dividend if it is lower as a cost of capital. This conclusion is decisive in the FIH, which instead bases its conclusions almost exclusively on the role that the bank has in financing the economic system and companies. Even companies, at least the more articulate ones, are inclined to sell subsidiaries or other assets given the high prices. In addition to this, there is another effect of a more macroeconomic nature that connects with monetary policy. Much of monetary policy operations are undertaken through the banking channel, as well as operations aimed at limiting real goods and services inflation. Margin operations, reserve requirements, and interest rates work to the extent that banks reduce or increase the propensity to lend money to the economy. In the case of CMI, as represented, this mechanism is weakened and applies only to short-term/deadline-oriented debt. The transmission of monetary policy impulses becomes less effective.

4.5 An Exercise on the Italian Market: Market Efficiency and Sustainability

The integration of Corporate Social Responsibility (CSR) and Environmental, Social, and Governance (ESG) scores has led to a notable overvaluation of stocks (Bofinger et al., 2022). This overvaluation stems from the increased attractiveness of firms with higher ESG ratings, resulting in greater inflows into mutual funds that prioritize sustainable investments. Essentially, CSR and ESG initiatives enhance market transparency by providing investors with more comprehensive information. This reduction in informational asymmetry fosters greater market efficiency. Moreover, the enhanced information availability aligns with the Stakeholder Theory (Freeman, 1984), which posits that considering the interests of all stakeholders, including the community and environment, can drive long-term value creation. Therefore, the indirect benefit of sustainability initiatives for firms lies in their ability to enhance corporate reputation, attract capital, and foster stakeholder trust, ultimately contributing to sustained financial performance and market valuation.

In the Italian context, the question of whether a market where companies are overvalued can be considered efficient raises several considerations. Market efficiency traditionally implies that prices of assets reflect all available information, implying that assets are neither overvalued nor undervalued. However, the integration of Corporate Social Responsibility (CSR) and Environmental, Social, and Governance (ESG) factors complicates this notion.

Firstly, the relationship between sustainability, information, and market valuations is crucial. The adoption of CSR and ESG practices provides additional information to investors beyond financial metrics alone. This broader set of data allows investors to assess not only the short-term financial health of a company but also its long-term sustainability and resilience. Consequently, companies with higher CSR and ESG ratings may attract more favorable valuations due to perceived lower risks and potential for sustainable growth.

Secondly, sustainability interacts with investor evaluations in significant ways. Investors increasingly consider sustainability factors as critical indicators of a company's management quality, risk management practices, and future prospects. Companies that prioritize sustainability often benefit from enhanced investor trust and access to capital, leading to potentially higher stock valuations.

Therefore, while a market where companies are overvalued might suggest inefficiency in traditional financial terms, the inclusion of sustainability factors introduces a broader perspective. Market efficiency in the context of CSR and ESG can be viewed through the lens of information transparency and the alignment of market valuations with long-term sustainability goals. Ultimately, the relationship between sustainability, information availability, and market valuations underscores the evolving understanding of market efficiency in today's economic landscape.

To construct an indicator comparing a company's market value to its fundamental value (true value), inspired by Bofinger et al. (2022), we can utilize the Residual Income Model (RIM). The market capitalization, which represents the current market value of the company based on its share price and outstanding shares, serves as the numerator in our indicator. The denominator incorporates the RIM, a model that estimates the true or fundamental value by considering expected future earnings and the cost of equity. This model accounts for the present value of residual incomes after deducting the cost of equity from the equity charge. The indicator itself is calculated as the ratio of market capitalization to the true value derived from the RIM. If the indicator is greater than 1, it suggests potential overvaluation, indicating that the market values the company higher than its fundamental value. Conversely, if the indicator is less than 1, it implies potential undervaluation. A ratio of 1 indicates alignment between market value and fundamental value as per the Residual Income Model. This indicator helps stakeholders gauge market efficiency and investor sentiment regarding the company's future prospects, though its accuracy depends on reliable earnings forecasts and the robustness of the RIM parameters used. Adjustments to the RIM can tailor the assessment to specific company characteristics and market conditions, offering deeper insights into market valuations and potential inefficiencies, as discussed by Bofinger et al. (2022).

$$Indicator_{t,i} = \frac{P_{i,t}}{V_{i,t}}$$

The inquiry focuses on assessing the impact of sustainability ratings on the market over/undervaluation ratio, specifically whether companies with higher sustainability scores (measured by ESG scores from Refinitiv) tend to be overvalued compared to those with lower sustainability scores. The analysis utilizes companies listed on the FTSE Italia All Share index, with the sample size constrained by data availability in the Refinitiv database. The period under scrutiny spans from 2013 to 2022. This investigation aims to explore correlations between sustainability metrics and market valuations, shedding light on whether investors assign higher market values to companies perceived as more sustainable.

Our dependent variable is the indicator highlighted before, while as independent variables, we consider one year lagged of: esg, envorimental, social and governance scores; return on equity (L.roe); debt of equity in percentage (L.debtequity); Google Seach Volume index on: Climate Change (L.gsvi_clim), ESG Invest (L.gsvi_esginv) and Global Warming (L.gsvi_global); CSR report (dummy variable, csrreport). In the following table we run a fixed effects regression on the available data. Results are reported in Tables 4.1, 4.2, 4.3 and 4.4.

4.5.1 Concluding Remarks

The findings of this study highlight that companies listed on the FTSE Italia All Share tend to be overvalued when they exhibit higher sustainability ratings, particularly concerning broader sustainability metrics measured by overall ESG scores from Refinitiv. These overvaluations are observed across companies without significant sector-specific patterns of over/undervaluation. Importantly, the size of the

Table 4.1 ESG overall score

VARIABLES	Indicator	Indicator	Indicator
L.esg	0.782**	0.782**	0.782**
	(0.396)	(0.396)	(0.396)
L.roe	0.221	0.221	0.221
	(0.306)	(0.306)	(0.306)
L.debtequity	−1.18e-05	−1.18e-05	−1.18e-05
	(0.0486)	(0.0486)	(0.0486)
L.gsvi_clim	0.603		
	(3.301)		
Csrreport	−21.35	−21.35	−21.35
	(36.40)	(36.40)	(36.40)
L.gsvi_esginv		0.950	
		(5.206)	
L.gsvi_global			1.724
			(9.443)
Constant	−31.23	−27.76	−83.79
	(54.46)	(41.77)	(331.4)
Observations	606	606	606
R-squared	0.0297	0.0294	0.0293
Years fixed effects	YES	YES	YES
Number of firms	124	124	124

Standard errors in parentheses
*** $p < 0.01$, ** $p < 0.05$, * $p < 0$

Table 4.2 Environmental score

VARIABLES	Indicator	Indicator	Indicator
L.env	0.514*	0.514*	0.514*
	(0.310)	(0.310)	(0.310)
L.roe	0.218	0.218	0.218
	(0.307)	(0.307)	(0.307)
L.debtequity	−0.00226	−0.00226	−0.00226
	(0.0489)	(0.0489)	(0.0489)
L.gsvi_clim	0.989		
	(3.320)		
Csrreport	−10.79	−10.79	−10.79
	(35.11)	(35.11)	(35.11)
L.gsvi_esginv		1.560	
		(5.235)	
L.gsvi_global			2.829
			(9.495)
Constant	−28.94	−23.25	−115.2
	(54.62)	(41.62)	(333.6)
Observations	606	606	606
R-squared	0.0247	0.0244	0.0243
Years fixed effects	YES	YES	YES
Number of firms	124	124	124

Standard errors in parentheses
*** $p < 0.01$, ** $p < 0.05$, * $p < 0.1$

Table 4.3 Social score

VARIABLES	Indicator	Indicator	Indicator
L.soc	0.650*	0.650*	0.650*
	(0.386)	(0.386)	(0.386)
L.roe	0.223	0.223	0.223
	(0.308)	(0.308)	(0.308)
L.debtequity	−6.87e-05	−6.87e-05	−6.87e-05
	(0.0487)	(0.0487)	(0.0487)
L.gsvi_clim	0.242		
	(3.305)		
Csrreport	−18.60	−18.60	−18.60
	(36.86)	(36.86)	(36.86)
L.gsvi_esginv		0.382	
		(5.212)	
L.gsvi_global			0.693
			(9.454)
Constant	−24.83	−23.44	−45.95
	(54.16)	(41.61)	(331.3)
Observations	606	606	606
R-squared	0.0397	0.0394	0.0393
Years fixed effects	YES	YES	YES
Number of firms	124	124	124

Standard errors in parentheses
*** $p < 0.01$, ** $p < 0.05$, * $p < 0.1$

company plays a crucial role, as overvaluation is more pronounced among larger companies with market capitalizations above the median. Specifically, companies in the first, second, and fourth quintiles show significant overvaluations compared to their fundamental values based on the Residual Income Model.

These findings suggest several implications for policymakers and market regulators. First, there is a need for enhanced transparency and disclosure regarding how sustainability ratings, such as ESG scores, are calculated and utilized in market valuations. Clearer guidelines on reporting standards and methodologies could mitigate potential misperceptions and speculative distortions in market valuations driven by sustainability metrics.

Second, policymakers should encourage the development of standardized frameworks for sustainability reporting across all sectors. This standardization could help investors make more informed decisions and reduce the variability in market perceptions of sustainability-related risks and opportunities.

Third, there is a role for regulatory bodies to monitor and possibly intervene in cases where market valuations significantly deviate from fundamental values based on misleading or unsubstantiated sustainability claims. This could involve periodic audits or assessments of ESG disclosures to ensure they accurately reflect the company's environmental, social, and governance practices. Lastly, promoting investor education on the nuances of sustainability ratings and their impact on market

Table 4.4 Governance score

VARIABLES	Indicator	Indicator	Indicator
L.gov	0.600*	0.600*	0.600*
	(0.317)	(0.317)	(0.317)
L.roe	0.157	0.157	0.157
	(0.303)	(0.303)	(0.303)
L.debtequity	0.00558	0.00558	0.00558
	(0.0485)	(0.0485)	(0.0485)
L.gsvi_clim	0.574		
	(3.302)		
Csrreport	−9.775	−9.775	−9.775
	(34.47)	(34.47)	(34.47)
L.gsvi_esginv		0.905	
		(5.206)	
L.gsvi_global			1.641
			(9.444)
Constant	−27.48	−24.18	−77.50
	(54.21)	(41.46)	(331.4)
Observations	606	606	606
R-squared	0.0307	0.0314	0.0303
Years fixed effects	YES	YES	YES
Number of firms	124	124	124

Standard errors in parentheses
*** $p < 0.01$, ** $p < 0.05$, * $p < 0.1$

valuations could empower investors to make more informed and responsible investment decisions. This education could focus on improving awareness of how sustainability factors contribute to long-term financial performance and risk management, thereby fostering a more sustainable and resilient market ecosystem.

In conclusion, while sustainability ratings provide valuable information for investors and stakeholders, careful consideration of their implications for market valuations is crucial to maintaining market efficiency and investor confidence. Policymakers play a pivotal role in shaping regulatory frameworks that enhance transparency, standardization, and accountability in sustainability reporting, ultimately contributing to more informed and sustainable investment decisions.

References

Aggarwal, R., & Rivoli, P. (1990). Fads in the initial public offering market? *Financial Management, 19*(4), 45. https://doi.org/10.2307/3665609

Aghamolla, C., & Thakor, R. T. (2022). Do mandatory disclosure requirements for private firms increase the propensity of going public? *Journal of Accounting Research, 60*(3), 755–804. https://doi.org/10.1111/1475-679X.12396

Al-Shaer, H., & Zaman, M. (2018). Credibility of sustainability reports: The contribution of audit committees. *Business Strategy and the Environment, 27*(7), 973–986. https://doi.org/10.1002/BSE.2046

Asker, J., Farre-Mensa, J., & Ljungqvist, A. (2015). Corporate investment and stock market listing: A puzzle? *The Review of Financial Studies, 28*(2), 342–390. https://doi.org/10.1093/RFS/HHU077

Barry, C. B., Muscarella, C. J., Peavy, J. W., & Vetsuypens, M. R. (1990). The role of venture capital in the creation of public companies: Evidence from the going-public process. *Journal of Financial Economics, 27*(2), 447–471. https://doi.org/10.1016/0304-405X(90)90064-7

Bernstein, S. (2015). Does going public affect innovation? *The Journal of Finance, 70*(4), 1365–1403. https://doi.org/10.1111/JOFI.1227

Blanchard, O, & Watson, M. (1982). *Bubbles, rational expectations and financial markets*, No 945, NBER Working Papers from National Bureau of Economic Research, Inc.

Bodnaruk, A., Kandel, E., Massa, M., & Simonov, A. (2008). Shareholder diversification and the decision to go public. *The Review of Financial Studies, 21*(6), 2779–2824. https://doi.org/10.1093/RFS/HHM036

Bofinger, Y., Heyden, K. J., & Björn, R. (2022). Corporate social responsibility and market efficiency: Evidence from ESG and misvaluation measures. *Journal of Banking & Finance, Elsevier, 134*(C), 106322. https://doi.org/10.1016/j.jbankfin.2021.106322

Brau, J. C., & Fawcett, S. E. (2006). Initial public offerings: An analysis of theory and practice. *The Journal of Finance, 61*(1), 399–436. https://doi.org/10.1111/J.1540-6261.2006.00840.X

Celikyurt, U., Sevilir, M., & Shivdasani, A. (2010). Going public to acquire? The acquisition motive in IPOs. *Journal of Financial Economics, 96*(3), 345–363. https://doi.org/10.1016/J.JFINECO.2010.03.003

Diba, B. T., & Grossman, H. I. (1982). Explosive Rational Bubbles in Stock Prices? *The American Economic Review, 78*(3), 520–530. (11 pages).

Doidge, C., Karolyi, G. A., & Stulz, R. M. (2013). The U.S. left behind? Financial globalization and the rise of IPOs outside the U.S. *Journal of Financial Economics, 110*(3), 546–573. https://doi.org/10.1016/J.JFINECO.2013.08.008

Ewens, M., & Farre-Mensa, J. (2020). The deregulation of the private equity markets and the decline in IPOs. *The Review of Financial Studies, 33*(12), 5463–5509. https://doi.org/10.1093/RFS/HHAA053

Fama, E. F., Fisher, L., Jensen, M. C., & Roll, R. J. (1969). The adjustment of stock prices to new information. *International Economic Review, 10.*

Farre-Mensa, J. (2017). The benefits of selective disclosure: Evidence from private firms. *SSRN Electronic Journal*. https://doi.org/10.2139/SSRN.1719204

Freeman, R. E. (1984). *Strategic management: A stakeholder approach*. Pitman.

Gao, X., Ritter, J. R., & Zhu, Z. (2013). Where have all the IPOs gone? *Journal of Financial and Quantitative Analysis, 48*(6), 1663–1692. https://doi.org/10.1017/S0022109014000015

Garber, P. M. (1990). Famous first bubbles. *The Journal of Economic Perspectives, 4*(2), 35–54. (20 pages).

Grossman, S., & Shiller, R. (1981). The determinants of the variability of stock market prices. *American Economic Review, 71*(2), 222–227.

Harasheh, M. (2023). Freshen up before going public: Do environmental, social, and governance factors affect firms' appearance during the initial public offering? *Business Strategy and the Environment, 32*(4), 2509. https://doi.org/10.1002/bse.3261

Harasheh, M., & Provasi, R. (2022). A need for assurance: Do internal control systems integrate environmental, social, and governance factors? *Corporate Social Responsibility and Environmental Management, ahead of print,* 1–18. https://doi.org/10.1002/CSR.2361

Hong Teoh, S., Welch, I., & Wong, T. J. (1998). Earnings management and the long-run market performance of initial public offerings. *The Journal of Finance, 53*(6), 1935–1974. https://doi.org/10.1111/0022-1082.00079

Miller, E. M. (1977). Risk, uncertainty, and divergence of opinion. *The Journal of Finance, 32*(4), 1151–1168. https://doi.org/10.1111/j.1540-6261.1977.tb03317.x
Minsky, H. P., (1992, May). The financial instability hypothesis Working Paper No. 74. *The Jerome Levy Economics Institute of Bard College.*
Pagano, M., Panetta, F., & Zingales, L. (1998). Why do companies go public? An empirical analysis. *Journal of Finance, 53*(1), 27–64. https://doi.org/10.1111/0022-1082.25448
Perera, W., Kulendran, N. (2016). Short-run underpricing and its deter- minants: Evidence from Australian IPOS. *Corporate Ownership and Control, 13*(3), 502–517. PMID: 10.22495/cocv13i3c3p9
Ritter, J. R. (1991). The long-run performance of initial public offerings. *The Journal of Finance, 46*(1), 3–27. https://doi.org/10.1111/j.1540-6261.1991.tb03743.x
Shiller, R. J. (1981, May). *The use of volatility measures in assessing market efficiency*. The Journal of Finance, Vol. 36, No. 2, Papers and Proceedings of the Thirty Ninth Annual Meeting American Finance Association, Denver, September 5–7, 1980, pp. 291–304 (14 pages) https://doi.org/10.2307/2327010.
Tirole, J. (1982). On the possibility of speculation under rational expectations. *Econometrica, 50*(5), 1163–1181. (19 pages). https://doi.org/10.2307/1911868
Tobin, J. (1984). On the efficiency of financial system. *Lloyds Bank Review.*
Toporowski, J. (1999). *Monetary policy in an era of capital market inflation.* Levy Economics Institute Working Paper.
Zingales, L. (1995). Insider ownership and the decision to go public. *The Review of Economic Studies, 62*(3), 425–448. https://doi.org/10.2307/2298036

Part II
Instruments and Methods

Chapter 5
Financial Instruments for Green Finance Tailored to SMEs

5.1 Introduction

The urgency of transitioning to a sustainable economy has never been greater. Central to this transition SMEs which are the backbone of many global economies. However, adopting green practices often requires substantial financial investment. To support SMEs in their journey toward sustainability, it is essential to consider a variety of innovative financial instruments tailored to their needs. This chapter delves into these instruments, exploring their roles, benefits, and implementation strategies.

SMEs are vital to the world economy, but they have a difficult time getting the funding they need to switch to sustainable practices. SMEs are accountable for 45% of the world's greenhouse gas (GHG) emissions, according to the OECD (2023b). Even while these companies have a significant influence, over half of them say that one of the biggest barriers to climate action is a lack of finance. Furthermore, almost 70% of SMEs state that they require more funding in order to initiate or expedite climate action. This chapter looks at the difficulties SMEs have getting widespread and sustainable credit, as well as the role public financial institutions play in easing these difficulties.

For SMEs, financing accessibility has long been a major concern. Their inability to obtain the required funds is hampered by a number of obstacles, which become more severe when considering sustainable finance.

Two of the biggest obstacles to SMEs obtaining financing are inadequate credit history and a lack of collateral. In order to reduce the risk of default, traditional lending banks sometimes need significant collateral, which many SMEs are unable to offer. Furthermore, it might be challenging for more recent SMEs to convince prospective lenders of their trustworthiness because they frequently lack a strong credit history (Hernández-Cánovas & Koëter-Kant, 2011; Benbekhti et al., 2021).

M. Aliano et al., *Sustainable Finance for SMEs*, Sustainable Finance,
https://doi.org/10.1007/978-3-031-74193-7_5

SMEs are frequently viewed by financial institutions as high-risk borrowers. This impression is the result of several things, such as the fact that businesses are usually run on a smaller scale, have fewer resources, and have greater failure rates than bigger corporations. It is difficult for SMEs to obtain inexpensive financing because of this perceived risk, which can result in increased interest rates or outright rejection of loan applications (Farinha & Félix, 2015; Jaabi, 2018). Loan and other financial product application procedures can be difficult and time-consuming. SMEs frequently lack the tools and knowledge necessary to successfully undergo these procedures, which lowers their chances of being approved for financing. For smaller companies with fewer employees, the administrative strain of creating thorough financial statements, business strategies, and other documentation might be too much to handle (Ismanto et al., 2022). SMEs and financial institutions frequently have a sizable information imbalance. It's possible that SMEs are unaware of all the funding alternatives accessible to them or are confused by the particular conditions and specifications of various financial instruments. However, financial institutions could not have a thorough understanding of the special demands and conditions of SMEs, which could result in expectations and requirements that are out of sync (Wang et al., 2020).

The chapter is organized as follows. Section 5.2 describes the main barriers to sustainable finance for SMEs. Public intervention is analyzed in Sect. 5.3. Section 5.4 highlights the structure of potential sustainable finance operations and outlines their main features. In Sect. 5.5, we discuss the gaps in the sustainability approach taken by providers of financial resources. Section 5.6 details the financial instruments and techniques used to offer these resources. Section 5.7 reviews global practices in sustainable finance. Finally, Section 5.8 concludes the chapter.

5.2 Barriers to Sustainable Finance for SMEs

SMEs encounter a unique set of challenges when trying to secure sustainable financing, over and above the usual difficulties associated with obtaining funds. Sustainable projects typically require higher upfront costs than regular initiatives. For example, consider an SME that wants to invest in energy-efficient machinery, implement sustainable supply chain processes, or install renewable energy systems like solar panels. These investments demand significant initial financial outlays. Given that many SMEs already operate with tight cash flows, setting aside funds for these substantial initial expenditures can be particularly difficult (Shaikh, 2024).

Moreover, SMEs often lack the necessary technical knowledge to identify, execute, and manage sustainable projects. This knowledge encompasses understanding the advantages of sustainable investments, navigating complex regulatory landscapes, and tracking and reporting sustainability metrics. Without this expertise, SMEs might hesitate to initiate sustainability projects due to fears of making errors or appearing incompetent (Ye & Kulathunga, 2019). For example, a small manufacturing business may not know how to assess the long-term benefits of switching to a more sustainable supply chain or how to comply with new environmental regulations.

The financial rewards from sustainable investments can also be less predictable and slower to materialize than those from traditional investments. This unpredictability can be a significant deterrent for SMEs, which often need to focus on maintaining short-term financial stability. For instance, while investing in renewable energy systems might promise long-term savings and sustainability benefits, the initial financial returns may be slow to appear, making the investment less appealing to an SME concerned with immediate financial health (Du, 2024).

Furthermore, SMEs frequently face market and regulatory barriers when seeking sustainable funding. These barriers can include the lack of government incentives for sustainable projects, stringent eligibility requirements for green finance products, and limited access to sustainable financing options in certain regions or industries (Kuteesa, 2024). For example, an SME in a rural area might find it difficult to access green financing due to a lack of local financial institutions offering such products, or due to stringent requirements that are hard to meet.

In conclusion, while sustainable projects offer significant long-term benefits, SMEs face substantial hurdles in securing the necessary financing. Higher upfront costs, a lack of technical expertise, uncertain financial returns, and various market and regulatory barriers all contribute to the challenges SMEs encounter. Overcoming these obstacles requires targeted support, both in terms of financial incentives and educational resources, to enable SMEs to contribute to a more sustainable economy.

5.3 The Role of Public Financial Institutions

Public financial institutions are essential in removing these obstacles and assisting SMEs in obtaining financing. Through grants or loans, they can directly assist SMEs, and indirectly, by offering assurances that bolster private financing.

SMEs can receive direct financial help from public financial institutions in the form of grants and low-interest loans that are intended for sustainable initiatives. These financial instruments have the potential to reduce the initial expenses of sustainability efforts and increase their accessibility for small and medium-sized enterprises. Grants, for instance, can be utilized to finance feasibility studies, pilot projects, and first investments, while low-interest loans can supply the money required for implementations on a wider scale (OECD, 2023a).

Guarantees from state financial institutions can greatly lower private lenders' perceptions of risk, enabling them to give loans to SMEs. In the event that the SME fails, these guarantees serve as a safety net, guaranteeing that a portion of the loan would be reimbursed. More advantageous loan conditions for SMEs, such as lower interest rates and less collateral requirements, may result from this risk minimization (Niranjala, 2020).

Public financial institutions may support SMEs in developing the skills required for sustainable projects by providing technical assistance and capacity-building initiatives, in addition to financial products. This might involve assistance with monitoring and reporting emissions, regulatory compliance advice, and training on sustainable practices.

By building the capacity of SMEs, public financial institutions can enhance their ability to implement and manage sustainable projects successfully (Saad et al., 2022).

Public financial institutions can work with other stakeholders and advocate for policies to help create settings that are supportive of sustainable financing. This may include encouraging industry norms for sustainability, collaborating with governments to create regulations that will support them, and fostering collaborations between SMEs, private investors, and other important participants in the sustainability ecosystem (Boutbhirt, 2023).

Numerous nations have effectively executed initiatives that showcase the significance of public financial institutions in facilitating small and medium-sized enterprises' access to sustainable financing. For example, the KfW Development Bank in Germany provides low-interest loans and subsidies for energy efficiency and renewable energy projects, among other green financing products, that are suited to the needs of SMEs. Comparably, the UK Green Investment Bank (now known as the Green Investment Group) has been instrumental in securing private funding for green infrastructure initiatives, frequently working with small and medium-sized enterprises (Du, 2024).

Addressing the barriers to sustainable finance for SMEs is crucial for enabling their transition to greener practices and contributing to global sustainability goals. While SMEs face significant challenges in accessing finance, especially for sustainable projects, public financial institutions can play a vital role in mitigating these barriers. Through direct financial support, risk mitigation mechanisms, technical assistance, and policy advocacy, public financial institutions can help SMEs overcome the hurdles to accessing sustainable finance and drive their journey toward sustainability. By doing so, they not only support the growth and resilience of SMEs but also contribute to broader environmental and social objectives.

5.4 A Scheme for Sustainable Finance

To delve deeper into the dynamics of demand and supply in sustainable finance, it's crucial to examine two distinct levels of interaction.

At the first level, we encounter the demand side, which encompasses stakeholders, savers, and investors seeking sustainable financial products. Here, financial intermediaries step in to fulfill this demand, either directly or indirectly. Directly, entities like funds and ETFs offer a variety of sustainable financial products tailored to meet the preferences of these stakeholders. However, the role of financial intermediaries extends beyond mere product provision. They also play a pivotal role in facilitating access to financial markets for companies engaged in sustainable initiatives. For instance, through the issuance of green bonds, banks and other intermediaries indirectly support sustainable finance. Furthermore, when banks extend loans to support green projects, they actively contribute to the economic transition towards sustainability. It's important to note that this level of interaction isn't solely driven by demand; rather, it represents a symbiotic relationship where stakeholders' preferences influence the offerings of financial intermediaries, thereby shaping the landscape of sustainable finance.

Moving to the second level, we shift our focus to the supply side of sustainable finance, primarily driven by banks, funds, and other financial intermediaries. Here, the dynamics become more intricate as financial institutions evaluate the sustainability credentials of companies seeking financial resources, particularly SMEs. However, this evaluation process is fraught with challenges, with one of the most significant hurdles being the lack of accessible information. SMEs, by nature, often lack the resources to generate comprehensive public data or historical records related to their sustainability performance. Moreover, the absence of robust organizational structures and processes further complicates the provision of this crucial information to financial intermediaries. Consequently, financial institutions face the daunting task of assessing the sustainability commitments of SMEs in the absence of reliable data points.

5.5 The Gap in Sustainability Implementation among Financial Institutions

While it is encouraging to note that most financial institutions have adopted sustainability strategies, a significant gap remains in their implementation. According to the OECD (2023b), nearly half of both public and private financial institutions have not developed specific emissions reduction targets or transition plans that outline concrete actions to achieve these targets. This gap is attributed to several critical constraints, including limited data, inadequate methodologies, and a lack of expertise related to measuring current and future emissions.

Sustainability strategies within financial institutions indicate a recognition of the importance of environmental responsibility. However, strategies alone are insufficient without actionable plans and measurable targets. Emissions reduction targets are essential for setting clear, quantifiable goals that institutions can strive to meet. Transition plans provide a roadmap for achieving these targets, detailing the steps, resources, and timelines required. Without these, sustainability strategies remain abstract commitments rather than actionable policies.

Accurate and comprehensive data on current emissions is a prerequisite for setting realistic reduction targets. Many financial institutions struggle with obtaining reliable data, particularly those related to indirect emissions (Scope 3), which include emissions from investments, lending, and supply chain activities. The complexity and scale of these indirect emissions make data collection a daunting task.

Even when data is available, methodologies for measuring and projecting emissions are often underdeveloped or inconsistent. Financial institutions need robust, standardized methodologies to assess their carbon footprints accurately. The lack of standardized approaches leads to inconsistencies in reporting and difficulties in benchmarking performance against peers.

The expertise required to develop and implement emissions reduction targets and transition plans is specialized and not always available within financial institutions. This expertise encompasses understanding carbon accounting, climate science, regulatory frameworks, and the financial implications of transitioning to a low-carbon economy. The shortage of such expertise hampers the ability of financial institutions to formulate effective and credible plans.

Emissions reduction targets and transition plans are vital components of a comprehensive sustainability strategy for several reasons. Targets provide a clear framework for accountability, enabling stakeholders to track progress and hold institutions responsible for their commitments. Investors are increasingly prioritizing ESG factors. Clear targets and transition plans can enhance investor confidence by demonstrating a commitment to managing climate risks and opportunities. As regulatory pressures around climate disclosures and emissions reductions increase, having concrete targets and plans ensures compliance and positions institutions favorably in the regulatory landscape. Institutions that proactively manage their environmental impact can differentiate themselves in the market, attracting environmentally conscious customers and partners.

Addressing these constraints requires a multifaceted approach. Financial institutions can collaborate with industry groups, regulators, and data providers to enhance the quality and availability of emissions data. Leveraging technology such as blockchain for transparent and accurate data collection can also be beneficial. Developing and adopting standardized methodologies for emissions measurement and reporting is crucial. Engaging with experts in carbon accounting, climate science, and related fields can provide the necessary expertise to formulate and implement effective emissions reduction targets and transition plans. Investing in training and capacity-building programs for staff can also help build the internal expertise needed to manage these complex issues effectively.

In essence, the interplay between demand and supply in sustainable finance operates at multiple levels, each characterized by its unique challenges and intricacies. While stakeholders drive the demand for sustainable financial products, financial intermediaries play a pivotal role in bridging the gap between investors and companies engaged in sustainable initiatives. However, the effective allocation of financial resources to SMEs remains a complex endeavor, largely due to the lack of transparency and information asymmetry inherent in this segment of the market. Addressing these challenges will be essential in unlocking the full potential of sustainable finance and fostering meaningful progress towards a more sustainable future.

5.6 Financial Instruments

5.6.1 Green Bonds for SMEs

One of the most promising financial instruments for fostering sustainability among SMEs is the green bond framework. Green bonds are debt securities designed to raise capital specifically for projects that yield positive environmental outcomes. These projects can include a wide array of initiatives, such as improvements in energy efficiency, waste-reduction efforts, and the development of sustainable supply chains.

For SMEs, green bonds can be tailored to finance smaller-scale projects, making them more accessible and relevant to these businesses. The process typically involves several key steps. Initially, an SME must identify projects that offer environmental benefits, such as upgrading to energy-efficient equipment or implementing waste management systems. Following this, the expected environmental benefits of these projects must be quantified to demonstrate their sustainability impact. Once the projects are clearly defined and their benefits assessed, green bonds can be issued to raise the necessary capital.

SMEs can derive substantial benefits from green bonds. For example, funding energy efficiency projects through green bonds can lead to significant cost savings for SMEs by reducing energy consumption and operational expenses. Furthermore, these projects can contribute to a smaller environmental footprint, aligning with broader global sustainability goals.

The advantages of green bonds for SMEs are multifaceted. They provide access to affordable capital, which is crucial for smaller enterprises that may struggle to secure funding through traditional means. Additionally, green bonds can enhance the reputation of SMEs by demonstrating a commitment to environmental sustainability, thereby attracting environmentally conscious investors and customers. Aligning with global sustainability trends through green bonds can also improve an SME's competitive edge in the market.

However, there are challenges associated with green bonds as well. One significant issue is the need for clear standards and guidelines to ensure that the projects funded are genuinely sustainable. Without robust standards, there is a risk that some projects might not achieve the intended environmental benefits, potentially leading to skepticism among investors and stakeholders. Moreover, SMEs may face difficulties in navigating the complexities involved in issuing green bonds. The process can be intricate, involving detailed documentation and compliance with various regulatory requirements. Therefore, SMEs often require support from financial advisors and institutions to successfully issue green bonds and manage the associated responsibilities. In summary, green bonds represent a valuable tool for SMEs seeking to invest in sustainable projects. By providing access to affordable capital and aligning with global sustainability trends, green bonds offer significant benefits. Nonetheless, addressing challenges such as the need for clear standards and the complexity of the issuance process is essential to fully realize their potential for promoting sustainability among SMEs.

5.6.2 Green Banks and Carbon Pricing

Another set of financial instruments crucial for SMEs are green banks and carbon pricing mechanisms. Green banks are specialized financial institutions focused on supporting green projects through various financial products, such as loans, guarantees, and credit enhancements.

Green banks play a pivotal role in mobilizing private capital for public good. They provide SMEs with the necessary financial resources to undertake green projects, often at more favorable terms than conventional banks. By offering tailored financial products, green banks can help bridge the gap between SME financing needs and available green finance. State-owned banks, alongside various social banks and financing organizations are encouraged to lower loan thresholds for SMEs and establish green financing mechanisms to propel economic recovery and sustainability (Su et al., 2022).

5.6.3 Are "Green Banks", Banks?

The Wall Street Journal article by Amrith Ramkumar, published on July 15, 2023,[1] reports that the Environmental Protection Agency (EPA) is establishing a national green bank, funded by $27 billion from last year's climate legislation. This initiative aims to support low-income communities in combating climate change. The funds are designed to address key areas such as battery storage, electric vehicle charging infrastructure, and building upgrades, which often struggle to attract private investment in economically disadvantaged areas.

EPA Administrator Michael Regan emphasized that this funding would enable communities that have previously been excluded from the clean energy transition to participate. The EPA aims to allocate these funds by September 2024. The green banks, which are not traditional banks but government-backed investment entities, will use loans, loan guarantees, and other financial tools to collaborate with private investors on clean energy projects. The goal is to reduce the risk for investors and stimulate private sector participation in these projects.

The EPA plans to allocate $20 billion of the green bank funding to national nonprofits, which will then distribute it through local networks. The remaining $7 billion will be directed towards a state solar program focusing on impoverished

[1] https://www.wsj.com/articles/epa-launches-green-bank-for-climate-funding-in-low-income-areas-13a59401

communities. This approach mirrors successful green fund models in states like New York and the U.K., where green funds have helped initiate significant clean energy projects.

Potential recipients of the funds include the Coalition for Green Capital, which manages a network of green funds, and the Justice Climate Fund, which represents minority communities. Some critics argue that the green fund program is redundant given existing tax credits and grants, while supporters believe it is essential for ensuring that the benefits of clean energy projects reach low-income populations.

According to this article, green banks are not traditional banks. Instead, they are specialized financial institutions that focus on funding and promoting clean energy and sustainable projects. Green banks are government-backed investment entities designed to accelerate private sector investment in clean energy and sustainable projects. They are typically established to address market gaps in financing, particularly for projects that may be too risky or too small for traditional lenders but are essential for achieving environmental and energy goals. Unlike traditional banks that operate primarily with private capital, green banks are often funded by government sources. This backing provides them with the financial stability and credibility needed to attract private sector investment.

Green banks use a variety of financial tools to support projects. These can include loans, loan guarantees, and other forms of debt financing. By leveraging government funds, green banks can offer more favorable terms to project developers and reduce the perceived risk for private investors. The primary mission of green banks is to finance projects that contribute to environmental sustainability. This can include investments in renewable energy, energy efficiency improvements, sustainable transportation, and other climate-related initiatives.

Green banks collaborate with private sector investors and financial institutions. By providing initial capital and reducing risk, green banks make it more attractive for private investors to participate in clean energy projects that might otherwise be too risky or not financially viable.

Green banks are designed to fill gaps in the market where traditional financing is lacking. This often includes small-scale projects or projects in underserved communities that have difficulty accessing capital from conventional sources.

For example, the Coalition for Green Capital, a prominent entity in the green bank network, operates as the American Green Bank Consortium. It has successfully helped establish green banks in various states and localities, facilitating funding for clean energy projects and leveraging both public and private investment.

In summary, green banks are not conventional banks but are specialized institutions with a mission to promote clean energy and sustainability. They leverage government funding and work with private investors to support projects that might otherwise struggle to attract investment.

5.6.4 Carbon Pricing

Carbon pricing mechanisms, such as carbon taxes and cap-and-trade systems, represent pivotal strategies in the global effort to mitigate climate change. These tools assign a monetary value to carbon emissions, creating economic incentives for businesses to reduce their greenhouse gas emissions. The underlying principle of carbon pricing is straightforward: by making carbon emissions costly, businesses are motivated to adopt cleaner technologies and practices to minimize their financial burden.

A carbon tax directly sets a price on carbon emissions by taxing each ton of CO2 emitted. This creates a clear financial incentive for businesses to lower their emissions, either by improving efficiency, switching to renewable energy sources, or investing in carbon capture technologies. The effectiveness of a carbon tax depends largely on its level—higher taxes create stronger incentives to reduce emissions.

Cap-and-trade systems, also known as emissions trading systems, cap the total level of greenhouse gas emissions allowed and permit industries with low emissions to sell their extra allowances to larger emitters. This creates a market for emission reductions and encourages businesses to innovate and reduce their emissions in the most cost-effective manner. The cap ensures that overall emissions stay within a defined limit, while the trading mechanism provides flexibility for businesses to meet their targets.

Boutbhirt (2023) highlights the dual benefits of carbon pricing mechanisms. On the environmental front, these tools are instrumental in achieving sustainability outcomes by directly addressing the economic cost of carbon emissions. By internalizing the external cost of emissions, businesses are driven to adopt practices and technologies that reduce their carbon footprint. This shift not only contributes to global climate goals but also supports the transition to a low-carbon economy. For investors, carbon pricing offers potential returns by creating a market for green technologies and sustainable practices. As businesses seek to minimize their carbon liabilities, they often invest in innovative solutions that align with carbon pricing frameworks. This opens up investment opportunities in sectors such as renewable energy, energy efficiency, and carbon capture technologies. Thus, carbon pricing can stimulate demand for green investments and provide attractive returns for investors.

While carbon pricing has significant potential, it is not without challenges. The design and implementation of carbon pricing mechanisms require careful consideration to avoid unintended economic consequences. For instance, carbon taxes that are too high may lead to increased costs for consumers and potentially harm economic competitiveness if not managed properly. Conversely, taxes that are too low might not provide sufficient incentive for substantial emissions reductions.

Cap-and-trade systems, while flexible, can face challenges related to market volatility and the allocation of emission allowances. Ensuring that the cap is set at an appropriate level and that the trading system is transparent and efficient is crucial for maintaining the system's effectiveness and credibility.

Additionally, for SMEs, the initial impact of carbon pricing can be more pronounced. SMEs often have fewer resources to invest in emissions reduction technologies and might face a higher financial burden compared to larger corporations. Therefore, supporting SMEs through transitional assistance, such as subsidies or access to green financing, can help them adapt to carbon pricing mechanisms and ensure that they can compete on a level playing field.

Integrating carbon pricing into broader environmental policies can enhance its effectiveness. For instance, combining carbon pricing with supportive measures such as grants for green technologies, energy efficiency programs, and research and development incentives can create a comprehensive framework for reducing emissions and promoting sustainable practices. Moreover, transparency and stakeholder engagement are key to successful carbon pricing implementation. Engaging businesses, investors, and the public in discussions about carbon pricing policies helps build support and ensures that the mechanisms are designed to address the needs and concerns of various stakeholders.

In summary, carbon pricing mechanisms like carbon taxes and cap-and-trade systems are critical tools for driving reductions in greenhouse gas emissions and fostering a transition to a sustainable economy. They create economic incentives for businesses to reduce their carbon footprints while offering investment opportunities in green technologies. However, successful implementation requires careful design to balance economic impacts and ensure that the benefits are widely distributed. Supporting SMEs through transitional measures and integrating carbon pricing with complementary policies can enhance its effectiveness and support the broader goal of sustainability.

5.7 Aligning Financial Products with Green Finance Principles: Global Practices in Sustainable Finance

According to Kuteesa (2024), aligning financial products with green finance principles is essential for enhancing the sustainability performance of both financial institutions and the SMEs they serve.

One of the central tenets of sustainable finance is the alignment of financial products with green finance principles. This involves developing and offering financial products that are specifically designed to support environmentally sustainable projects and practices. Green finance principles typically focus on projects that contribute to reducing carbon emissions, improving energy efficiency, and fostering the development of renewable energy sources.

Kuteesa (2024) emphasizes that financial institutions must tailor their offerings to meet these green finance principles to enhance their own sustainability performance and better support SMEs.

Aligning financial products with green finance principles not only benefits SMEs but also enhances the sustainability performance of financial institutions themselves.

Institutions that are proactive in sustainable finance can strengthen their reputation and differentiate themselves in the market. This can attract environmentally conscious investors and clients, providing a competitive edge in an increasingly green-conscious marketplace.

By focusing on sustainable finance, institutions can better manage environmental and financial risks. Investing in green projects can reduce exposure to risks associated with climate change, such as regulatory changes or physical impacts, and align with global trends towards stricter environmental regulations.

5.7.1 Global Best Practices in Sustainability

Successful green finance initiatives often involve collaboration between public and private sectors. For example, national green banks and development finance institutions can partner with private financial institutions to leverage public funding and scale up investments in green projects. Global standards and certifications for green finance, such as the Green Bond Principles or the Climate Bonds Standard, help ensure that projects financed are genuinely sustainable. Adopting these standards can provide credibility and assurance to investors and SMEs alike.

Exploring innovative financing models, such as impact investing or blended finance, can enhance the effectiveness of green finance. These models combine different sources of capital and risk-sharing mechanisms to support projects that might otherwise struggle to secure funding.

Building the capacity of SMEs and financial institutions through education and training is crucial. Programs that focus on understanding green finance principles, project evaluation, and reporting can help both SMEs and financial institutions effectively navigate the green finance landscape.

Global practices in sustainable finance underscore the importance of aligning financial products with green finance principles to support SMEs in their green transition. By offering green bonds, sustainable investment funds, and tailored financial instruments, financial institutions can help SMEs access the capital they need to implement environmentally sustainable projects. Additionally, such alignment enhances the sustainability performance of financial institutions themselves, providing reputational, risk management, and financial benefits. Drawing on global best practices and insights can further strengthen these efforts, ensuring that the transition to a sustainable economy is both effective and inclusive.

5.7.2 The Role of Financial Literacy

Encouraging financial literacy is essential to helping SMEs become more sustainable. Establishing good capital structures that optimize long-term gains and reduce expenses is made possible for SMEs by a deep grasp of sustainable practices and financial instruments. According to Ye and Kulathunga (2019), SMEs may create a sustainable culture in their operations by using increased financial literacy to assist them make well-informed decisions regarding funding sustainable initiatives.

There are a number of ways that may be used to increase financial literacy. These consist of seminars, online classes, and consulting services designed with SMEs' unique requirements in mind. Financial organizations may make a big difference by providing instructional materials that outline the advantages and workings of green finance.

Enhancing financial literacy may significantly influence the long-term growth of small and medium-sized enterprises. SMEs may improve resource management, lower operating expenses, and invest in long-term, sustainable initiatives by learning how to use financial instruments successfully. This helps them achieve more social and environmental objectives in addition to improving their financial security.

5.7.3 *Islamic Finance as a Tool for Sustainability*

Islamic banking offers special structures that can effectively meet SME funding needs. These structures conform to principles such as the prohibition of interest (riba), the emphasis on risk-sharing, and ethical investing. Islamic finance may be a potent instrument for SMEs, offering competitive and efficient financing options that can result in the creation of jobs and economic growth, according to Benbekhti et al. (2021).

Islamic finance instruments, including Murabaha, Ijarah, and Mudarabah, offer unique advantages that align closely with the needs of SMEs. These instruments provide flexible and ethical financing options that are particularly relevant in the context of SMEs, which often face significant financial constraints and challenges in accessing traditional financing.

Murabaha, or cost-plus financing, operates on the principle of selling an asset at a profit margin agreed upon in advance. Unlike conventional loans, which typically involve interest payments, Murabaha structures the financing as a sale, where the cost and profit are predetermined and clearly outlined. This arrangement provides SMEs with a predictable repayment plan and avoids the financial burden of interest. For small businesses, which may struggle with cash flow issues and financial uncertainty, the clarity and stability offered by Murabaha can be particularly beneficial.

Ijarah, or leasing, allows SMEs to acquire assets without needing to purchase them outright. Instead, the company leases the asset from the financier for a specified period. This arrangement can be highly advantageous for SMEs that require equipment or property but lack the capital to make a full purchase. Ijarah provides flexibility, enabling SMEs to use the asset while managing their cash flow more effectively. Additionally, because Ijarah agreements do not involve interest, they align with Islamic financial principles and can appeal to businesses operating in regions where interest-based transactions are less acceptable.

Mudarabah, or profit-sharing, is another Islamic finance instrument that is well-suited to SMEs. In a Mudarabah agreement, one party provides the capital while the other provides expertise and management. Profits from the venture are shared according to a pre-agreed ratio, but the loss is borne only by the capital provider. This model supports SMEs by allowing them to access financing without taking on debt or interest obligations. Mudarabah can also foster entrepreneurial activity, as it encourages the pooling of resources and sharing of risks and rewards. For SMEs with innovative ideas but limited capital, Mudarabah can provide an avenue for growth and development.

Overall, Islamic finance instruments align well with the needs of SMEs by offering financing options that adhere to ethical principles and avoid the pitfalls of interest-based loans. These instruments not only reduce financial strain but also support the growth and sustainability of SMEs by providing flexible, asset-based, and risk-sharing financial solutions. By integrating these Islamic finance principles, SMEs can better navigate their financial challenges while adhering to ethical standards, making these instruments a valuable addition to the financing landscape for small and medium-sized enterprises.

SMEs might benefit from a special mechanism provided by waqf, a traditional Islamic financial instrument, especially in areas where Islamic financing is widely prevalent. According to Saad et al. (2022), there is a great deal of opportunity for Waqf—which is the endowment of assets for philanthropic and communal purposes—to offer SMEs long-term and sustainable finance.

In order to assist a variety of objectives, including social and economic development, assets, such as cash, land, or real estate, can be donated to a charity organization under the Waqf idea. After it is created, the endowed assets in the Waqf fund yield returns or revenue that is allocated to the stated objective. With the help of this framework, an endless stream of money is created that may be used to support ongoing efforts and projects.

Waqf may be very helpful for SMEs since it adheres to the values of community development and sustainability. Because of their size, perceived risk, or lack of collateral, SMEs frequently have trouble obtaining traditional funding. These businesses can access funding intended for social and economic development by utilizing Waqf. In addition to helping SMEs meet their capital needs, this kind of funding incorporates their operations into larger community and development objectives.

One of Waqf's main benefits to SMEs is its capacity to offer a reliable, long-term source of capital. Waqf funds, in contrast to traditional loans or equity investments, are meant to be used over a longer period of time and do not have an instant return requirement. With no imminent financial commitments or interest payments to worry about, SMEs may benefit from a more stable financial climate as a result.

Additionally, using Waqf to encourage SME growth is consistent with the core values of Islamic finance, which include social responsibility and moral corporate conduct. Funds from the waqf can be allocated to businesses that support community development, environmental sustainability, and social welfare. This has a favorable effect on the larger social framework in which these enterprises operate in addition to the specific businesses.

Nevertheless, there are obstacles and factors to take into account when putting Waqf for SME support into practice. Careful planning and governance are necessary for the establishment and management of a Waqf fund in order to guarantee that the assets are used responsibly and that the fund will endure over time. Additionally, SMEs must manage the administrative and legal requirements for obtaining Waqf money, which might change based on the area and the specific Waqf structure. According to Saad et al. (2022), cooperation between financial institutions, community groups, and legislators is necessary for the effective integration of Waqf into SME finance. Through collaborative efforts, these parties can establish structures and procedures that enable the efficient use of Waqf funds, guaranteeing their usage for the advancement of sustainable development and SMEs' expansion.

To sum up, Waqf presents a viable way to help SMEs by giving them access to a sustainable and moral finance solution. By utilizing Waqf, SMEs can have access to funding specifically designed to help their expansion and align with more general objectives of social and economic development. To maintain Waqf's long-term impact and optimize its advantages, many stakeholders must work together and exercise rigorous management.

5.7.4 Supply Chain Finance[2]

Supply chain financing, or SCF, is essential to supporting SMEs' sustainable development. SCF is an umbrella term for a range of financial strategies that use the creditworthiness of bigger, more reliable purchasers to reduce financial risks and maximize cash flow. SCF greatly improves SMEs' financial capability, allowing them to adopt sustainable practices and support their growth and stability (Wang et al., 2020).

SCF methods are essential for SMEs looking to manage their working capital more effectively. These mechanisms include factoring, reverse factoring, and dynamic discounting. Reverse factoring enables SMEs to obtain early payment on their bills through agreements signed by their purchasers, whereas factoring entails selling receivables to a financial institution at a discount in return for instant cash.

Discounts on bills are given via dynamic discounting in return for early payment. Every one of these methods contributes to increased liquidity, which lowers the requirement for outside borrowing. SMEs are better positioned to participate in sustainable projects without jeopardizing their financial stability by improving their cash flow.

The increase in cash flow is one of SCF's main advantages for SMEs. SCF procedures help SMEs better fulfill their operational demands and seize development

[2] See also Chap. 1.

opportunities by expediting the availability of working cash. Better cash flow makes it possible for SMEs to make investments in environmentally friendly activities that may otherwise be unaffordable, including upgrading waste management procedures or implementing energy-efficient technology.

Furthermore, SCF lowers SMEs' financial risks by lessening the effects of late payments and erratic market circumstances. Compared to conventional borrowing methods, SCF enables SMEs to get funding at a reduced risk and expense by leveraging the creditworthiness of bigger customers. For SMEs dealing with erratic payment schedules or working in turbulent markets, this risk minimization is very beneficial.

Moreover, SCF improves the connections within the supply chain by encouraging increased cooperation between SMEs and their bigger consumers. SMEs may improve their integration and resilience in the supply chain by aligning their operations with the demands and expectations of their bigger partners through SCF initiatives. SMEs are now better positioned to invest in sustainability and are more resilient to changes in the market.

To sum up, SCF is an essential tool for assisting SMEs in developing sustainably. SCF methods help SMEs engage in and implement sustainable practices by boosting cash flow, lowering financial risks, and strengthening supply chain linkages. According to Wang et al. (2020), SCF is a crucial part of contemporary financial strategies for small and medium-sized businesses as it supports the expansion and stability of SMEs and is consistent with larger sustainability objectives.

5.7.5 The Role of Innovation: Digital (Inclusive) Finance

Digitally inclusive finance has become a key tool for promoting green innovation among SMEs. It provides financial services via the use of digital technology. Du (2024) asserts that digital banking increases access to financial resources, reduces expenses, and improves service efficiency to effectively relieve financing restrictions encountered by SMEs.

Peer-to-peer lending, crowdsourcing, and mobile banking are just a few of the digital tools and platforms that give SMEs new opportunities to get money. For SMEs operating in poor nations where traditional banking infrastructure may be undeveloped or unavailable, these digital alternatives are extremely beneficial. SMEs may monitor their accounts and conduct financial transactions from a distance with the help of mobile banking, which lessens their need for physical bank branches. Peer-to-peer lending platforms eliminate traditional financial middlemen by putting SMEs and individual investors directly in contact. SMEs can receive modest sums of money from a large number of individuals through crowdfunding, sometimes in exchange for prizes or equity. By lowering financial obstacles, these digital breakthroughs provide a more welcoming financial climate that encourages the testing and uptake of environmentally friendly activities and technology.

Digital inclusive finance encourages an innovative culture that is vital for sustainable development by lowering the cost and increasing the accessibility of financial services. These digital financial services may be used by SMEs, who are frequently at the forefront of implementing new practices and technology, to invest in and carry out green solutions. For instance, SMEs may be able to create and implement energy-efficient equipment, renewable energy systems, or other ecologically beneficial inventions with the help of peer-to-peer lending or crowdfunding.

Apart from digital inclusive finance, financial intermediaries and leasing businesses provide novel lending solutions that tackle ongoing funding obstacles faced by small and medium-sized enterprises. Jaabi (2018) emphasizes how important these technologies are in giving SMEs the funding they need to develop sustainable projects. For example, leasing is a different kind of finance that SMEs may use to buy assets without having to make large upfront payments. For SMEs looking to invest in expensive green technology like solar panels or cutting-edge energy-efficient systems, this is especially advantageous. By lessening their initial financial load, SMEs may adopt sustainable practices without exhausting their cash reserves thanks to leasing.

Moreover, by lowering information asymmetry through creative credit rating methods, financial institutions can improve SME access to financing. Ismanto et al. (2022) draw attention to the possibility that these models—which use sophisticated analytics and non-traditional data sources—could yield a more precise evaluation of SME creditworthiness. Conventional credit scoring techniques sometimes fall short of providing a complete picture of a tiny or newly established company's financial situation, especially when it comes to its credit history. Financial organizations are able to provide more accurate and customized credit assessments by employing advanced analytics and alternative data. This enhanced evaluation makes it easier and more advantageous for SMEs to obtain finance, which encourages them to engage in sustainable practices and green technology.

In conclusion, creative lending technologies and digitally inclusive financing play a critical role in helping SMEs make the transition to a greener economy. By increasing capital accessibility, cutting expenses, and improving service effectiveness, digital finance solutions empower SMEs to invest in and develop sustainable technology. In a similar vein, alternative financing options such as leasing and sophisticated credit rating models remove important funding obstacles, enabling SMEs to undertake green projects more easily and confidently. SMEs may more effectively manage their financial difficulties and support larger sustainability objectives by using these financial solutions.

5.8 Conclusion

The landscape of financial instruments available for green finance tailored to SMEs is diverse and evolving. From green bonds and Islamic finance to supply chain finance and digital inclusive finance, SMEs have access to a wide array of tools to support their sustainability efforts. By leveraging these instruments and aligning them with green principles, SMEs can drive their own sustainable development while contributing to broader environmental and social goals. This comprehensive approach not only helps SMEs mitigate the impacts of climate change but also enhances their competitiveness and resilience in a rapidly changing economic landscape. As SMEs continue to play a crucial role in global economies, ensuring they have access to appropriate green finance is essential for achieving sustainable development worldwide. By adopting innovative financial instruments and enhancing financial literacy, SMEs can navigate the complexities of sustainable finance and position themselves as leaders in the green economy.

References

Benbekhti, S., Boulila, H., & Bouteldja, A. (2021). Islamic finance, small and medium enterprises and job creation in Turkey: Empirical evidence (2009-2017). *International Journal of Islamic Economics and Finance (Ijief), 4*(SI). https://doi.org/10.18196/ijief.v4i0.10490

Boutbhirt, N. (2023). Financial innovation of small and medium enterprises in Morocco in the area of energy optimization: State of the art. *E3s Web of Conferences, 412*, 01084. https://doi.org/10.1051/e3sconf/202341201084

Du, C. (2024). Research on the impact of digital inclusive finance on green innovation of smes. *Sustainability, 16*(11), 4700. https://doi.org/10.3390/su16114700

Farinha, L., & Félix, S. (2015). Credit rationing for portuguese smes. *Finance Research Letters, 14*, 167–177. https://doi.org/10.1016/j.frl.2015.05.001

Hernández-Cánovas, G., & Koëter-Kant, J. (2011). Sme financing in europe: Cross-country determinants of bank loan maturity. *International Small Business Journal Researching Entrepreneurship, 29*(5), 489–507. https://doi.org/10.1177/0266242611402569

Ismanto, H., Pratiwi, T., Zulianti, N., & Qofur, A. (2022). The role of competencies, financial planning, and access to finance in explaining smes financial innovation. *Jurnal Manajemen Dan Kewirausahaan, 24*(1), 44–51. https://doi.org/10.9744/jmk.24.1.44-51

Jaabi, S. (2018). Sme finance and economic development paradox: The case of fish industry in The Gambia. *Advances in Social Sciences Research Journal, 5*(9). https://doi.org/10.14738/assrj.59.4790

Kuteesa, K. (2024). Exploring global practices in providing small and medium enterprises access to sustainable finance solutions. *World Journal of Advanced Science and Technology, 5*(2), 035–051. https://doi.org/10.53346/wjast.2024.5.2.0034

Niranjala, S. A. U. (2020). Financial Innovations for SMEs in Sri Lanka. *Journal of Economics and Sustainable Development, 11*(20) www.iiste.org

OECD. (2023a). *Financing SMEs for sustainability: Challenges and opportunities*. OECD Publishing.

OECD (2023b). *Financing SMEs for sustainability—Financial institution strategies and approaches financing SMES for sustainability results of an OECD survey of public and private financial institutions*.

Saad, A., Mohammed, M., Al-Jubari, I., & Ahamed, F. (2022). The prospect of waqf in financing small and medium enterprises (smes) in Yemen. *Qijis (Qudus International Journal of Islamic Studies), 10*(2), 381. https://doi.org/10.21043/qijis.v10i2.9689

Shaikh, S. (2024). Impact of green corporate governance and green finance on sustainable performance: a case of manufacturing smes of pakistan. *Contemporary Issues in Social Sciences and Management Practices, 3*(1), 221–230. https://doi.org/10.61503/cissmp.v3i1.129

Su, W., Guo, X., Ling, Y., & Fan, Y. (2022). China's smes developed characteristics and countermeasures in the post-epidemic era. *Frontiers in Psychology, 13*. https://doi.org/10.3389/fpsyg.2022.842646

Wang, K., Yan, F., Zhang, Y., Xiao, Y., & Gu, L. (2020). Supply chain financial risk evaluation of small- and medium-sized enterprises under smart city. *Journal of Advanced Transportation, 2020*, 1–14. https://doi.org/10.1155/2020/8849356

Ye, J., & Kulathunga, K. (2019). How does financial literacy promote sustainability in smes? A developing country perspective. *Sustainability, 11*(10), 2990. https://doi.org/10.3390/su11102990

Chapter 6
Initial Coin Offering as a Possible Way to Obtain Financial Resources

6.1 Introduction

In this chapter, we analyze the role of Initial Coin Offerings (ICOs) in financing companies and SMEs, particularly when they are engaged in sustainability challenges. To raise the money required to finance a business initiative, initial coin offerings, or ICOs, are akin to crowdfunding and initial public offerings (IPOs). They are sometimes referred to as "token sales" since Fisch (2019) describes them as "a fundraising method used by new companies to raise capital by selling tokens to a crowd of investors." In contrast to conventional funding methods, ICOs entail the creation of digital coins or tokens as opposed to conventional financial instruments like shares that are made available to investors. These tokens can be bought using fiat money or, increasingly often, cryptocurrencies like Ether and Bitcoin. Distributed ledger technology (DLT) is used for the creation, issuance, and transfer of these tokens. An ICO may involve tokens with a range of features and rights for the holder, including using rights that grant access to a service, property rights that signify ownership, and rights to a physical object on the blockchain. The majority of tokens offered in ICOs are utility tokens, which may be used to pay for an issuer's good or service. An ICO is typically publicized by publishing a document called a "White Paper," which includes a wealth of information about the project, the underlying blockchain, the project's operation, the rights of the holders, and the value of the issued tokens. In addition, ICOs may have a presale stage exclusive to major investors, succeeded by an open public sale whereby a restricted quantity of tokens are typically distributed (Gutmann & Schückes, 2020). In the wake of the 2008 financial crisis, ICOs have become a novel means of funding for businesses, especially startups and SMEs. Due to the exorbitant risks attached to subprime mortgages, the international financial system was severely harmed during the crisis, which hindered banks from lending enough money to market participants and created issues with financing availability. This resulted in a fall in the amount of credit

M. Aliano et al., *Sustainable Finance for SMEs*, Sustainable Finance,
https://doi.org/10.1007/978-3-031-74193-7_6

that financial institutions were willing to provide to consumers and businesses, particularly SMEs. This was due to the financial institutions' incapacity and unwillingness to lend money, rather than a decline in demand. This occurrence, commonly referred to as the "credit crunch," made the crisis worse and caused the production of the economy to decline significantly (Boreiko & Sahdev, 2018). Venture capital has become more consolidated as a result of its growing acceptance since the 1980s as a viable alternative to bank loans for startups with strong growth potential. Businesses looking for finance to launch or grow started going to venture capitalists more frequently than they were going to traditional banks. Even while venture capital is riskier than standard bank loans, investors might potentially receive larger returns if the firm is successful. Apart from providing funding, venture capitalists frequently offer assistance, counsel, and guidance from professionals in the field. They also own vast networks of connections and assets that they may make accessible to firms they have backed. For businesses that are just getting started or are expanding, this is quite beneficial as it helps them grow and succeed. But after the financial crisis of 2008, investors started to be much more selective and careful when lending money to start-up businesses, since they saw them as high-risk ventures.

In order to safeguard investors and avert further financial disasters, the amount of market liquidity was reduced throughout those years, and new laws and regulations were implemented. This made it harder for businesses to get bank loans or venture capital to get the money they needed. In essence, a more restricted environment was produced by the combination of these three variables (high risk, less liquidity, and regulatory reforms), which limited the funding alternatives for businesses with potential for development.

Token offers emerged specifically in this setting, hoping to give a fresh and creative approach to obtaining the capital required to launch and grow company ventures. By facilitating the direct fundraising of capital from the investor community via the digital token sale, these offers lowered reliance on conventional financial institutions. This gave businesses new options and made it possible for them to easily and swiftly obtain capital without having to go through the drawn-out and expensive procedures that are usually connected with traditional financing. The introduction of Bitcoin, blockchain, and other cryptocurrencies, which brought about the creation of a new financial system and a new means of transferring value through peer-to-peer transactions outside the established system, also contributed to the growth of ICOs. The decentralized blockchain technology removed the need for intermediaries and allowed for the safe and transparent issuance and trade of digital tokens, opening up ICOs to a worldwide audience. In addition, the utilization of cryptocurrencies as a mode of payment expedited and enhanced the effectiveness of transactions.

6.2 ICO and Sustainability

With the advent of cryptocurrency token sales, ICOs have become a cutting-edge way to fund development and provide prospects for creative fundraising methods in the digital age (Howell et al., 2018). Researchers are examining how ICOs might propel sustainable and social finance into its own asset class, as the relationship between ICOs and sustainability has gained more and more attention (Brochado & Troilo, 2021). Research has examined what drives ICO activity, including what influences digital start-ups' tweeting habits when they use ICOs to raise capital (Moro et al., 2023).

Furthermore, ICO research is becoming more and more popular, which emphasizes the necessity for comprehensive investigation of this financing strategy and its implications for future research orientations (Brochado & Troilo, 2021).

When it comes to sustainability, ICOs present a special way to fund initiatives that support social and environmental objectives. Preliminary data indicates a favorable correlation between financing quantities in utility token offerings and ESG disclosure (Bongini et al., 2022). This suggests that ICO marketplaces have the ability to stimulate sustainable finance.

Additionally, the use of ICO data might promote a new wave of investment in ecologically aware enterprises by helping to marketize sustainable and social finance (Bongini et al., 2022). Companies may reach a wide range of investors who are eager to fund projects that put sustainability and social responsibility first by utilizing ICOs. Beyond only financial factors, there is a link between sustainability and ICOs that includes wider environmental consequences and initiatives to mitigate climate change. To improve urban development and handle ecological concerns, research has highlighted the significance of investigating the real-world applications of smart and sustainable cities (Angelidou et al., 2017). Furthermore, research has demonstrated the need for tracking vegetation state and ecosystem dynamics over time by utilizing cutting-edge technology like phenocams to monitor environmental changes (Brown et al., 2016). Researchers can improve our knowledge of the effects of climate change and ecosystem functioning by combining data from many networks and sources. This will help with sustainable resource management and well-informed decision-making (Brown et al., 2016). In summary, the developing field of ICOs offers a viable way to advance environmental projects and encourage sustainability through creative funding methods. Through investigating the relationship between ICOs and sustainability objectives, scholars might find novel avenues for financing ecologically aware initiatives and promoting efforts to mitigate climate change. It is possible to transform conventional financial models and hasten the shift to a more robust and sustainable future by fusing ICO findings with sustainability practices.

6.3 The Attractiveness of ICOs for Companies: Motivations and Gains

Generally, the need to secure funding is the primary reason driving the establishment of an ICO. Unlike traditional fundraising methods, ICOs enable companies to overcome the geographical limitations often associated with conventional financing channels and reach a wide base of investors globally, rather than relying solely on institutional investors or high-net-worth individuals (Kotiloglu & Ometto, 2024).

Their digital nature allows investors from all corners of the world to participate easily via the internet platform, facilitating faster transactions and shorter fundraising periods. This eliminates the need for financial intermediaries, which typically involve longer collection times and higher transaction costs. Consequently, ICOs are perceived as a superior form of crowdfunding, as they do not require an intermediary platform and thereby accelerate the fundraising process.

Compared to seeking angel investors or venture capitalists, an ICO is considered a quicker and less cumbersome way to raise initial capital. This is one of the main reasons companies are inclined towards this fundraising instrument. Angel investors and venture capitalists both provide funding during a company's startup phase, but they differ in terms of investment size, involvement in the company, and investment goals (Hellmann et al., 2021). Specifically, angel investors (or business angels) are private individuals who use their own capital; however, their investments tend to be smaller than those of venture capitalists, who manage funds raised from institutional investors and invest larger sums. VCs generally take a more active role in the strategic management of the company.

Traditional investors often conduct a more thorough decision-making process before committing to an investment, as these are riskier and larger in monetary terms compared to an ICO. For instance, business angels often invest in early stages of a company where both risk and growth potential are high. This leads to a more detailed evaluation of the business model, development prospects, and company leadership, as well as other critical factors, but it lengthens the timeframe compared to the faster and broader-reaching ICO. Furthermore, ICOs are preferred as a funding method because they allow companies to retain decision-making control, unlike the approach taken by venture capitalists.

Startups also use ICOs as a method to assess the market potential of their ideas and business models. For example, by selling utility tokens for a product or service under development, they can test market demand and evaluate the purchasing readiness of future customers without making additional investments in research and development. Thus, ICOs can also be considered a way to generate interest in launching new products and services, efficiently attracting consumer attention and avoiding excessive marketing costs. Additionally, through the direct participation of users in the project, ICOs can create a closer bond between investors and the company, as well as a community of innovators and users who contribute their knowledge and experience to the project's development. This community then plays a crucial role as beta testers, providing timely feedback on product or service features, allowing for the identification of any weaknesses. A study conducted in 2020 by German researchers Schückes and Gutmann highlighted that in some cases, the decision to launch an ICO is not justified solely by economic factors but is also influenced by personal and ideological reasons. These are often linked to shared ideals of collaboration that steer entrepreneurs towards token offerings, driven by the desire to promote collaboration, make investments more accessible to a broader audience, and contribute to socially positive goals.

6.3.1 Risks Associated with ICOs

ICOs can present significant risks for contributors, which can be categorized in various ways according to Chebukhanova et al. (2021). The first category includes analytical risks, which pertain to the potential failure of funded projects, often due to the lack of comprehensive and accurate information provided by the issuer about the project. This makes it difficult to assess the potential for success. Unlike established businesses, ICO projects are characterized by significant asymmetry and opacity of information and rely on the so-called White Paper prepared by project promoters. While some are more technical and complete, others provide only a partial amount of information (Adhami et al., 2018). The second category encompasses technical risks, which are related to the negligent management of funds and potentially fraudulent activities, as token offerings are conducted online and in a decentralized manner through blockchain technology.

Finally, there are financial risks associated with the extreme volatility of cryptocurrencies, which can lead to substantial fluctuations in the value of the issued tokens. Financial risks are the most challenging to predict.

To effectively address and mitigate the potential risks associated with ICOs, it is essential to develop a detailed White Paper that accurately describes the project, objectives, development team, and involved parties. This approach aims to provide clear, complete, and transparent information to potential investors, thereby reducing information asymmetries and promoting informed decision-making based on a thorough understanding of the project and its implications.

6.3.2 Classification of Tokens

Tokens are traditionally distinguished between cryptocurrencies and crypto-assets. Cryptocurrencies include payment tokens and stable coins, while crypto-assets are categorized into security tokens and utility tokens. Based on the economic function performed by the instrument, we can distinguish three main categories of tokens according to the EBA (2019). Payment tokens encompass cryptocurrencies and stable coins. Stable coins are a particular type of virtual currency that maintains a stable value over time because they are linked to the value of a legal tender currency or a commodity. Payment tokens do not grant rights to the holder (unlike investment or utility tokens) but are used as a means of exchange (e.g., for buying or selling goods provided by an entity other than the token issuer), for investment purposes, or for value storage. Notable examples include Bitcoin and Litecoin. Utility tokens generally provide access to the issuer's future products or services and typically require the use of blockchain infrastructure; however, they are not accepted as a means of payment for other products or services. In this sense, utility tokens act as a smart contract between the buyer and the seller, where the buyer has the right to early access to the company's new products or services, often designed with integrated functionalities through smart contracts that define the rules and conditions of use. Security tokens grant economic, or property rights linked to the performance of a business initiative (e.g., the right to participate in the distribution of future profits) or administrative rights (such as voting rights on certain matters) to the issuer. Generally, security tokens represent rights to underlying assets such as cash flows or real estate; they are also known as "equity tokens" or "investment tokens." These three distinct types of tokens can combine to create mixed or hybrid tokens. For the same project, a company may issue multiple types of tokens. The choice of the ideal token to issue for each project depends on various factors, such as funding needs, agency problems, and platform characteristics.

In addition to the fungible tokens described above, there are also Non-Fungible Tokens (NFTs), which are unique tokens representing an individual asset and utilizing blockchain technology. Unlike traditional cryptocurrencies like Bitcoin or Ethereum, which are fungible, NFTs represent unique assets that cannot be replaced by another equivalent. Their use is widespread in various fields, such as the art market or sports content, where they are used to certify the authenticity and ownership of assets such as digital artworks, music, and so on. Generally, the most frequently issued tokens in initial coin offerings are utility tokens, which, unlike security tokens, do not offer an actual monetary ownership stake in a company but simply allow access to the company's products or services. Besides utility tokens, the other most common ones are equity tokens; these represent a form of equity participation in an organization or project and are used like shares or participation quotas whose value is linked to the performance of the issuing company.

6.3.3 Example of Token in Boosting Sustainability for SMEs

Because ICOs provide a decentralized means of obtaining cash, companies may avoid using conventional financial middlemen. This is especially helpful for SMEs that struggle to get sustainable financing because of their high startup costs and onerous regulatory requirements. SMEs may raise money through ICOs from a worldwide pool of investors who are becoming more and more interested in funding green initiatives. This essay addresses the wider implications for sustainable finance and looks at many instances of ICOs that have effectively promoted sustainability in small and medium-sized enterprises.

One well-known ICO that supports sustainability as an example of a token in the energy sector, is Power Ledger. In order to build a blockchain-based platform for peer-to-peer energy trading, Australia-based Power Ledger conducted an ICO in 2017 and raised $34 million. Individuals and businesses may conduct direct transactions for renewable energy using the platform. This decentralized approach encourages the adoption of sustainable energy sources by making it easier for consumers to acquire renewable energy and for producers to sell excess energy. Power Ledger issues tokens that stand in for energy credits in order to make the platform easier to use. By enabling the exchange of these tokens, the platform establishes a transparent and functional green energy market. This idea promotes the utilization of renewable energy sources while also democratizing the energy market. This model not only promotes the use of clean energy but also democratizes the energy market, making it more accessible and affordable for everyone.[1]

WePower,[2] a blockchain-based green energy trading platform, also used an ICO to fund its activities in the same industry. Through its ICO in 2018, WePower collected $40 million to build a platform that allows renewable energy producers to generate finance by selling energy tokens, or future energy output, up front. Consumers may then exchange or utilize these tokens, establishing a direct line of communication between producers and consumers of green energy. WePower's strategy has two advantages: it allows customers the chance to make direct investments in green energy while also giving renewable energy companies the capital they need to grow. This technique assists in removing the financial obstacles that frequently obstruct the growth of renewable energy initiatives, especially for smaller producers.

An example of using ICOs to finance solar energy projects is the South African business, Sun Exchange. The startup makes solar cell leasing and purchases easier by utilizing blockchain technology. Users of the website can purchase solar cells for use in a variety of projects and rent them out to companies, educational institutions, and other organizations in developing nations. This strategy gives the local population access to inexpensive, clean energy while producing lease income for the owners of solar cells. Sun Exchange held an ICO in 2018 to seek money for business expansion. More solar projects were constructed with the help of money, expanding the supply of clean energy and encouraging sustainable development in impoverished areas. This approach also provides a novel way for investors to participate in the green economy, aligning financial returns with positive environmental impact.

To develop a blockchain-based carbon credit trading market, CarbonX held an ICO. By improving the market's efficiency and transparency, the platform hopes to make carbon credits more available to small and medium-sized businesses. CarbonX provides a new way for companies to offset their carbon emissions and adopt sustainable practices by tokenizing carbon credits. Users may trade and measure

---

[1] https://www.powerledger.io/company/power-ledger-whitepaper

[2] https://whitepaper.io/document/202/wepower-whitepaper

emissions reductions in real time on the CarbonX platform. This openness guarantees the authenticity of the credits and the accuracy of the stated reductions. This implies SMEs will have an easier time taking part in carbon offsetting, as it can be a complicated and expensive process when using traditional techniques.[3]

Another initiative that promotes sustainable supply chain practices using blockchain technology is EcoChain. EcoChain collected money through an ICO to create a platform that monitors and confirms the sustainability of goods across the supply chain. Customers are able to make better decisions because to this openness, which also motivates businesses to use more environmentally friendly methods. Tokens representing confirmed sustainable activities are distributed via the EcoChain platform. Businesses and consumers may exchange these tokens, establishing a sustainable market. This encourages businesses to enhance their environmental policies and gives customers a clear indication of how sustainable the products they buy.[4]

CarbonX, Eco-Chain, WePower, Power Ledger, and Sun Exchange are a few instances of how ICOs may be used to advance sustainable supply chains, encourage renewable energy, and improve carbon trading. These initiatives demonstrate how ICOs have the power to democratize financial access, draw impact-focused investors, and create open, effective marketplaces for sustainability. Although the ICO market has some dangers, they may be reduced with appropriate regulation and due diligence, guaranteeing that ICOs will remain a useful instrument for fostering sustainability in SMEs. The importance of novel financing techniques like ICOs will only increase in tandem with the growing need for sustainable finance. ICOs can facilitate the shift to a more sustainable economy by arming SMEs with the resources they require to carry out environmentally friendly initiatives.

References

Adhami, S., Giudici, G., & Martinazzi, S. (2018). Why do business go crypto? An empirical analysis of initial coin offerings. *Journal of Economic and Business, 2018.*

Angelidou, M., Psaltoglou, A., Komninos, N., Kakderi, C., Tsarchopoulos, P., & Panori, A. (2017). Enhancing sustainable urban development through smart city applications. *Journal of Science and Technology Policy Management, 9*(2), 146–169. https://doi.org/10.1108/jstpm-05-2017-0016

Bongini, P., Osborne, F., Pedrazzoli, A., & Rossolini, M. (2022). A topic modelling analysis of white papers in security token offerings: Which topic matters for funding? *Technological Forecasting and Social Change, 184*, 122005. https://doi.org/10.1016/j.techfore.2022.122005

Boreiko D., & Sahdev N. (2018). *To ICO or not to ICO–empirical analysis of initial coin offerings and token sales, social science research network*, papaers.ssrn.com.

Brochado, A., & Troilo, M. (2021). Initial coin offerings: An emergent research area. *Digital Policy Regulation and Governance, 23*(2), 113–131. https://doi.org/10.1108/dprg-06-2020-0084

[3] https://carbonx.ca

[4] https://ecochain.com

Brown, T., Hultine, K., Steltzer, H., Denny, E., Denslow, M., Granados, J., et al. (2016). Using phenocams to monitor our changing earth: Toward a global phenocam network. *Frontiers in Ecology and the Environment, 14*(2), 84–93. https://doi.org/10.1002/fee.1222

Chebukhanova, L. V., Blokhina, T. K., & Karpenko, O. A. (2021). The Initial Coin Offering (ICO) process: Regulation and risks. *Journal of Risk and Financial Management.*

European Banking Authority. (2019). *Report with advice for the European Commission on crypto-assets, 2019.*

Fisch, C. (2019). Initial coin offering (ICOs) to finance new ventures. *Journal of Business Venturing, 34*, 1–22.

Gutmann, T., & Schückes, M. (2020). Why do startups pursue initial coin offerings (ICOs)? The role of economic drivers and social identity on funding choice. *Small Business Economy, 57*, 1027–1052.

Hellmann, T., Schure, P., & Vo, D. H. (2021). Angels and venture capitalists: Substitutes or complements? *Journal of Financial Economics, 141*, 454–478.

Howell, S., Niessner, M., & Yermack, D. (2018). Initial coin offerings: financing growth with cryptocurrency token sales. *The Review of Financial Studies, 38*, 3925–3974. https://doi.org/10.3386/w24774

Kotiloglu, S., & Ometto, M. P. (2024). An exploratory look at the role of ownership in initial coin offerings (ICO): Different audiences and ICO success. *Journal of Business Venturing Insights, 21*, e00438.

Moro, A., Radic, N., & Truong, V. (2023). To tweet or not to tweet? The determinants of tweeting activity in initial coin offerings. *British Journal of Management, 35*(1), 243–258. https://doi.org/10.1111/1467-8551.12709

Chapter 7
Greenwashing

7.1 Introduction

In the last decade, increasing pollution and its environmental impacts have heightened awareness of sustainability (Liu et al., 2023). Stakeholders—whether consumers, investors, or governments—demand that companies adopt environmentally friendly practices (Chen & Chang, 2012; de Freitas Netto et al., 2020), aligning with sustainable economic development, which involves creating surplus value while avoiding environmental harm. The European Commission defines sustainable development as "development that meets the needs of the present without compromising the ability of future generations to meet their own needs". This concept encompasses three main pillars: economic growth, social inclusion, and environmental protection. Sustainable development aims to achieve a balanced approach where economic activities do not deplete natural resources or cause long-term environmental damage.

Transitioning to sustainable production is complex and slow. Companies must not only change production activities but also instill sustainability values within their boards, employees, and third parties, including suppliers and investors. Sustainable production thus requires a system change, affecting the entire supply chain.

Adapting to sustainable development is multidimensional, necessitating commitment across all levels of the production value chain. This systemic change requires time for two main reasons: (1) shifting from viewing production solely as a means of creating surplus value to integrating environmental respect (Polonsky et al., 1997), and (2) the higher economic commitment required for sustainable investments.

Often, the priority for firms, and for those in the value chain, is market satisfaction rather than real environmental responsibility (Guo et al., 2018). This can lead to greenwashing, where there is a discrepancy between communicated and actual

M. Aliano et al., *Sustainable Finance for SMEs*, Sustainable Finance,
https://doi.org/10.1007/978-3-031-74193-7_7

environmental commitments (Bernini et al., 2023). Greenwashing, a widespread deceptive practice, can take many forms: false, omitted, exaggerated, or incomplete information, all leading to a distorted perception of reality (ESMA, 2023).

Examples of greenwashing practice includes Chevron case, whose corporate responsibility is shown to be sensitive to environmental change. It promoted campaigns in favor of reducing emissions—the main cause of climate change—to have a positive impact on the planet, when in reality the company releases quantities of CO_2 that increase every year and contributes to increasing oil production: sustainable information was more a marketing strategy than a real green commitment. The same situation occurred with Ryanair, when in 2020 it was accused of greenwashing because it promoted a campaign claiming to be the European low-cost airline with the lowest CO_2 emissions, when in fact an EU report listed it among the ten most polluting companies (in terms of emissions). Furthermore, Ryanair could not be included amongst the virtuous companies, in terms of sustainability, because it had used data from 2011 in order to meet the 'low emissions' criteria. This data is obviously obsolete for an analysis carried out in 2019. These are just a few examples that clearly state the practice of misleading the market for personal financial reporting.

Greenwashing is hard to spot because it's purposefully misleading; it can take many different forms, making it difficult to describe, recognize, and standardize; literature also has a hard time coming up with a single definition for it.

This chapter aims to describe greenwashing, exploring its various facets across the value chain and identifying the internal and external forces that contribute directly or indirectly to the creation and escalation of deception. The analysis will begin by defining greenwashing, exploring its various forms, and detailing the methods through which it is implemented. Then we will describe the actors of greenwashing, both those actively involved in deception—greenwashing promoters and drivers—and those passively involved—drivers and receivers. After giving an overall view of the forces that lead to greenwashing, the analysis will be deepened by breaking down the practice on the different levels of the value chain.

The study is structured in three different levels of analysis: through a *bottom-up approach*, the phenomenon will be investigated starting with *greenwashing at product level* (*first level analysis*), where the company deceives the consumer to increase sales; we will proceed with *greenwashing at firm level* (*second level analysis*), where the (un)green policies promoted by companies and the motivations behind their choices are analyzed; the final step is *greenwashing on financial markets* (*third level analysis*), which frames the phenomenon of greenwashing in a macro environment by analyzing the market in its entirety.

Studying the components of deception—actors, methods, forms and channels of implementation—each of the three levels allows us to understand how greenwashing moves along the entire production chain and how deception can be perpetuated directly or indirectly, voluntarily or involuntarily.

The growth of greenwashing may be fueled by the lack of clear definitions and standards, and by insufficient guidelines and sanctions from authorities, potentially promoting deception themselves.

7.2 Greenwashing and SMEs

Greenwashing, the practice of falsely presenting an environmentally responsible image while engaging in harmful environmental activities, presents significant challenges and concerns, particularly within the context of SMEs. This deceptive practice undermines genuine sustainability efforts and misleads stakeholders, posing a threat to the credibility of environmental initiatives across various sectors. Although SMEs are often perceived as less likely to engage in greenwashing compared to larger corporations, the risk remains, and its implications warrant a thorough examination.

Several studies have underscored the risks and implications of greenwashing within the SME sector. Bos-Brouwers (2009) highlights the issue of "window dressing" or greenwashing in corporate sustainability practices. The author emphasizes the challenges posed by the lack of measurability and the potential misrepresentation of environmental efforts. This lack of clarity and transparency can lead to stakeholders being misled about a company's true environmental impact. The misrepresentation not only damages trust but also hinders the progress of genuine sustainability initiatives.

Balasubramanian et al. (2020) further elaborate on how larger firms might engage in greenwashing to project an appearance of environmental responsibility without delivering substantial benefits. This practice can significantly impact the environmental sustainability of supply chains. The pressure to appear environmentally responsible often leads large corporations to invest more in marketing their supposed green credentials than in implementing current sustainable practices. This creates a ripple effect, influencing smaller companies within their supply chains to either adopt similar deceptive practices or struggle to compete without genuine sustainable credentials.

Contrary to the practices of larger corporations, SMEs are often perceived as more authentic and less likely to engage in greenwashing. Wickert (2014) argues that due to their size and structure, SMEs are more likely to provide genuine reports on their environmental practices. This authenticity is crucial in maintaining credibility and trust with stakeholders. SMEs, with their closer-knit structures and direct stakeholder interactions, often find it more feasible to adopt and report on authentic sustainable practices. Their smaller scale operations make it easier to implement and monitor sustainable initiatives genuinely, without the extensive bureaucratic hurdles faced by larger corporations.

However, the perception of authenticity in SMEs is not always guaranteed. Hunter (2023) explores the occurrence of greenwashing even within certified SMEs, raising questions about the prioritization of environmental performance over social performance in obtaining certifications like the B Corp certification. This indicates that even well-intentioned certification programs can be manipulated or misused, leading to greenwashing. Certifications, while designed to assure stakeholders of a company's commitment to sustainability, can sometimes become tools for misleading claims if not rigorously enforced and audited.

Despite these challenges, SMEs have significant potential to engage in meaningful sustainability practices. Jenkins (2008) highlights the potential for SMEs to engage in commercially viable activities that advance both environmental and social sustainability. This perspective aligns with the notion that SMEs can make substantial contributions to sustainability without resorting to greenwashing practices. By focusing on commercially viable sustainability, SMEs can integrate environmental and social goals into their core business strategies, ensuring that their sustainability efforts are both genuine and beneficial to their bottom line.

Moreover, Enz et al. (2021) suggest that SMEs, by adopting individual and traceable sustainability measures, can generate a competitive advantage without the need for greenwashing tactics. These measures, when transparent and verifiable, build trust with stakeholders and differentiate SMEs from competitors who may rely on deceptive practices. Traceable sustainability measures provide a clear and accountable way for SMEs to demonstrate their commitment to environmental responsibility, making it easier for stakeholders to verify and trust their claims.

Nonetheless, the risk of greenwashing remains a concern for SMEs. Ling (2024) warns that greenwashing compromises the effectiveness of green finance initiatives, emphasizing the importance of transparency and credibility in sustainability efforts. For green finance to be effective, there must be assurance that the funds are genuinely contributing to sustainable outcomes. SMEs engaging in greenwashing not only risk damaging their reputation but also undermine the broader green finance ecosystem, making it harder for genuinely sustainable businesses to attract necessary investments.

Tshuma Zahoor et al. (2023) highlight that SMEs avoiding greenwashing are more likely to succeed as they do not face the risk of backlash from stakeholders. This suggests that authentic sustainability efforts, while potentially more challenging to implement, offer long-term benefits in terms of trust and business resilience. Stakeholders are becoming increasingly vigilant and informed about sustainability claims, and companies found guilty of greenwashing face severe reputational damage, legal consequences, and loss of customer trust.

In conclusion, while SMEs are generally perceived as less likely to engage in greenwashing compared to larger corporations, the risk still exists within the sector. It is essential for SMEs to prioritize authenticity, transparency, and genuine sustainability efforts to build trust with stakeholders and contribute meaningfully to environmental and social responsibility. As the scrutiny of corporate sustainability practices intensifies, SMEs that focus on genuine, verifiable, and transparent sustainability measures will be better positioned to navigate the challenges of greenwashing and leverage their sustainability initiatives for competitive advantage. This approach not only benefits the SMEs in terms of reputation and stakeholder trust but also contributes to the broader goal of achieving sustainable development and environmental stewardship.

7.3 What Is Greenwashing Practice? Types and Methodologies

Greenwashing is defined as the discrepancy between reported and actual environmental commitments. Over the years, numerous studies have highlighted the complex, dynamic, and multidimensional nature of greenwashing (Bernini et al., 2023). Due to these characteristics, while greenwashing is recognized as a gap between communication and reality, it remains challenging to standardize within a single definition (Seele & Gatti, 2017).

For instance, Delmas and Cuerel Burbano (2011) describe greenwashing as "poor environmental performance and positive communication about environmental performance", whereas Lyon and Maxwell (2011) define it as the "selective disclosure of positive information about a company's environmental or social performance without full disclosure of negative information, creating an overly positive corporate image". Furthermore, Lyon and Montgomery (2015) describe it as "a range of communication that misleads people into adopting overly positive beliefs about an organization's environmental performance". Essentially, greenwashing represents a gap between symbolic and substantive commitments to environmental issues (Walker & Wan, 2012).

Due to the lack of a unique definition in literature and the multidimensional nature of greenwashing, the first step in this chapter is to propose a standardization of the phenomenon by making clear distinctions. In line with the distinction proposed by Gatti et al. (2021) we assert that the gap in greenwashing arises from the nature of the information provided, which can be either through false disclosures (active deception) or selective disclosures (passive deception).

False disclosures leave no room for interpretation; the deception is direct, with statements that contradict reality. Selective disclosures, in contrast, allow for multiple interpretations. While false information is objectively untrue, selective information involves disseminating only certain facts to create a distorted view of reality.

The following Table 7.1 shows the diversification of the two types of greenwashing and the various connotations they can take on.

Based on this distinction, the following classification of *selective disclosures* implies that the dissemination of deception occurs in a 'hidden' manner. In this

Table 7.1 Greenwashing's typologies

TYPOLOGIES OF GREENWASHING (How greenwashing is generated?)	False Disclosures	Disclosure of false information. The connotation of "false" must be intend in the strict sense of the term, as "opposite of truth".
	Selective Disclosures	Disclosure of specific information—selected precisely. Information is false in the wider sense of the term.

"False", in the strict sense of the term, is to be interpreted in a literal way, i.e. "not true"
"False" in the wider sense of the term does not mean false information but information that leads to error

case, information is not falsified but selectively presented to induce the receiver into a distorted view of reality, thereby conveying deception indirectly. This type of greenwashing can manifest in several ways:

1. Selective disclosure as omission: partially true information is provided, omitting un-green practices, leading receivers to overestimate green commitments.
2. Selective disclosure as ambiguity: unspecific disclosures mislead receivers. For example, paper packaging does not necessarily mean a product is more sustainable.
3. Selective disclosure as no proof: disclosures are not substantiated by verifiable information.
4. Selective disclosure as irrelevance: True but irrelevant information is highlighted to appear environmentally committed.
5. Selective disclosure as unfocused: true information is used to divert attention from negative environmental impacts, such as an oil company promoting minor green initiatives while ignoring its core polluting activities.

Selective disclosures can be more insidious than false ones because they involve the omission of detrimental information rather than outright falsehoods. Both forms of deception aim to protect a company's economic performance and image.

The phenomenon of greenwashing is further complicated by the different ways it can be executed. Misleading information, whether false or selective, can be communicated directly or indirectly. In the first case, it is referred to as claimed greenwashing, while in the second case, it is known as executional greenwashing (Table 7.2).

Claim greenwashing is a form of deception perpetuation, where misleading information is communicated through textual language and word is the transmission channel (de Freitas Netto et al., 2020).

Executional greenwashing, on the other hand, has evocation as its transmission channel. In other words, misleading communication comes from the use of images, colours, sounds (and the like) that are directly associated with ESG themes (e.g. use of the colour green, logos depicting nature, etc.) (Parguel et al., 2015; Ende et al., 2023). Although there is no direct statement (through language) about environmental commitment, this is evoked by exploiting the cognitive bias of the receivers.

Executional greenwashing, like selective disclosures, is subtler and harder to detect, relying on the receiver's information and cognitive background.

Understanding these mechanisms is crucial for identifying and addressing the pervasive issue of greenwashing in sustainability communications.

Table 7.2 Greenwashing's methodologies of implementation

METHODOLOGIES OF GREENWASHING (How to implement greenwashing?)	Claim Greenwashing	Deception is transmitted through word language (direct transmission channel)
	Executional Greenwashing	Deception is transmitted through evocation (indirect transmission channel)

7.3.1 *How Greenwashing Is Transmitted? Drivers*

When discussing the spread and transmission of deception, the drivers of greenwashing come into play. These are the subjects, means, and vehicles that enable greenwashing to occur and proliferate within the market. In its Progress Report on Greenwashing (European Securities and Markets Authority, 2023), the European Securities and Market Authority (ESMA) defined three categories of greenwashing drivers: triggers, spreaders, and receivers.

Triggers are the initiators of the deception. They are individuals who voluntarily engage in misleading behaviour with the aim of deceiving the receivers of the information. Spreaders represent the vehicles through which the deception is transmitted to the market. Receivers are the recipients of the deception itself.

For example, consider a company promoting its environmental commitment through an ESG report. The ESG manager acts as the trigger, the report itself is the spreader, and the stakeholders, such as investors and suppliers, are the receivers.

Delmas and Cuerel Burbano (2011) showed that greenwashing is difficult to manage due to a poorly defined regulatory environment and market sensitivity to sustainability. Regulatory activity around sustainability reporting, mandatory green practices, and sanctions for greenwashing is limited. This lack of clarity, combined with the complex nature of greenwashing, can incentivize those looking to exploit sustainability claims for undeserved benefits. Moreover, increased market focus on the environment pressures companies to greenwash to satisfy stakeholders quickly and cheaply.

This creates a vicious cycle: heightened environmental awareness leads to greater green demand, which, due to management challenges, tempts companies into deceptive practices.

In the following paragraphs, the concepts expressed so far will be deepened, distinguishing the levels of study mentioned above: understanding the dynamics at the product level (*first level*) is useful for understanding the motivations behind corporate choices about the environmental policies that are (or are not) implemented (*second level*) and the resulting effects on the financial market (*third level*).

7.4 Greenwashing at Product Level

Greenwashing at the product level relies on consumers' growing awareness of sustainability issues (Antunes et al., 2015). This increased environmental concern drives individuals to act responsibly and seek sustainable products. As a result, their heightened sensitivity translates into a greater demand for green products from companies (Zhang et al., 2018).

"Green" has become a focal point of new consumer demand. Firms are increasingly asked to produce and offer products and services that are environmentally friendly (de Freitas Netto et al., 2020). However, it is not easy for firms to promptly and effectively manage the supply of products with "green" characteristics. Shifting to sustainable production involves significant effort in terms of both costs and organization. Green production requires an increase in production costs and a change in the internal organizational structure to align with new environmental values (Polonsky et al., 1997). This process is gradual and requires careful adaptation.

To meet new customer demands quickly and remain competitive, some companies may choose to bypass the adaptation phase and rapidly market products with purported eco-friendly features that are not entirely genuine (Zhang et al., 2018). This leads to the concept of greenwashing at the product level.

Greenwashing at product level is defined as the act of misleading consumers regarding the environmental benefits of a product (or a service) issued by firms. While selling green products allows companies to meet market demands, increase product value, and create a responsible image (Chen, 2010), through greenwashing they achieve the same results but in an illicit manner.

However, greenwashing is not always a deliberate practice. In the first level analysis, the consumer assumes a central role as the direct receiver of the products or services offered by firms (Liu et al., 2023; Montgomery et al., 2023). Consequently, the consumer's perception and judgment determine the transition *from green to greenwashing*. This opens up to a dual definition of the phenomenon, which is no longer an *act of misleading* but a *perceived deception* (Lyon & Montgomery, 2015).

This section aims to analyze all elements that constitute *first level greenwashing*. First, the phenomenon will be described from an "objective" point of view, identifying the different types of greenwashing and its implementation methodologies. Then, the motives that drive a company to greenwash (in cases of voluntary practice) will be examined, identifying the main drivers. Finally, the strategies employed to carry out deceptive activities will be described.

Next, a "subjective" analysis will explore greenwashing as a matter of "consumer perception" and its impact on firms. Greenwashing can be an easy way for companies to achieve customer satisfaction quickly and at a lower cost. Promoting a "green" product attracts consumers who reward the company by purchasing its products. However, companies might underestimate the reputational risk and potential damage to their image if their claims do not align with reality. This section will provide an overview of the relationships and dynamics behind *product level greenwashing*, analyzing the benefits and the risks of the practice. The first level analysis is the first step in understanding the practice of greenwashing. The primary market actors involved are companies (triggers) and consumers (receivers). The vehicle of deception (spreaders) is the advertising behind the promotion of a product. By understanding these dynamics, we can better grasp the motivations behind greenwashing and its implications for both companies and consumers. This analysis will set the stage for deeper investigations into greenwashing at the firm and market levels.

7.4.1 *Typologies of Greenwashing*

As stated in the previous paragraphs, under the condition of voluntariness, firms can generate misleading information at the product level through two different channels: communication and evocation.

The communication channel is the so-called claim greenwashing. Here, companies mislead consumers through "vocabulary" by providing incomplete, vague, irrelevant, or false information about a product or service, leading consumers to believe a product is greener than it is.

A notable example of claim greenwashing is the case of ENI in 2020 with its "ENIdiesel+" campaign. ENI, an Italian company involved in the production, transportation, processing, and marketing of oil and natural gas, ran an environmentally friendly campaign from 2016 to 2019. The campaign promoted "ENIdiesel+," a diesel fuel that was claimed to have a 15% renewable component, reduces fuel consumption by 4%, and lower emissions by 40%. The advertisements suggested that using this fuel would not only extend the life of a car but also contribute to environmental protection.

However, Legambiente, Movimento Difesa del Cittadino, and Transport & Environment (T&E) filed complaints with the Italian Antitrust Authority, which in 2020 ruled that ENI's advertising constituted an "unfair business practice." The promotional campaign leveraged terms like "green" and "renewable" to market a product and a commitment to environmental protection that was not substantiated. The claimed emission reductions and the renewable component of the diesel were not fully demonstrated, resulting in a fine of five million euros due to the severity and duration of the violation. The company exploited consumer awareness of environmental issues with the message "using it, you do it too," without fully supporting the green claims made.

Evocation, instead, is the channel of executional greenwashing, where misleading information is implicitly generated through the use of images, colors, and sounds directly associated with sustainability themes. This form of greenwashing leverages the cognitive biases of consumers. Products or services are promoted using eco-prototype characteristics, such as green or brown colors, high prices, and other eco-friendly symbols, triggering a direct association with sustainability and eco-friendliness. Typically, executional greenwashing accompanies misleading claims, reinforcing the sustainable message through visual and auditory cues.

The common element of both channels, whether direct (claim greenwashing) or indirect (executional greenwashing), is the promulgation or association of information about a product whose green characteristics are more symbolic than substantial. Both forms of greenwashing aim to create a falsely positive perception of a product's environmental benefits, thus misleading consumers and protecting the company's economic performance and image.

7.4.2 Green(Washing) Marketing

Due to increasing consumer awareness of sustainability, firms are often induced to incorporate greenwashing into their marketing strategies (Lyon & Montgomery, 2015), making it a mechanism through which they can build a competitive advantage in the market and benefit from improved business and financial performance (Siano et al., 2017; Guo et al., 2018).

Greenwashing marketing could be considered the "dark side" of green marketing. Green marketing is a legitimate strategy aimed at producing, designing, promoting, and selling environmentally friendly products or services (Shao et al., 2023). The goal is to influence consumer behavior towards respecting the environment (Polonsky et al., 1997) while establishing a reputation as a sustainable company.

In contrast, "*greenwashing marketing*" focuses on creating market credibility and exploiting increased economic revenues. It neglects the genuine motivation behind sustainable strategies, which is environmental commitment. As long as the deception goes undetected, consumers will still be influenced by the company's purported environmentally friendly behaviour. However, this allows companies to take undue and improper advantage of the market (Chen, 2010; Guo et al., 2018).

Whether through 'claim' greenwashing or 'executional' greenwashing, greenwashing marketing communication incorporates a deceptive intent.

7.4.3 Perception

At this point, greenwashing has been referred to as an act of misleading, thus emphasizing the willingness of companies to act unfairly towards consumers. However, first-level greenwashing is not limited to intentional deception alone. Product-level analysis is fundamentally based on the relationship between "consumer" and "product," meaning the final judgment of a product's sustainability depends on how the consumer perceives it.

Drawing on the study by Seele and Gatti (2017), which constructed a greenwashing matrix to better delineate and describe the phenomenon, including its subjective aspects (i.e., perception), we propose the following reflection.

Most common in the product-level literature is the consideration of greenwashing as a phenomenon based on a causal relationship, where the misleading intention of the company is a condition for the consumer's accusation of deception. However, perception can actually break this cause-and-effect relationship, giving new connotations to the phenomenon. Based on the definition of greenwashing outlined above, the greenwashing matrix is presented below.

The greenwashing matrix simplifies the understanding of greenwashing by showing how it varies based on the combination of two factors: the company's intention to mislead and consumer perception (Fig. 7.1).

		COMPANIES	
		MISLEADING	NO MISLEADING
COSTUMER	PERCEPTION	*REAL* GREENWASHING	*FALSE* GREENWASHING
	NO PERCEPTION	*POTENTIAL* GREENWASHING	NO GREENWASHING

Fig. 7.1 Greenwashing matrix

The first quadrant corresponds to *real greenwashing*. The misleading and deceptive intention of the company is perceived by the consumer, who condemns the practice, damaging the company's image and sales. An example of real greenwashing is the famous "Dieselgate" scandal. The car manufacturer Volkswagen was accused in 2014 of falsifying information about the emissions of their cars. Their cars had failed pollutant assessment tests, with emissions' levels far exceeding legal limits. Volkswagen denied these allegations and conducted their own tests to prove compliance. However, in 2015, the EPA exposed the use of software that falsified emission levels during tests. Volkswagen had to admit guilt, compensate deceived customers, and face financial and criminal consequences.

The second quadrant represents *potential greenwashing*, where the company's deceptive actions are not perceived by the public. Greenwashing, according to the above definition, does not occur as long as the deception remains undetected. Companies illicitly enjoy economic and image benefits from their false environmental claims. However, if the misleading intent is eventually perceived, the phenomenon transitions from potential to real greenwashing. For instance, if Volkswagen's emissions tests had not been re-evaluated, "Dieselgate" would have remained in the potential greenwashing category.

The third quadrant is that of *false greenwashing*. Here, the consumer perceives a deception that was never intended or enacted by the company. Despite the absence of an actual misleading campaign, the company suffers the same negative impacts as real greenwashing. An example is the case of H&M. The clothing company was accused in 2021 of greenwashing for its "Conscious Choice" campaign, promoting clothing made from "50% sustainable materials." Although the company faced allegations of misleading advertising, it proved that the information provided did not claim their garments were fully sustainable but rather made from more sustainable materials than their other collections. The charges were dropped, showing this was a case of false greenwashing.

The fourth and final quadrant is categorized as *no greenwashing*, where neither misleading claims nor perceived deception are present.

The analysis of the matrix shows how (mis)perception of the exterior generates market malfunctions. The subjectivity of greenwashing in product-level analysis can breach the necessary causal relationship of real greenwashing, creating two "pathological" dimensions. While the potential dimension benefits firms and undermines sustainable economic development, false greenwashing unfairly punishes firms due to consumer misjudgment.

Relating greenwashing strictly to perception makes it a subjective phenomenon, where "socially responsible" and "socially irresponsible" depend on the *eye of the beholder*.

7.4.4 Risks

At the moment deception is perceived—whether real or false—the firm undergoes losses on two different levels: reputational and financial.

In the case of real greenwashing, the firm consciously chooses the path of deception, using greenwashing as a strategy to consolidate its market position both reputational and financial. The firm's goal is to leverage consumers' environmental concerns to increase sales and revenue. However, when the malpractice is revealed (or perceived), the competitive advantage improperly created turns into a *boomerang effect*. Just as emotional participation builds consumer loyalty to green-oriented firms, the reverse occurs when deception is uncovered (Lyon & Montgomery, 2015; Ende et al., 2023). The company that deceives undermines its own credibility and professional reliability, generating a reaction of distrust (Lyon & Montgomery, 2015) that starts with consumers and spreads like wildfire to other stakeholders and the market in general.

As a result of the deception, consumers lose trust in the company that issued the (un)green product and are strongly discouraged from making future purchases from the same brand. A direct consequence is the loss of investors, whose association with the offending firm could also negatively affect their credibility and reputation. Reduced purchases and investments reflect negatively on financial performance and business continuity. Starting with stakeholders—both consumers and investors—the impact of greenwashing then extends to the entire market.

The increasing episodes of greenwashing create a situation of green scepticism (Torelli et al., 2020; Bernini et al., 2023), in which consumers question companies' statements about their environmental policies (Shao et al., 2023). Skepticism might motivate consumers to inquire more about the products they are offered and develop a greater critical sense. On the other hand, companies that implement a real commitment to the environment might also be questioned, discouraging them from their efforts.

In potential greenwashing, the company encounters the same negative effects as in real greenwashing without having engaged in any misbehavior, or at least not voluntarily. The repercussions on the firm's reputation and finances are similar, even though the deceptive intent was not present.

In the unintentional dimension, the only way to avoid, as far as possible, external misperception is to choose transparent communication that leaves no room for possible misrepresentation. Clear and honest communication helps prevent the misperception of greenwashing and maintains consumer trust.

Given the extent of the damage, companies that implement real and concrete green policies often choose not to communicate their ESG commitment in order to avoid overexposing themselves (Cheng et al., 2024). Such practice is called *greenhushing*.

7.5 Greenhushing

Greenhushing is defined as a voluntary act by companies to under-report their sustainable policies and commitments (Falchi et al., 2022). It is an aspect of greenwashing that involves a firm deciding to hide and not communicate certain implemented pro-sustainability information. While this phenomenon is not exactly the same as greenwashing, greenhushing also has characteristics of deception, particularly in its omission of claims.

At first glance, greenhushing might seem paradoxical. Consumers' awareness of sustainability makes them more likely to buy green products, even at higher prices than conventional products (Zhang et al., 2018), so hiding sustainability efforts might seem unreasonable. However, greenhushing can be advantageous.

Consider the case of H&M. The well-known Swedish brand's advertising campaign was subject to external misperception, leading to a court defense against charges of misleading advertising. Although H&M proved its innocence, it found itself under the spotlight for a fault it did not commit.

A company perceived as a greenwasher, regardless of whether the deceptive advertising charge is confirmed, suffers image damage (Zhang et al., 2018). Reputation and credibility depend not only on the presence or absence of misconduct but also on word of mouth (WOM) (Zhang et al., 2018).

WOM refers to verbal communication between consumers and others (e.g., relatives and friends) about a product or service (Chen et al., 2014) issued by firms. It is termed "green" (green WOM) when the object of communication is the company's sustainable commitment (Chen et al., 2014). Green WOM can be either positive or negative. Positive WOM involves customers praising the environmental efforts of firms, which can lead to increased sales. Negative WOM concerns consumers' distrust of corporate green policies, which can have a disastrous impact on reputation (Zhang et al., 2018).

The main characteristic of word-of-mouth (WOM) is the speed at which information is transmitted. The swiftness of information flow directly impacts communication effectiveness, providing the enterprise with immediate advantages (positive WOM) or disadvantages (negative WOM). WOM is based on communicating the consumer's perception of the enterprise. Given the rapid transmission of information, it may be more convenient for the enterprise to remain in the shadows to avoid false accusations of greenwashing. WOM gives the enterprise considerable exposure, which is further amplified if the information is transmitted through mass media channels (Sajid et al., 2024).

Greenhushing is motivated by the risks of misperception. While greenwashing involves omission with a misleading goal, greenhushing involves under-reporting that is not fraudulent, as it is not used to push consumers to buy more. Greenhushing can be seen as a 'trap' rather than outright deception. The growth of greenwashing cases and the outrage they create can instill fear in truly green companies of being falsely accused of greenwashing and suffering undeserved consequences.

A deceived consumer perceives the company's wrongdoing as a 'betrayal,' resulting in loss of trust, brand avoidance, and negative WOM (NWOM) (Sajid et al., 2024). Given this perspective and considering that consumers are not always rational, omitting information to safeguard against potential or false greenwashing might seem the best choice for companies.

Although the goal of greenhushing is "company protection," it can also hinder sustainable economic development (Falchi et al., 2022). Firms with genuine sustainable commitments should act as examples, encouraging responsible behaviour. However, greenhushing reduces the visibility of true sustainability efforts, potentially slowing progress toward broader sustainable practices in the market.

7.6 Greenwashing at Firm Level

Product-level analysis is the first step in describing the phenomenon of greenwashing in all its facets and dimensions. While necessary, it is not sufficient to understand how deception is presented to the market and how it is transmitted. This analysis focuses on the final stage of the transmission of deception, where a company presents a product or service to the market with only apparently 'green' characteristics. What has been omitted is the intent that drives the company to promote an environmental commitment that it does not possess or does not possess to the extent it claims, especially considering the negative effects that the discovery of deception could generate. To gain a deeper understanding of the motives and reasons, we move on to the second level of analysis: greenwashing at the firm level.

Greenwashing at the firm level refers to activities where the positive environmental actions communicated by a company do not match the negative activities actually implemented (Torelli et al., 2020). As mentioned in previous sections, transitioning from conventional to sustainable production is not immediate. Companies need an adaptation phase, in which they must (1) recognize that sustainable development is a necessary choice motivated by ethical reasons rather than economic needs, (2) understand their sustainability targets and incorporate these values into the company culture, and (3) transmit these values to employees and collaborators, ensuring that sustainability is seen not as a market imposition but as a normal step in the company's evolution.

The concept of corporate culture should not be underestimated. To ensure a genuine transition to green production, the entire corporate apparatus needs a 'change of course.' Any minor 'mismatch' or 'non-conformance' within the supply chain can directly or indirectly, voluntarily or involuntarily, trigger or transmit deception, and hence greenwashing.

In this second phase of analysis, we will address issues related to market demands, analyzed not solely as a force and stimulus to greenwashing, but also investigating how this pressure is assimilated and managed by companies. Every stimulus derives a reaction that can be right—green—or not right—greenwashing. The analysis will no longer focus solely on external market and demand factors but will also take a closer look at the governance component, from which the policies considered best for the company are implemented. Given the more internalized analysis and the shifted focus on corporate governance, the role of shareholders—rather than stakeholders dealt with in the first level—will be explored in greater depth, and how they themselves are often 'triggers' of deception.

7.6.1 Mechanisms of greenwashing's Trigging

The importance of the CSR claim has already been emphasized, it represents the means by which companies show their commitment to their stakeholders while also creating expectations for their present and future productive activity: the stakeholders link the value of the company to the CSR activities (Arouri et al., 2021). Given the importance placed on reporting, sustainable commitment, and market awareness, companies are under pressure (Delmas & Cuerel Burbano, 2011) because, on one hand, they have to respond to stakeholder demand, and on the other, they have to deal with internal processes related to the company policies to be implemented and how to implement them (Liu et al., 2023). Greenwashing at the firm level is therefore triggered by two different mechanisms, one of external origin and one of internal origin within the firm.

7.7 External Mechanism

The external mechanism refers to the need for companies to respond to demands and adapt to what political powers, consumers, and the media require. Everything must be done to gain the approval of external stakeholders and build an environmental image and credibility in the market (Liu et al., 2023). The components of the external mechanism also include the cultural beliefs, values, norms, and customs of a society.

According to legitimacy theory, companies must obtain legitimacy for their activities from the market and thus conform to and adapt to the demands of the stakeholders (Roulet & Touboul, 2015). Legitimacy theory claims that businesses act and behave according to the limits, values, and norms defined by societies (Suchman, 1995). This means that if society is sensitive to sustainability and environmental issues, companies must act in a way that legitimizes their commitment on this front. The lower the environmental profile of a company within society, the greater the need for them to seek and obtain legitimacy, hence the instrumentalization of CSR to obtain legitimacy and credibility as quickly as possible (Roulet & Touboul, 2015; Zhang et al., 2023). Conversely, if the company has a high environmental profile and credibility in the market, there will be less need for greenwashing, as there is no additional legitimacy to be gained (Delmas & Cuerel Burbano, 2011; Roulet & Touboul, 2015; Liu et al., 2023). In other words, legitimacy theory applied to the concept of social responsibility predicts that companies adapt their activities in order to be accepted by society and social values.

7.8 Internal Mechanism

The internal mechanism includes factors such as the structure, board composition, and characteristics of shareholders that influence the decision to implement greenwashing. As noted by Liu et al. (2023), various internal forces play a role in the choice to adopt greenwashing. Chief among these is top management, followed by the board and its characteristics.

Regarding the board and its diversification, several studies have confirmed that the board plays a role in the decision to engage in greenwashing, though findings are not always in agreement. For instance, Chen and Dagestani (2023) highlight that greater diversification in terms of gender, age, and education reduces the likelihood of greenwashing. Conversely, Taglialatela et al. (2024) show that the larger and more heterogeneous the board, the greater the probability of greenwashing. Similarly, Ghitti et al. (2024) found results that contrast with those of Chen and Daghestani, indicating that the characteristics of the board significantly influence the likelihood of greenwashing. These differing outcomes are likely due to the different study samples, such as listed companies in China for Chen and Daghestani, and companies from 58 countries for Taglialatela. In any case, there is a clear correlation between greenwashing and the board.

7.9 Some Considerations

From the analysis of the external and internal mechanisms behind firm-level greenwashing, it is evident that the incentive to choose deception always depends on market demands, and the means of implementation are mainly related to CSR. Through CSR, the company creates a relationship of trust and expectation with stakeholders. However, demand management and its response depend on internal factors such as the corporate board, the manager, and major shareholders. The tendency to greenwash depends on the characteristics, values, and background of these internal actors.

A company with a good environmental profile and a high ESG score does not need to legitimize itself to stakeholders as it already enjoys credibility in the market. However, companies with a low ESG score must prove their worth and establish credibility, often turning to greenwashing for a quick solution. If the board lacks independence and the manager is solely profit-driven, deceptive practices become a viable strategy.

In conclusion, the influence of stakeholders, shareholders, and corporate governance is the determinant of firm-level greenwashing. External pressure from market demands and internal pressure from low board independence and heterogeneity drive companies to deceive the market, accepting the associated risks.

7.10 The Role of *Green Finance* in First Level Greenwashing

Although the first-level analysis focuses on the consumer's perception of the product, another important category of stakeholders to consider are financiers. For companies, securing financing is crucial to carrying out their productive activities. Whether from private individuals or banks, companies must demonstrate their reliability and credibility to ensure trust for future projects and productions.

In the context of sustainable development, stakeholders are more inclined to finance companies with socially and environmentally responsible projects rather than those with a neutral stance on climate change. The ESG information provided by companies plays a decisive role in stakeholders' decisions on which projects to support and which companies to promote (Teichmann et al., 2023). This leads to the concept of *green finance*, where investments and resources are directed towards eco-friendly projects, promoting economic growth that aligns with environmental objectives.

7.10.1 Introduction to the Concept of Green Finance

Green finance differs from traditional finance in that it aims to promote projects with benefits that extend beyond economic growth to include environmental respect and responsibility (Luo & Liu, 2022). In 2016, the G20 launched the Sustainable Finance Working Group (SFWG), which defined green finance as the '*financing of investments that provide environmental benefits in the broader context of environmentally sustainable development.*'.

Since financial resources are directed toward projects aimed at adapting to and mitigating climate change, green finance serves the environment, playing a crucial role in the ecological transition and promoting environmental responsibility.

Green finance employs products like green loans or credits, through which financial institutions provide resources to companies, provided these funds are used for environmentally friendly activities (Liu et al., 2024). To ensure the smooth functioning of green finance, lending institutions consider companies' environmental commitments in their decision-making processes, thereby directing finances responsibly. Green finance serves as a tool for implementing sustainable development through the promotion of 'clean' projects (Zhang, 2023). Consequently, it can be considered a catalyst for sustainable development by prompting companies to adapt their activities to obtain financing. Green finance incentivizes ESG commitment: if stakeholders prefer socially and environmentally responsible projects, companies will adapt their performance to meet ESG targets to secure financing (Zhang, 2023) and enhance their ESG reputation.

7.11 Green Finance Reacts to Greenwashing at Product Level

As green finance is a tool for achieving sustainability goals, it is essential that it is used appropriately. If corporate governance does not genuinely embrace environmental responsibility, the green commitment of financing institutions could be undermined. CSR claims attract financiers' interest, and companies may promote projects with only apparent green characteristics to secure necessary financing and build 'environmental credibility' in the market. Consequently, green finance, designed to foster sustainable economic growth, can inadvertently become a vehicle for spreading greenwashing.

Given that the lending process depends on a company's perceived responsibility, discovering that a company is greenwashing should prompt financial institutions to distance themselves from it and exercise greater caution in future client selection. Non-professional lenders may be more susceptible to public opinion and could distance themselves from a brand due to negative word-of-mouth (NWOM) (Zhang et al., 2018), even in cases of potential greenwashing. For professional lenders, the mechanism may take on different connotations. A financial institution, unlikely to be swayed by accusations of greenwashing or misleading advertisements, should distance itself from a brand only in cases of real greenwashing.

In both scenarios, whether the deception is discovered or merely perceived, and whether the greenwashing is real or potential, companies risk undermining the trust relationship with investors, discouraging them from future collaborations (Gatti et al., 2021). The value of a company, in the eyes of stakeholders, is linked to CSR commitments (Ioannou et al., 2022). If CSR is exploited to illegally obtain funding, investors become victims of deception. This leads to broken trust and loyalty between the funders and recipients. Greenwashing thus results in a loss of market credibility, investor trust, and current funding, while also disincentivizing future investments. Disappointed expectations and betrayed trust exacerbate green skepticism, impacting not only the final consumer but also investors at the initial stages of production.

7.12 Conclusion

Greenwashing is a widespread issue in sustainable development, making it harder for genuine efforts to succeed. This chapter has explored the multidimensional and multifaceted nature of greenwashing, detailing its various forms, methods of implementation, and the complex network of actors involved. From product-level deception aimed at consumers to firm-level policies and the broader financial market dynamics, greenwashing impacts every part of the value chain, creating challenges for stakeholders seeking true sustainability.

The analysis highlights the difficulties in identifying greenwashing due to its deliberate and complex nature. The lack of clear definitions, standards, and strong regulatory frameworks makes this problem worse, allowing these deceptive practices to be unchecked. As companies try to shift to sustainable production, there is an urgent need for systemic changes that go beyond just marketing strategies.

To mitigate greenwashing, it is essential to increase transparency, accountability, and strict oversight. Stakeholders, including consumers, investors, and regulatory bodies, must collaborate to develop and enforce rigorous guidelines and standards. These standards should be designed to ensure that companies' environmental claims can be verified and that any discrepancies are promptly addressed through appropriate penalties.

Achieving sustainable development necessitates a systemic commitment to integrating environmental, social, and governance (ESG) criteria into all facets of production and business operations. This requires the adoption of comprehensive reporting frameworks, such as Global Reporting Initiative (GRI) and Task Force on Climate-related Financial Disclosures (TCFD), which provide clear metrics and benchmarks for sustainability performance.

Additionally, financial markets play a key role in promoting real sustainability. By incorporating ESG factors into investment decisions, asset managers and institutional investors can direct capital towards companies demonstrating authentic environmental commitments. This transition in investment priorities can create a market-driven incentive for businesses to adopt sustainable practices, thereby reducing greenwashing.

Addressing the root causes of greenwashing also involves enhancing corporate governance structures to prioritize long-term environmental impacts over short-term profits, ensuring that sustainability goals are embedded within the strategic objectives of the organization.

In conclusion, moving towards true sustainable development requires a multifaceted approach that combines stringent regulatory frameworks, robust reporting standards, and market-based incentives.

References

Antunes, D., Santos, A., & Hurtado, A. (2015). The communication of the LCA: The need for guidelines to avoid greenwashing. *Espacios, 36*(5), 1.

Arouri, M., El Ghoul, S., & Gomes, M. (2021). Greenwashing and product market competition. *Finance Research Letters, 42*, 101927. https://doi.org/10.1016/j.frl.2021.101927

Balasubramanian, S., Shukla, V., & Chanchaichujit, J. (2020). Firm size implications for environmental sustainability of supply chains: Evidence from the UAE. *Management of Environmental Quality an International Journal, 31*(5), 1375–1406. https://doi.org/10.1108/meq-01-2020-0004

Bernini, F., Giuliani, M., & La Rosa, F. (2023). Measuring greenwashing: A systematic methodological literature review. *Business Ethics, the Environment & Responsibility, 00*, 1–19. https://doi.org/10.1111/beer.12631

Bos-Brouwers, H. (2009). Corporate sustainability and innovation in SMEs: Evidence of themes and activities in practice. *Business Strategy and the Environment, 19*(7), 417–435. https://doi.org/10.1002/bse.652

Chen, P., & Dagestani, A. A. (2023). Greenwashing behavior and firm value: From the perspective of board characteristics. *Corporate Social Responsibility and Environmental Management.* https://doi.org/10.1002/csr.2488

Chen, Y. S. (2010). The drivers of green brand equity: Green brand image, green satisfaction, and green trust. *Journal of Business Ethics, 93*(2), 307–319. https://doi.org/10.1007/s10551-009-0223-9

Chen, Y. S., Lin, C. L., & Chang, C. H. (2014). The influence of greenwash on green word-of-mouth (green WOM): The mediation effects of green perceived quality and green satisfaction. *Quality & Quantity, 48*(6), 2411–2425. https://doi.org/10.1007/s11135-013-9898-1

Chen, Y., & Chang, C. (2012). Enhance green purchase intentions: The roles of green perceived value, green perceived risk, and green trust. *Management Decision, 50*(3), 502–520. https://doi.org/10.1108/00251741211216250

Cheng, H., Dong, D., & Feng, Y. (2024). Corporate greenhushing and stock price crash risk: Evidence from China. *Environmental Development and Sustainability.* https://doi.org/10.1007/s10668-024-04935-5

de Freitas Netto, S. V., Sobral, M. F. F., Ribeiro, A. R. B., & Soares, G. R. L. (2020). Concepts and forms of greenwashing: A systematic review. *Environmental Sciences Europe, 32*(19). https://doi.org/10.1186/s12302-020-0300-3

Delmas, M. A., & Cuerel Burbano, V. (2011). The drivers of greenwashing. *California Management Review, 54*(1), 64–87.

Ende, L., Reinhard, M. A., & Göritz, L. (2023). Detecting greenwashing! The influence of product colour and product price on consumers' detection accuracy of faked bio-fashion. *Journal of Consumer Policy, 46*(2), 155–189. https://doi.org/10.1007/s10603-023-09537-8

Enz, C., Škodová-Parmová, D., & Wolf, P. (2021). *Co2 neutrality of small and medium-sized hotels—Publicity stunt or sustainable competitive advantage?.* 585-604. https://doi.org/10.31410/tmt.2021-2022.585

European Securities and Markets Authority. (2023). *Progress report on greenwashing*. ESMA.

Falchi, A., Grolleau, G., & Mzoughi, N. (2022). Why companies might under-communicate their efforts for sustainable development and what can be done? *Business Strategy and the Environment, 31*(5), 1938–1946. https://doi.org/10.1002/bse.2991

Gatti, L., Pizzetti, M., & Seele, P. (2021). Green lies and their effect on intention to invest. *Journal of Business Research, 127*, 228–240. https://doi.org/10.1016/j.jbusres.2021.01.028

Ghitti, M., Gianfrate, G., & Palma, L. (2024). The agency of greenwashing. *Journal of Management & Governance, 28*, 905–941. https://doi.org/10.1007/s10997-023-09683-8

Guo, R., Zhang, W., Wang, T., Li, C. B., & Tao, L. (2018). Timely or considered? Brand trust repair strategies and mechanism after greenwashing in China—From a legitimacy perspective. *Industrial Marketing Management, 72*, 127–137. https://doi.org/10.1016/j.indmarman.2018.04.001

Hunter, J. (2023). The environmental performance of b corp smes and the occurrence of greenwashing. *Sinergie Italian Journal of Management, 41*(3), 49–69. https://doi.org/10.7433/s122.2023.03

Ioannou, I., Kassinis, G., & Papagiannakis, G. (2022). The impact of perceived greenwashing on customer satisfaction and the contingent role of capability reputation. *Journal of Business Ethics, 185*, 1–20. https://doi.org/10.1007/s10551-022-05151-9

Jenkins, H. (2008). A 'business opportunity' model of corporate social responsibility for small- and medium-sized enterprises. *Business Ethics a European Review, 18*(1), 21–36. https://doi.org/10.1111/j.1467-8608.2009.01546.x

Ling, X. (2024). Green behavior strategies in the green credit market: Analysis of the impacts of enterprises' greenwashing and blockchain technology. *Sustainability, 16*(11), 4858. https://doi.org/10.3390/su16114858

Liu, C., Wang, J., Ji, Q., & Zhang, D. (2024). To be green or not to be: How governmental regulation shapes financial institutions' greenwashing behaviors in green finance. *International Review of Financial Analysis, 93*, 103225. https://doi.org/10.1016/j.irfa.2024.103225

Liu, Y., Li, W., Wang, L., & Meng, Q. (2023). Why greenwashing occurs and what happens afterwards? A systematic literature review and future research agenda. *Environmental Science and Pollution Research, 30*, 1–15. https://doi.org/10.1007/s11356-023-30571-z

Luo, Z., & Liu, H. (2022). Research on debt financing efficiency and influencing factors of smes in China. *BCP Business & Management, 20*, 277–291. https://doi.org/10.54691/bcpbm.v20i.976

Lyon, T. P., & Maxwell, J. W. (2011). Greenwash: Corporate environmental disclosure under threat of audit. *Journal of Economics & Management Strategy, 20*(1), 3–41. https://doi.org/10.1111/j.1530-9134.2010.00282.x

Lyon, T. P., & Montgomery, A. W. (2015). The means and end of greenwash. *Organization & Environment, 28*(2), 223–249. https://doi.org/10.1177/1086026615575332

Montgomery, A. W., Lyon, T. P., & Barg, J. (2023). No end in sight? A greenwash review and research agenda. *Organization & Environment., 37*, 221–256. https://doi.org/10.1177/10860266231168905

Muhammed Sajid, K. A., Zakkariya, N. M. S., & Islam, J. U. (2024). When going green goes wrong: The effects of greenwashing on brand avoidance and negative word-of-mouth. Journal of Retailing and Consumer Services, 78, 103773. https://doi.org/10.1016/j.jretconser.2024.103773

Parguel, B., Benoit-Moreau, F., & Russell, C. A. (2015). Can evoking nature in advertising mislead consumers? The power of 'executional greenwashing'. *International Journal of Advertising, 34*(1), 107–134. https://doi.org/10.1080/02650487.2014.996116

Polonsky, M. J., Carlson, L., Grove, S., & Kangun, N. (1997). International environmental marketing claims: Real changes or simple posturing? *International Marketing Review, 14*(4), 218–232. https://doi.org/10.1108/02651339710173426

Roulet, T. J., & Touboul, S. (2015). The intentions with which the road is paved: Attitudes to liberalism as determinants of greenwashing. *Journal of Business Ethics, 128*(2), 305–320. http://www.jstor.org/stable/24702872

Sajid, M., Abdulkhader, Z., Mohd Suki, N., & Islam, J. U. (2024). When going green goes wrong: The effects of greenwashing on brand avoidance and negative word-of-mouth. *Journal of Retailing and Consumer Services, 78*, 103773. https://doi.org/10.1016/j.jretconser.2024.103773

Seele, P., & Gatti, L. (2017). Greenwashing revisited: In search of a typology and accusation-based definition incorporating legitimacy strategies. *Business Strategy and the Environment, 26*(2), 239–252. https://doi.org/10.1002/bse.1912

Shao, X., Jeong, E., Zhang, X., & Jang, S. (2023). Green marketing versus demarketing: The impact of individual characteristics on consumers' evaluations of green messages. *Journal of Hospitality & Tourism Research, 0*(0), 109634802211470. https://doi.org/10.1177/10963480221147054

Siano, A., Vollero, A., Conte, F., & Amabile, S. (2017). "More than words": Expanding the taxonomy of greenwashing after the Volkswagen scandal. *Journal of Business Research, 71*, 27–37. https://doi.org/10.1016/j.jbusres.2016.11.002

Suchman, M. C. (1995). Managing legitimacy: Strategic and institutional approaches. *The Academy of Management Review, 20*(3), 571–610. https://doi.org/10.2307/258788

Taglialatela, J., Miroshnychenko, I., Barontini, R., & Testa, F. (2024). Talk or walk? The board of directors and firm environmental strategies. *Business Strategy and the Environment, 33*(4), 2890–2910. https://doi.org/10.1002/bse.3628

Teichmann, F. M. J., Wittmann, C., & Sergi, B. S. S. (2023). What are the consequences of corporate greenwashing? A look into the consequences of greenwashing in consumer and financial markets. *Journal of Information, Communication and Ethics in Society, 21*(3), 290–301. https://doi.org/10.1108/JICES-10-2022-0090

Torelli, R., Balluchi, F., & Lazzini, A. (2020). Greenwashing and environmental communication: Effects on stakeholders' perceptions. *Business Strategy and the Environment, 29*(2), 407–421.

Walker, K., & Wan, F. (2012). The harm of symbolic actions and green-washing: Corporate actions and communications on environmental performance and their financial implications. *Journal of Business Ethics, 109*(2), 227–242. https://doi.org/10.1007/s10551-011-1122-4

Wickert, C. (2014). "Political" corporate social responsibility in small- and medium-sized enterprises. *Business & Society, 55*(6), 792–824. https://doi.org/10.1177/0007650314537021

Zahoor, N., Khan, H., Donbesuur, F., Khan, Z., & Rajwani, T. (2023). Grand challenges and emerging market small and medium enterprises: The role of strategic agility and gender diversity. *Journal of Product Innovation Management, 41*(2), 473–500. https://doi.org/10.1111/jpim.12661

Zhang, D. (2023). Does green finance really inhibit extreme hypocritical ESG risk? A greenwashing perspective exploration. *Energy Economics, 121*, 106688. https://doi.org/10.1016/j.eneco.2023.106688

Zhang, K., Pan, Z., Janardhanan, M., et al. (2023). Relationship analysis between greenwashing and environmental performance. *Environment, Development and Sustainability, 25*, 7927–7957. https://doi.org/10.1007/s10668-022-02381-9

Zhang, L., Li, D., Cao, C., & Huang, S. (2018). The influence of greenwashing perception on green purchasing intentions: The mediating role of green word-of-mouth and moderating role of green concern. *Journal of Cleaner Production., 187*, 740–750.

Chapter 8
Italian SMEs' Sustainability Scores

8.1 Introduction

In recent years, the focus on sustainability and corporate responsibility has intensified across various sectors, including Small and Medium Enterprises (SMEs). Recognizing the pivotal role of SMEs in the economy, this chapter embarks on an analytical journey based on a comprehensive survey conducted by the University of Ferrara in 2019 and 2021. The primary objective is to estimate a sustainability score for Italian SMEs, utilizing advanced statistical methodologies.

The survey addresses critical aspects of the Circular Economy, patent innovations, product and process improvements, waste reduction, and labor force conditions. These dimensions are crucial for understanding the sustainability initiatives undertaken by SMEs. To enrich the analysis, survey data is integrated with balance sheet information sourced from AIDA Bureau Van Dijk. This integration allows for a multifaceted examination of sustainability, transcending mere qualitative assessments.

While Environmental, Social, and Governance (ESG) scores, such as those provided by Eikon Refinitiv, are prevalent in assessing corporate sustainability, this chapter adopts a different approach. Specifically, the scores developed herein do not incorporate the governance aspect. This decision stems from the observation that many Italian SMEs lack complex or articulated governance structures, making traditional governance metrics less applicable.

Despite the exclusion of governance in the sustainability scores, the regulatory landscape in Italy underscores its importance. The implementation of corporate governance and Enterprise Risk Management (ERM) practices has become essential for the viability of SMEs. The introduction of the Insolvency and Crisis Code (IC-Code) mandates that Italian family SMEs establish appropriate organizational, management, and accounting bodies to ensure sustainability and regulatory compliance (Riva et al., 2021). This regulatory framework highlights the significance of

M. Aliano et al., *Sustainable Finance for SMEs*, Sustainable Finance,
https://doi.org/10.1007/978-3-031-74193-7_8

governance mechanisms in mitigating risks and ensuring the long-term success of SMEs in Italy.

The chapter also delves into the adoption of strategic leadership and innovation among Italian SMEs. This area has garnered significant research attention, emphasizing the need for supportive policies that incentivize innovation and create an enabling environment for SMEs. The interplay between strategic leadership, innovation, and sustainability forms a core component of the analysis.

To analyze the survey data, a combination of Correspondence Analysis (CA) and Principal Component Analysis (PCA) is employed. CA is applied to qualitative responses, while PCA is used for quantitative data. This dual approach facilitates a comprehensive understanding of the factors influencing sustainability. The analysis further extends to balance sheet determinants using panel regression and quantile regression techniques. Additionally, propensity score analysis is conducted to explore the impact of innovations.

The chapter is organized as follows. Section 8.2 describes the survey sample and presents the main descriptive statistics, addressing issues related to data gaps and their implications for the analysis. Section 8.3 presents the methodologies applied to the data, covering the rationale behind choosing specific statistical techniques and how they are implemented. Section 8.4 presents the results of the sustainability score analysis, discussing key findings and their implications for SMEs. Section 8.5 applies panel and quantile regression analyses to understand the balance sheet determinants of the sustainability scores, discussing the main findings and their significance. Finally, Section 8.6 concludes with a propensity score analysis to assess the impact of innovations on sustainability, summarizing the key insights and highlighting areas for future research. Through this structured approach, the chapter aims to provide a comprehensive and scientifically robust assessment of sustainability in Italian SMEs, contributing valuable insights to the broader discourse on corporate sustainability and innovation.

8.2 Survey Features and Sample Composition

According to the most important sustainability score provided by very important data providers, such as Eikon Refinitiv, for this chapter we use a survey of qualitative e quantitative on a sample of SMEs.

The empirical investigation focused on Italian small and medium enterprises (SMEs) across two periods: 2017–2018 and 2019–2020. The primary aim was to assess the current state of the Circular Economy (CE) transition at the firm level in Italy, with a special emphasis on the role of innovation and the implementation of eco-innovative practices. To gather the necessary data, two national surveys were conducted in 2020 and 2021. These surveys utilized the Computer Assisted Web Interview (CAWI) method, where firms were given a structured questionnaire. This approach facilitated efficient and uniform data collection from a large number of respondents.

The study's main objective was to understand how firms are transitioning to CE, focusing specifically on the role of innovation in this process and the extent to which eco-innovative practices are being implemented. The data collection targeted various aspects of firm behavior and practices related to CE, aiming to provide a comprehensive overview of the current situation.

The sample for the study was carefully stratified to ensure it was representative of different segments within the Italian economy. The stratification was based on three main criteria: geographical localization, sectoral classification, and firm size. Geographical localization followed the macro areas defined by Istat, the Italian National Institute of Statistics. The sectoral classification was based on the technological intensity categories established by Eurostat. Firm size was categorized into three groups: small firms with 10–49 employees, medium firms with 50–249 employees, and larger firms with more than 250 employees. The final dataset comprised 4565 firms for the 2017–2018 period and 4649 firms for the 2019–2020 period. Notably, 2305 firms responded to both surveys, providing a rich longitudinal dataset that enhances the robustness of the analysis. This large and detailed dataset allowed for a thorough examination of the CE transition among Italian SMEs.

A significant focus of the study was on innovation and eco-innovative practices. The researchers aimed to identify the types of innovations being adopted by firms, such as product, process, and organizational innovations, and to what extent these innovations were environmentally friendly or contributed to sustainable practices. Additionally, the study explored the barriers and drivers that firms face in adopting eco-innovative practices. From this detailed analysis, a sustainable score was derived, which quantifies the level of sustainability practices and CE adoption at the firm level. This sustainable score provides a measurable indicator of how well firms are integrating CE principles into their operations.

The importance of this empirical investigation lies in its potential implications for policymakers, businesses, and academics. For policymakers, the findings can provide valuable insights into the current state of CE transition, informing the design of targeted interventions to promote sustainable practices. Businesses can use the results to benchmark their practices against industry standards, identifying areas for improvement in their own CE efforts. Academically, the study contributes to the existing literature by providing empirical evidence from a significant sample of SMEs in Italy, offering practical insights into the challenges and opportunities associated with CE implementation.

In conclusion, this empirical investigation offers a comprehensive analysis of the CE transition among Italian SMEs. By focusing on innovation and eco-innovative practices, it provides a detailed understanding of how firms are adapting to CE principles and the factors influencing this transition. The sustainable score derived from the data serves as a valuable tool for assessing and promoting sustainability within firms, highlighting the progress and areas for further development in the journey towards a circular economy.

Our investigation centers on the dataset gathered during extensive surveys conducted in 2020 and 2021, specifically targeting firms classified as small and medium enterprises (SMEs) according to the European Commission's stringent criteria.

These criteria delineate SMEs as entities with fewer than 250 employees, annual revenues not surpassing 50 million euros, and total assets under 43 million euros.

This targeted approach ensures a focused analysis on firms that typify the SME sector, crucial for understanding their role and practices within the broader economic landscape. By adhering to these standardized thresholds, we streamline our dataset to include only those firms that align with the European Commission's definition of SMEs, thus ensuring consistency and comparability in our subsequent analyses. The rationale behind this selection criteria lies in the distinct characteristics of SMEs, which often exhibit unique operational dynamics, responsiveness to market changes, and resource limitations compared to larger enterprises. This segmentation allows for a nuanced examination of how SMEs navigate challenges related to sustainability practices, innovation adoption, and regulatory compliance, particularly pertinent within the context of transitioning towards a Circular Economy (CE).

Moreover, by focusing on SMEs meeting these specific criteria, our study aims to uncover trends and patterns in their approaches to sustainable development, technological innovation, and eco-friendly practices. This approach not only enriches the empirical understanding of SME behavior in relation to CE principles but also contributes valuable insights for policymakers, stakeholders, and academia seeking to support and promote sustainable business practices within SME ecosystems.

Our sample is composed by 1772 Italian SMEs which operated in the follow sectors (Table 8.1).

Totally, the survey is characterized by 156 questions. The questionnaire is structured into several sections to comprehensively gather information from participating businesses. Section 0 focuses on gathering details about the company itself and the respondent executives. It serves as a foundational section to understand the organizational context and the individuals' responses. Section 8.1 delves into the characteristics of the company, aiming to capture key aspects such as size, sector, and market positioning. This section provides essential background information that contextualizes the subsequent analysis of the survey data. Section 8.2 explores innovation and investment activities within the company, covering areas such as research and development (R&D), investments in green and circular economy practices, and advancements related to Industry 4.0 technologies. This section aims to assess the company's approach to technological and sustainable innovation. Section 8.3 is dedicated to exploring the company's engagement with Circular Economy principles. It investigates strategies, practices, and initiatives implemented to promote resource efficiency, waste reduction, and sustainable production processes. Section 8.4 examines organizational aspects, including structures, training programs, and industrial relations within the company. This section provides insights into how the company manages its workforce, fosters skills development, and maintains productive industrial relationships. Finally, Section 8.5 addresses the impact and scenarios arising from the COVID-19 crisis. It investigates how the pandemic has affected the company's operations, strategies, and future outlook, providing valuable insights into resilience and adaptation strategies.

Table 8.1 Sample composition by industries

Sector	firms
Other manufacturing industries	38
Retail trade (excluding automotive retail)	2
Wholesale trade (excluding automotive wholesale)	3
Apparel manufacturing; leather and fur goods manufacturing	82
Manufacture of other transport equipment	19
Manufacture of other non-metallic mineral products	79
Manufacture of electrical equipment and non-electrical household appliances	70
Manufacture of rubber and plastic products	127
Manufacture of leather and similar products	65
Manufacture of motor vehicles, trailers, and semi-trailers	20
Manufacture of paper and paper products	41
Manufacture of coke and refined petroleum products	2
Manufacture of computers and electronic and optical products; Electromedical and precision equipment; watches and clocks	53
Manufacture of machinery and equipment N.E.C. (not elsewhere classified)	205
Manufacture of furniture	81
Manufacture of chemicals	34
Manufacture of basic pharmaceutical products and pharmaceutical preparations	1
Manufacture of fabricated metal products (excluding machinery and equipment)	421
Wood and Cork industry (excluding furniture); manufacture of straw and plaiting materials	54
Beverage industry	13
Food industry	126
Textile industry	73
Specialized construction activities	1
Metallurgy	30
Repair, maintenance and installation of machinery and equipment	72
Printing and reproduction of recorded media	60
Total	1772

Together, these sections form a comprehensive framework for evaluating various dimensions of participating businesses, facilitating a deeper understanding of their operational dynamics, strategic orientations, and responses to contemporary challenges and opportunities.

8.3 Methodologies

The increasing emphasis on sustainability and corporate social responsibility (CSR) has necessitated the development of robust methodologies to evaluate companies' performance in these areas. This paragraph discusses the application of two different methodologies to obtain an environmental and social responsibility score, which incorporates both qualitative and quantitative data. This dual approach aims to provide a comprehensive assessment of a company's efforts in sustainability and CSR.

The evaluation process begins by categorizing the questions into qualitative and quantitative types, following a methodology similar to that employed by Eikon Refinitiv. This initial categorization is crucial because it allows for the appropriate application of statistical techniques tailored to the nature of the data (Refinitiv, n.d.).

For qualitative data analysis, the questions are designed to capture aspects such as investment in waste reduction, research and development (R&D), emission reduction, employee training, career development, skills enhancement, and overall labor conditions. To analyze these qualitative aspects, Correspondence Analysis (CA) is employed. CA is a multivariate graphical technique designed to explore relationships among categorical variables. It provides a means of displaying or summarizing a set of data in two-dimensional graphical form. By applying CA to qualitative questions, we can visualize the relationships between different qualitative variables and identify patterns or trends within the data (Greenacre, 2017). Specifically, two separate correspondence analyses are performed to capture different dimensions of qualitative data. The first analysis focuses on aspects related to environmental sustainability, such as investments in reducing waste, R&D for sustainable practices, and emission reduction initiatives. The second analysis targets social responsibility elements, including training programs, career development opportunities, skill enhancement initiatives, and overall labor conditions. Once the correspondence analyses are completed, the scores obtained from CA are normalized. Normalization is essential to standardizing the scores, ensuring that they are comparable across different metrics and scales. This normalization process involves transforming the CA scores into a range from 0 to 1. The normalized scores from the two correspondence analyses are then combined to form a comprehensive qualitative score.

For quantitative data analysis, Principal Component Analysis (PCA) is utilized. PCA is a statistical technique used to reduce the dimensionality of a dataset while retaining most of the variance present in the data. It identifies principal components, which are new variables constructed as linear combinations of the original variables. These principal components capture the maximum variance within the dataset (Jolliffe, 2002). In this study, PCA is applied to quantitative variables to extract two principal components. The first principal component represents activities related to recycling and re-use of resources, while the second principal component encompasses investment in R&D for product and process improvements. The selection of these components is guided by their communalities, which indicate the proportion of each variable's variance that is accounted for by the principal components (Jolliffe, 2002).

After extracting the principal components, the scores are also normalized to ensure comparability. The normalization of PCA scores follows a similar transformation process as used in the qualitative analysis, converting the scores to a range from 0 to 1.

To arrive at a final comprehensive score, the normalized scores from both qualitative and quantitative analyses are combined. The combination process assigns different weights to the qualitative and quantitative scores, reflecting their relative importance in the overall assessment. In this methodology, the qualitative score is given a weight of 70%, while the quantitative score is assigned a weight of 30%. This weighting scheme acknowledges the greater emphasis on qualitative aspects, which often capture more nuanced and impactful elements of CSR and sustainability practices.

The combined score, ranging from 0 to 1, provides a holistic measure of a company's performance in environmental and social responsibility. This integrated approach leverages the strengths of both qualitative and quantitative analyses, offering a balanced and comprehensive assessment. By employing advanced statistical techniques such as CA and PCA, the methodology ensures that the scores are derived from a rigorous and scientifically sound process, enhancing their reliability and validity.

8.4 Details of Analysis

Correspondence Analysis (CA) is particularly effective for qualitative data as it can handle the categorical nature of the data and uncover underlying structures. In our application, CA was used to evaluate two distinct aspects of corporate sustainability: environmental initiatives and social responsibility. For the environmental initiatives, questions might include whether the company has implemented a waste reduction program, the extent of R&D efforts aimed at sustainable practices, and measures taken to reduce emissions. The CA helps in visualizing how these different initiatives relate to each other and to overall company performance. In terms of social responsibility, CA examines questions related to employee training programs, career development opportunities, skill enhancement initiatives, and overall labor conditions. By analyzing the relationships between these factors, CA provides a comprehensive view of a company's commitment to its workforce. The scores derived from CA are then normalized. Normalization here involves adjusting the range of scores to a common scale of 0 to 1. This step is crucial as it allows for the combination of scores from different analyses, ensuring that each score contributes equally to the final assessment.

PCA is employed to distill the quantitative data into principal components that represent the most significant sources of variance in the data. In this study, PCA was applied to questions measuring quantitative aspects such as recycling activities, resource re-use, and investments in R&D for product and process improvements.

The first principal component (PC1) captures the variance associated with recycling and resource re-use. This component indicates how well a company manages its material resources and its commitment to reducing waste through recycling efforts. The second principal component (PC2) is related to investments in R&D. This component reflects the company's focus on innovation and improvements in product and process sustainability. Higher scores in this component suggest a stronger emphasis on sustainable development and innovation. The extraction of these components simplifies the complexity of the dataset while retaining the essential information needed for a robust evaluation. The PCA scores are then normalized to a scale of 0 to 1, ensuring they are comparable to the qualitative scores obtained from CA.

The final step involves combining the normalized scores from CA and PCA. Given the different nature and significance of qualitative and quantitative aspects, they are weighted differently. The qualitative scores, reflecting nuanced aspects of CSR and sustainability, are given a weight of 70%. In contrast, the quantitative scores, which provide concrete numerical measures of a company's sustainability efforts, are assigned a weight of 30%.

This weighting scheme is designed to reflect the importance of qualitative factors in evaluating CSR. Qualitative factors often capture more nuanced and complex dimensions of a company's practices that quantitative measures might miss. However, the inclusion of quantitative data ensures that the evaluation is grounded in concrete, measurable outcomes. The final score, ranging from 0 to 1, is a comprehensive measure of a company's performance in both environmental and social responsibility. This score can serve as a valuable tool for stakeholders, including investors, regulators, and consumers, to assess the sustainability and CSR performance of companies (Fig. 8.1).

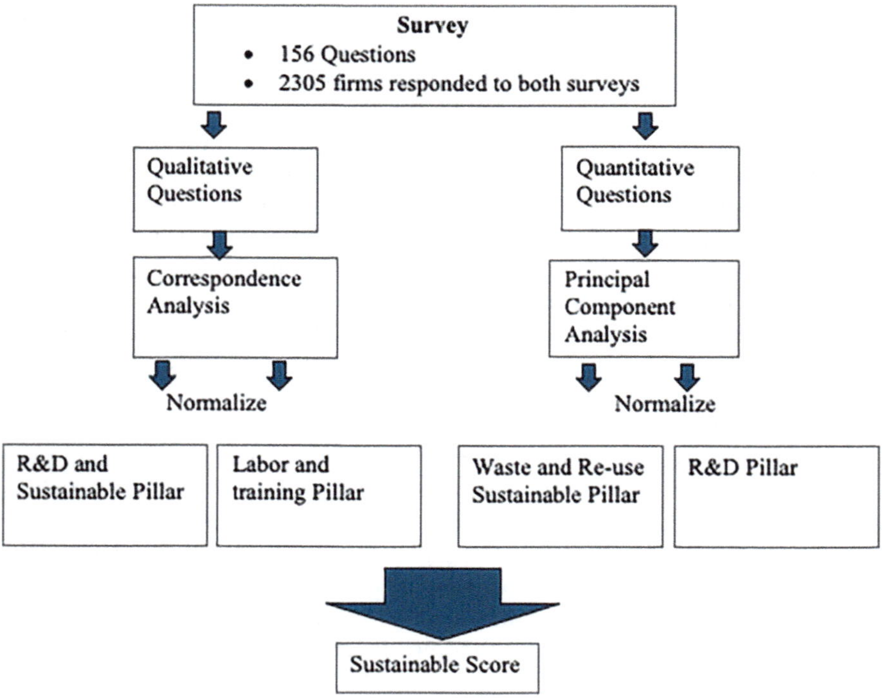

Fig. 8.1 Calculation of score

In conclusion, the dual methodology described in this chapter represents a robust framework for evaluating companies' environmental and social responsibility. By systematically categorizing questions, applying correspondence analysis to qualitative data, and principal component analysis to quantitative data, and combining the normalized scores with appropriate weights, this approach provides a comprehensive and balanced assessment. The resulting score serves as a valuable tool for stakeholders to gauge the sustainability and CSR performance of companies. Future research could refine this methodology further by incorporating additional variables and exploring alternative weighting schemes to enhance its applicability and accuracy in different contexts.

8.5 Determinants of Sustainable Score

To evaluate the characteristics of companies with high and low sustainable performance, we calculated scores using fundamental balance sheet data from the AIDA database. This required excluding some companies due to insufficient or incomplete data. Our analysis primarily centers on the balance sheet indices provided by AIDA, aiming to capture the fundamental aspects of each company. By focusing on these indices, we aim to identify the key financial metrics that differentiate companies based on their sustainability performance. The following table provides a detailed description of the variables utilized in the regression analysis (Table 8.2), offering insights into the specific balance sheet items and financial ratios considered in our

Table 8.2 Determinants 'description

Variable	Description
NCE	Net capital employed turnover ratio
EBITDA%	EBITDA on total turnover
ROE	Return on equity
CR	Current ratio
LT	Long-term index
AGE	Age of the company
EXP	Export yes = 1 export no = 0
TA	Total assets
EMP	Employees
GCE	Gross capital employed turnover ratio
ROA	Return on asset
LI	Liquidity index
FINEXP	Financial expense on revenues
ST	Short term debt index
EQUITY	Equity ratio
EBITFIN	Ebit on financial expenses

Table contains the description of the variables used as determinants in the chapter study. This approach ensures a comprehensive understanding of the financial underpinnings that contribute to a company's sustainability profile.

To thoroughly investigate the determinants of sustainable performance among companies, our analysis began with a fixed effects panel regression. This technique was chosen because it effectively controls for unobserved heterogeneity by examining within-company variations over time, thus providing a more accurate assessment of the individual contributions of each variable. This approach helps isolate the impact of time-invariant characteristics and focus on the dynamic changes within companies, ensuring that our estimates are not biased by omitted variable bias that could arise from unobserved heterogeneity.

Following the initial regression, we recognized the presence of heterogeneity in our data, which could affect the reliability of our standard error estimates. To address this issue, we employed the covariance and variance clustering method (VCE method). By clustering the standard errors, we account for potential correlations within clusters, thus providing robust standard error estimates that are less likely to be influenced by heteroskedasticity or autocorrelation within the data. This step is crucial for obtaining valid statistical inferences, as it corrects for the potential biases introduced by heterogeneity in the error terms.

In addition to these steps, we incorporated sector effects into our regression analysis. Including sector effects allows us to control for industry-specific influences that might impact the variables of interest. Different sectors can have varying operational practices, regulatory environments, and market conditions, all of which could affect the financial and sustainability metrics of companies. By accounting for these sector-specific factors, we ensure that our results more accurately reflect the intrinsic relationships between the variables and sustainable performance, independent of the broader industry context.

Overall, this comprehensive approach—combining fixed effects regression, robust error clustering, and sector controls—provides a nuanced and reliable evaluation of the factors influencing sustainable performance in companies. The following table details the variables used in the regression analysis, offering insights into the specific balance sheet items and financial ratios that were considered in our study. This methodology enables a deeper understanding of the financial underpinnings that contribute to a company's sustainability profile.

The analysis reveals that the current ratio is negatively related to higher sustainability scores, indicating that companies with greater liquidity tend to be less sustainable (see next Table 8.3). This counterintuitive result might be explained by several factors. Companies with high liquidity ratios may be focusing on short-term financial stability and flexibility, possibly at the expense of long-term sustainable investments. Such firms might prioritize immediate returns and maintaining cash reserves over committing resources to sustainability initiatives, which often require significant upfront investments and a longer-term perspective. Similarly, the negative relationship between the liquidity ratio and sustainability scores reinforces this notion. High liquidity might reflect a conservative financial strategy aimed at maintaining ample cash reserves, which could limit the funds available for sustainability projects. Alternatively, it might suggest that companies with extensive investments

Table 8.3 Regression results

	Fixed Effects			Cluterized Errors			Fixed effects sector		
	score	score	score	score	score	score	score	score	score
NCE	0.00131			−5.53e-05			0.000196		
	(0.00224)			(0.00162)			(0.00161)		
ROE	−1.34e-05			−1.56e-05			−1.31e-05		
	(2.88e-05)			(2.91e-05)			(2.90e-05)		
CR	−0.00253**			−0.00170*			−0.00166*		
	(0.00112)			(0.000898)			(0.000886)		
LT	0.00332			0.00308			0.00331		
	(0.00565)			(0.00576)			(0.00577)		
GCE		−0.000352			−0.00102			−0.000827	
		(0.00124)			(0.00113)			(0.00114)	
ROA		−1.49e-07			4.36e-05			3.44e-05	
		(0.000102)			(9.46e-05)			(9.49e-05)	
LI		−0.00179			−0.00214**			−0.00192**	
		(0.00116)			(0.000899)			(0.000906)	
FINEXP		0.00122*			0.00106			0.00113	
		(0.000687)			(0.000734)			(0.000734)	
ST			0.00619			0.00252			0.00320
			(0.00560)			(0.00556)			(0.00559)
EQUITY			−0.000415***			−0.000153**			−0.000165**
			(9.63e-05)			(7.17e-05)			(7.09e-05)
EBITFIN			6.44e-06			−2.18e-06			−4.71e-06
			(1.51e-05)			(1.30e-05)			(1.29e-05)
EBITDA%	0.000120	0.000121	3.70e-05	7.23e-05	7.99e-05	0.000135	7.56e-05	8.60e-05	0.000154

(continued)

Table 8.3 (continued)

	Fixed Effects			Cluterized Errors			Fixed effects sector		
	score	score	score	score	score	score	score	score	score
	(7.80e-05)	(8.09e-05)	(0.000155)	(6.35e-05)	(8.69e-05)	(0.000139)	(6.31e-05)	(8.86e-05)	(0.000140)
AGE	0.000204***	0.000216***	0.000183**	0.000257***	0.000260***	0.000286***	0.000242***	0.000244***	0.000268***
	(7.46e-05)	(7.30e-05)	(8.17e-05)	(6.78e-05)	(6.90e-05)	(7.25e-05)	(6.76e-05)	(6.91e-05)	(7.23e-05)
EXP	−0.00205	−0.00189	−0.00106	0.00215	0.00218	0.00326	0.00128	0.00136	0.00231
	(0.00135)	(0.00132)	(0.00143)	(0.00204)	(0.00202)	(0.00214)	(0.00205)	(0.00203)	(0.00215)
TA	−3.17e-07***	−3.31e-07***	−2.71e-07***	2.12e-07***	2.12e-07***	2.03e-07***	1.88e-07***	1.89e-07***	1.80e-07***
	(9.45e-08)	(9.28e-08)	(9.56e-08)	(6.80e-08)	(6.73e-08)	(6.65e-08)	(6.41e-08)	(6.35e-08)	(6.25e-08)
EMP	4.07e-06**	4.09e-06**	4.27e-06**	5.35e-06***	5.39e-06***	5.38e-06***	5.28e-06***	5.34e-06***	5.32e-06***
	(1.85e-06)	(1.85e-06)	(1.84e-06)	(6.51e-07)	(6.84e-07)	(6.57e-07)	(6.15e-07)	(6.50e-07)	(6.34e-07)
Constant	0.298***	0.297***	0.303***	0.290***	0.291***	0.288***	0.284***	0.285***	0.280***
	(0.00446)	(0.00418)	(0.00596)	(0.00398)	(0.00406)	(0.00571)	(0.00829)	(0.00830)	(0.00945)
Observations	6609	6779	5895	6609	6779	5895	6609	6779	5895
R-squared	0.007	0.007	0.009	0.0664	0.0503	0.0534	0.1002	0.1088	0.1080
Number of id.	1731	1740	1648	1731	1740	1648	1731	1740	1648

The table presents the results of panel estimations. Columns 1 to 3 display the fixed effects model estimations. Columns 4 to 6 include standard errors clustered by variance and covariance (VCE). The last three columns provide additional model specifications. Standard errors are reported in parentheses. All independent variables are one year lagged. Statistical significance is denoted by *** $p < 0.01$, ** $p < 0.05$, * $p < 0.1$

in sustainability initiatives have lower liquidity because such projects tie up capital that would otherwise contribute to liquid assets.

Another finding is that companies with more equity have lower sustainability scores. This could be due to the fact that firms with substantial equity might be investing heavily in growth and expansion rather than sustainability. Equity-rich companies might also have more financial flexibility to pursue a variety of strategic goals, some of which may not align with sustainability.

Conversely, the positive relationship between age and sustainability scores suggests that older companies tend to be more sustainable. This could be because established companies have more experience and resources to implement and benefit from sustainability practices. They may also face greater scrutiny from stakeholders, including investors and regulators, pushing them to adopt more sustainable practices.

The number of employees is also positively related to sustainability scores. Larger workforces could be indicative of larger companies that have more resources and greater capacity to invest in sustainability. Additionally, companies with more employees may be more motivated to pursue sustainable practices to maintain their reputation and appeal as employers.

Interestingly, the total asset size is negatively related to sustainability scores. This might be because larger companies, despite having more resources, also have more complex operations that can be harder to manage sustainably. These companies might also face more significant challenges in transitioning to sustainable practices due to their scale and the legacy systems they have in place.

In summary, the findings suggest that liquidity and equity-richness might be associated with lower sustainability due to a focus on short-term financial goals and expansion over long-term sustainable development. In contrast, older companies and those with larger workforces tend to be more sustainable, possibly due to their greater experience, resources, and stakeholder pressures. Meanwhile, the negative relationship between total assets and sustainability might reflect the complexities and challenges larger companies face in implementing sustainable practices.

Quantile regression is employed as a robustness check in applications to SMEs because it offers a more nuanced view of how explanatory variables impact various points of the distribution of the dependent variable, rather than just the mean. This approach is particularly useful for SMEs, which often exhibit significant variability in performance metrics. By analyzing different quantiles of the distribution, quantile regression can reveal whether the effects of variables on sustainability are consistent across different performance levels or if they vary significantly. This method helps address the limitations of traditional mean-based regression models, which may be skewed by outliers or extreme values (Koenker, 2005; Buchinsky, 1998). For instance, in studies of firm performance and sustainability, quantile regression has been shown to provide more robust and detailed insights by examining the impact of variables on both low and high-performing firms (Cade & Noon, 2003). By incorporating quantile regression, we ensure that our findings are not disproportionately influenced by outliers and better capture the diverse experiences of SMEs, leading to a more comprehensive understanding of the factors affecting their sustainability.

Contrary to previous regressions, the percentage of EBITDA relative to total revenue is positively related to sustainability scores (see next table). This indicates that companies with higher profitability margins are more likely to invest in and achieve higher sustainability scores. Higher profitability provides the financial resources and flexibility necessary for significant investments in sustainability initiatives, which may not yield immediate financial returns but are crucial for long-term sustainability.

The positive relationship between company age and sustainability scores is confirmed, as suggested in previous analyses. Older companies are likely to have more established sustainability practices and a deeper understanding of the long-term benefits of sustainability, driven by their historical experience and regulatory or market pressures.

The liquidity index continues to show a negative relationship with sustainability scores, as previously found. This suggests that companies with higher liquidity might prioritize short-term financial stability and flexibility over long-term sustainable investments. These companies might prefer to maintain cash reserves and immediate returns rather than committing resources to sustainability projects that require significant upfront investment.

Export activities show a positive relationship with sustainability scores. Companies involved in export markets might face higher environmental and social standards, driven by international regulations and market expectations. Consequently, these companies may adopt more sustainable practices to meet global market demands and enhance their competitive advantage.

Long-term debt has a weak but positive relationship with sustainability scores. This suggests that companies utilizing long-term debt financing are investing in long-term projects, which could include sustainability initiatives. Long-term debt provides the necessary capital for substantial investments, such as sustainable technologies or processes, though the weak relationship suggests this is not a predominant trend.

EBIT relative to financial expenses is positively related to sustainability scores. Companies that efficiently manage their financial expenses and maintain higher EBIT are likely to be in a better position to invest in sustainability. This efficiency reflects good management practices and financial health, enabling more resources to be allocated toward sustainable practices.

Interestingly, the total assets variable shows a positive relationship with sustainability scores in this analysis, differing from previous regressions. This shift might be due to non-linear relationships and the impact of outliers. Larger companies with significant assets may indeed have more capacity to invest in sustainability, but this relationship can be complex. The positive sign in this regression suggests that, when managing outliers or considering non-linear effects, the overall capacity of large companies to engage in sustainable practices becomes more apparent.

In summary, the findings in the following table several factors influencing sustainability (Table 8.4). Higher profitability, involvement in export activities,

Table 8.4 Quantile regression

VARIABLES	score	score	score
NCE	0.000106		
	(0.00189)		
EBITDA%	−7.59e-05	−2.80e-05	0.000336**
	(0.000101)	(0.000103)	(0.000160)
ROE	−2.02e-05		
	(4.20e-05)		
CR	−0.000677		
	(0.000806)		
LT	0.0101*		
	(0.00523)		
AGE	0.000174***	0.000192***	0.000257***
	(4.35e-05)	(4.21e-05)	(4.49e-05)
EXP	0.0157***	0.0148***	0.0168***
	(0.00178)	(0.00177)	(0.00184)
TA	2.87e-07***	2.64e-07***	2.31e-07***
	(2.69e-08)	(2.64e-08)	(2.76e-08)
EMP	1.20e-05***	1.93e-05***	1.19e-05***
	(3.36e-06)	(3.36e-06)	(3.29e-06)
GCE		−0.00154	
		(0.00117)	
ROA		0.000144	
		(0.000130)	
LI		−0.00217**	
		(0.000908)	
FINEXP		0.00174**	
		(0.000678)	
ST			−0.00171
			(0.00549)
EQUITY			−7.74e-05
			(5.55e-05)
EBITFIN			−2.97e-05*
			(1.79e-05)
Constant	0.271***	0.273***	0.269***
	(0.00384)	(0.00364)	(0.00521)
Observations	6609	6779	5895

The table presents the results of quantile regression analyses. All independent variables are one year lagged. Statistical significance is denoted by *** $p < 0.01$, ** $p < 0.05$, * $p < 0.1$

efficient financial management, and older company age positively impact sustainability scores. While the negative relationship between liquidity and sustainability persists, long-term debt shows a weak positive influence. The shift in the relationship between total assets and sustainability underscores the importance of considering non-linear relationships and outliers in financial analysis.

8.6 Propensity Match Score

In this section, we apply propensity score matching methodologies to evaluate the impact of patent innovations on the sustainability scores calculated in the previous analysis. By categorizing companies with patents and green patents as the treated group, we aim to assess the net effect of these innovations on sustainability. We acknowledge the limitations of this approach, particularly the potential endogeneity problem due to the use of patents in CA, which could affect the robustness of our findings. Despite these concerns, the method allows us to isolate and evaluate the impact of patents on sustainability scores more clearly.

The findings indicate that companies holding generic patents experience a net increase of 6.86% in their sustainability scores (Table 8.5). This suggests that the presence of patents, in general, correlates with improved sustainability performance. More strikingly, companies with green patents show an even more significant increase, with their sustainability scores rising by 15.3%. This notable boost reflects the additional value that green patents bring, highlighting their crucial role in enhancing sustainable practices within companies.

These results have important policy implications. The positive correlation between green patents and sustainability scores suggests that policies encouraging innovation in environmentally friendly technologies can lead to substantial improvements in corporate sustainability. By fostering an environment that supports the development and adoption of green technologies, policymakers can drive more companies toward greater sustainability. Furthermore, the significant impact of green patents underscores the need for targeted incentives and support for research and development in this area. Such measures can accelerate the economic transition toward more sustainable practices and enhance overall environmental performance across industries.

Table 8.5 Propensity match score

VARIABLES	score	score
Patents	0.0685***	
	(0.00566)	
Green patents		0.153***
		(0.00646)
Observations	6803	6803

This table presents the results of the propensity score matching estimation assessing the impact of patents and green patents on sustainability scores. The treatment model employed is a logit regression. Other variables included in the analysis are AGE, EXP (Experience), and TA (Total Assets). Standard errors are reported in parentheses. Statistical significance is denoted by *** $p < 0.01$, ** $p < 0.05$, * $p < 0.1$

Appendix

In this appendix, we adjust the dependent variable by normalizing the sustainability score, enabling us to categorize companies into quintiles (see Table 8.6). This transformation provides a clearer comparative framework for analyzing the distribution and relative performance of companies based on their sustainability scores.

The analysis reveals that ROE is negatively related to the sustainability score (Table 8.7). This negative relationship suggests that companies with higher profitability, as measured by ROE, may not necessarily prioritize or perform well in terms of sustainability. This could imply a trade-off where firms focusing heavily on maximizing shareholder returns might allocate fewer resources toward sustainable practices, which often require significant investments and may not yield immediate financial returns. Liquidity is found to have no significant effect on the sustainability score. This indicates that a company's ability to cover short-term liabilities with its short-term assets does not directly influence its sustainability performance. The lack of correlation suggests that liquidity, while crucial for operational stability, is not a key driver of sustainability initiatives or outcomes.

The age of companies and their propensity to export positively affect the sustainability score, but only in a few cases. This limited impact may be due to various factors. Older companies might have more established sustainability practices and experience, but this is not uniformly the case across all firms. Similarly, companies involved in export activities might adopt higher sustainability standards to meet international regulations and market demands, but this positive influence is not widespread. These findings suggest that while age and export activities can contribute to better sustainability performance, their effects are not consistently significant across all companies.

The number of employees shows a similar pattern, positively affecting the sustainability score in only a few cases. This could indicate that larger companies, which typically have more employees, may have more resources to invest in sustainability. However, the sporadic significance of this relationship suggests that simply having a larger workforce does not automatically lead to better sustainability outcomes. The effectiveness of sustainability initiatives likely depends on how well these companies leverage their human resources toward sustainable practices.

These findings suggest several policy implications. The negative relationship between ROE and sustainability scores highlights the need for policies that encourage companies to balance profitability with sustainability. Policymakers could consider introducing incentives for firms that successfully integrate sustainable practices without compromising financial performance.

The lack of a significant relationship between liquidity and sustainability suggests that policies aimed at improving corporate liquidity might not directly influence sustainability outcomes. Instead, targeted policies that directly support sustainable investments may be more effective.

Given the limited but positive impact of age, export activities, and the number of employees on sustainability scores, policymakers should consider providing

Table 8.6 Quintile analysis by sub-sector

	Quintile				
Sector	1	2	3	4	5
Other manufacturing industries	0.00%	1.58%	8.80%	45.77%	43.85%
Retail trade (excluding automotive retail)	0.00%	0.00%	0.00%	14.41%	85.59%
Wholesale trade (excluding automotive wholesale)	0.00%	0.00%	0.00%	79.67%	20.33%
Apparel manufacturing; leather and fur goods manufacturing	1.68%	1.24%	5.40%	54.80%	36.88%
Manufacture of other transport equipment	0.00%	1.48%	16.87%	47.33%	34.32%
Manufacture of other non-metallic mineral products	0.00%	1.47%	9.10%	54.14%	35.29%
Manufacture of electrical equipment and non-electrical household appliances	0.00%	5.63%	16.06%	39.22%	39.09%
Manufacture of rubber and plastic products	1.70%	7.98%	16.60%	43.53%	30.19%
Manufacture of leather and similar products	0.00%	1.10%	11.07%	53.35%	34.48%
Manufacture of motor vehicles, trailers, and semi-trailers	0.00%	0.00%	14.71%	57.72%	27.57%
Manufacture of paper and paper products	2.14%	5.76%	14.85%	35.37%	41.88%
Manufacture of coke and refined petroleum products	0.00%	0.00%	0.00%	52.38%	47.62%
Manufacture of computers and electronic and optical products; Electromedical and precision equipment; watches and clocks	0.68%	7.12%	22.19%	57.14%	12.87%
Manufacture of machinery and equipment N.E.C. (not elsewhere classified)	0.23%	2.46%	20.74%	43.12%	33.45%
Manufacture of furniture	0.00%	4.04%	11.59%	48.65%	35.72%
Manufacture of chemicals	1.76%	7.00%	13.97%	41.47%	35.80%
Manufacture of basic pharmaceutical products and pharmaceutical preparations	0.00%	0.00%	0.00%	100.00%	0.00%
Manufacture of fabricated metal products (excluding machinery and equipment)	0.00%	1.89%	6.45%	43.90%	47.76%
Wood and Cork industry (excluding furniture); manufacture of straw and plaiting materials	1.40%	7.54%	12.45%	46.75%	31.87%
Beverage industry	0.00%	4.98%	36.22%	43.74%	15.06%
Food industry	0.99%	3.88%	9.62%	52.70%	32.83%
Textile industry	1.00%	2.36%	10.47%	59.83%	26.34%
Specialized construction activities	0.00%	0.00%	0.00%	0.00%	100.00%
Metallurgy	0.00%	2.11%	3.94%	44.16%	49.79%
Repair, maintenance and installation of machinery and equipment	0.00%	0.55%	6.71%	45.58%	47.16%
Printing and reproduction of recorded media	0.00%	0.68%	14.05%	46.74%	38.53%
Total	0.48%	3.10%	11.59%	46.97%	37.86%

Table 8.7 Robustness with changing in dependent variable

	Fixed Effects			Cluterized Errors			Fixed effects sector		
VARIABLES	score2	score2	score2	score2	score2	score2	score2	score2	score2
NCE	0.00751			0.00504			0.00366		
	(0.00742)			(0.00422)			(0.00427)		
ROE	−0.000182*			−0.000182**			−0.000180**		
	(9.52e-05)			(8.42e-05)			(8.43e-05)		
CR	0.000992			0.00117			0.00157		
	(0.00371)			(0.00181)			(0.00182)		
LT	−0.0188			−0.0160			−0.0186		
	(0.0187)			(0.0123)			(0.0125)		
FINEXP		−5.84e-06			−0.00194			−0.00169	
		(0.00228)			(0.00135)			(0.00139)	
ST			0.0202			0.0156			0.0172
			(0.0186)			(0.0125)			(0.0127)
EQUITY			0.000419			6.10e-05			8.89e-05
			(0.000319)			(0.000155)			(0.000156)
EBITFIN			3.26e-05			5.61e-05			5.41e-05
			(5.01e-05)			(4.05e-05)			(4.05e-05)
EBITDA%	5.52e-05	−0.000180	−0.000420	−0.000103	−0.000268	−0.000558	−7.14e-05	−0.000233	−0.000477
	(0.000258)	(0.000268)	(0.000514)	(0.000166)	(0.000170)	(0.000363)	(0.000158)	(0.000169)	(0.000365)
AGE	−7.74e-05	−0.000101	−8.79e-05	0.000226**	0.000227**	0.000217**	0.000198*	0.000203**	0.000191*
	(0.000247)	(0.000242)	(0.000270)	(0.000104)	(0.000102)	(0.000109)	(0.000105)	(0.000103)	(0.000110)
EXP	0.00625	0.00698	0.00469	0.0114***	0.0119***	0.0101***	0.0100***	0.0104***	0.00899**
	(0.00446)	(0.00438)	(0.00475)	(0.00348)	(0.00347)	(0.00377)	(0.00352)	(0.00349)	(0.00382)
TA	3.95e-08	1.52e-08	−8.02e-08	1.81e-07	1.80e-07	1.77e-07	1.77e-07	1.75e-07	1.77e-07

(continued)

Table 8.7 (continued)

	Fixed Effects			Cluterized Errors			Fixed effects sector		
VARIABLES	score2	score2	score2	score2	score2	score2	score2	score2	score2
	(3.14e-07)	(3.09e-07)	(3.18e-07)	(1.47e-07)	(1.46e-07)	(1.55e-07)	(1.46e-07)	(1.45e-07)	(1.54e-07)
EMP	9.94e-06	9.73e-06	1.02e-05*	1.44e-05***	1.43e-05***	1.50e-05***	1.48e-05***	1.46e-05***	1.52e-05***
Constant	0.264***	0.262***	0.246***	0.253***	0.261***	0.244***	0.274***	0.283***	0.264***
	(0.0147)	(0.0138)	(0.0197)	(0.00868)	(0.00835)	(0.0116)	(0.0181)	(0.0181)	(0.0214)
Observations	6584	6754	5871	6584	6754	5871	6584	6754	5871
R-squared	0.002	0.001	0.002	0.054	0.0554	0.053	0.102	0.110	0.103
Number of id	1725	1734	1642	1725	1734	1642	1725	1734	1642

The table presents the results of panel estimations for modified score variable. Columns 1 to 3 display the fixed effects model estimations. Columns 4 to 6 include standard errors clustered by variance and covariance (VCE). The last three columns provide additional model specifications. Standard errors are reported in parentheses. All independent variables are one year lagged. Statistical significance is denoted by *** $p < 0.01$, ** $p < 0.05$, * $p < 0.1$

support and resources tailored to different types of companies. For older firms and exporters, enhancing existing sustainability practices and ensuring compliance with international standards can be beneficial. For companies with larger workforces, initiatives that encourage the active participation of employees in sustainability programs could be more effective.

Overall, these insights underscore the complexity of factors influencing corporate sustainability and the need for nuanced, targeted policy interventions to drive meaningful improvements in sustainability performance.

The analysis (see next Table) reveals that net capital employed has a weak effect on the sustainability score. This indicates that the amount of capital a company uses for its operations is not a strong determinant of its sustainability performance. The weak relationship suggests that while net capital employed is important for operational efficiency and growth, it does not significantly drive sustainable practices.

Interestingly, the relationship between long-term debt and the sustainability score has inverted. In previous analyses, long-term debt showed a positive but weak relationship with sustainability, whereas now it appears to be negative. This inversion could imply that high levels of long-term debt might limit a company's ability to invest in sustainability initiatives due to the financial burden of servicing debt. Alternatively, it might reflect a strategic focus on debt reduction over sustainable investment.

The positive relationships of age, export activities, and total assets with sustainability scores are confirmed (Table 8.8). Older companies, those involved in export markets, and those with larger asset bases tend to have higher sustainability scores. These findings reinforce the notion that established firms with significant resources and international exposure are better positioned to implement and benefit from sustainable practices. Older companies are likely to have more experience and established processes for sustainability, exporters must meet international standards, and companies with larger assets have more resources to invest in sustainability.

Short-term debt is positively related to sustainability scores, which is a notable finding. This positive relationship suggests that companies taking on short-term debt might be doing so to finance immediate sustainability projects or operational improvements that contribute to better sustainability performance. Unlike long-term debt, which may constrain resources due to long-term financial commitments, short-term debt can be used more flexibly and promptly for sustainable initiatives.

Overall, these findings highlight the complex interplay between financial metrics and sustainability performance, emphasizing the need for nuanced analysis when evaluating the factors that contribute to corporate sustainability.

The analysis shows that only green patents significantly affect sustainability scores and improve performance (Table 8.9). This finding suggests that the development and implementation of environmentally friendly technologies are critical drivers of corporate sustainability. Green patents are likely to represent substantial innovations that directly contribute to reducing environmental impact, enhancing energy efficiency, or improving resource management, all of which are core components of sustainable performance.

Table 8.8 Robustness quantile regression

VARIABLES	score2	score2	score2
NCE	0.00775*		
	(0.00418)		
EBITDA%	−3.40e-05	−0.000158	−0.000109
	(0.000223)	(0.000232)	(0.000354)
ROE	−6.73e-05		
	(9.29e-05)		
CR	0.000398		
	(0.00179)		
LT	−0.0202*		
	(0.0116)		
AGE	0.000188*	0.000131	0.000170*
	(9.65e-05)	(9.50e-05)	(9.94e-05)
EXP	0.0111***	0.0112***	0.0104**
	(0.00395)	(0.00399)	(0.00408)
TA	2.97e-07***	2.97e-07***	2.80e-07***
	(5.99e-08)	(6.00e-08)	(6.16e-08)
EMP	2.16e-05***	2.15e-05***	2.15e-05***
	(7.44e-06)	(7.56e-06)	(7.28e-06)
GCE		0.00175	
		(0.00264)	
ROA		−0.000146	
		(0.000293)	
LI		−0.000635	
		(0.00205)	
FINEXP		−0.00244	
		(0.00153)	
ST			0.0201*
			(0.0122)
EQUITY			−0.000200
			(0.000123)
EBITFIN			8.44e-05**
			(3.96e-05)
Constant	0.219***	0.229***	0.213***
	(0.00850)	(0.00821)	(0.0115)
Observations	6584	6754	5871

The table presents the results of quantile regression analyses. All independent variables are one year lagged. Statistical significance is denoted by *** $p < 0.01$, ** $p < 0.05$, * $p < 0.1$

The exclusive impact of green patents on sustainability scores highlights the importance of focusing on innovations that are specifically designed to address environmental challenges. While generic patents might contribute to overall technological advancement, they do not necessarily align with the goals of sustainability. Green patents, on the other hand, are explicitly aimed at creating sustainable solutions, making their impact on sustainability scores more pronounced.

Table 8.9 Tab propensity match score (robustness)

VARIABLES	score	score
Patents	−0.0104	
	(0.00869)	
Green patents		0.0382*
		(0.0220)
Observations	6803	6803

This table presents the results of the propensity score matching estimation assessing the impact of patents and green patents on sustainability scores. The treatment model employed is a logit regression. Other variables included in the analysis are AGE, EXP (Experience), and TA (Total Assets). Standard errors are reported in parentheses. Statistical significance is denoted by *** $p < 0.01$, ** $p < 0.05$, * $p < 0.1$

This finding underscores the role of targeted innovation in achieving sustainability objectives. Companies that invest in green technologies not only enhance their sustainability performance but also position themselves as leaders in the transition towards a more sustainable economy. This can lead to competitive advantages, as consumers, investors, and regulators increasingly prioritize environmental responsibility.

In summary, the significant positive impact of green patents on sustainability scores and performance emphasizes the necessity for companies to invest in environmentally focused innovations. It also illustrates that sustainable performance is closely linked to the adoption of green technologies, which directly address and mitigate environmental issues.

References

Buchinsky, M. (1998). Recent advances in quantile regression models: A practical guideline for empirical research. *Journal of Human Resources, 33*(1), 88–126.

Cade, B. S., & Noon, B. R. (2003). A gentle introduction to quantile regression for ecologists. *Frontiers in Ecology and the Environment, 1*(8), 412–420.

Koenker, R. (2005). *Quantile Regression*. Cambridge University Press.

Greenacre, M. (2017). *Correspondence analysis in practice*. CRC Press.

Jolliffe, I. T. (2002). *Principal component analysis*. Springer Series in Statistics.

Refinitiv, E. (n.d.). *Environmental, Social and Governance (ESG) Data and Scores*. Retrieved from https://www.refinitiv.com/en/sustainable-finance/esg-scores

Riva, P., Comoli, M., & Garelli, A. (2021). *Corporate governance and erm for smes viability in italy*. https://doi.org/10.5772/intechopen.96688.

Part III
Companies Crisis

Chapter 9
Business Crisis and Bankruptcy Prediction Models: The Other Side of Sustainability

9.1 Business Crisis

9.1.1 The Phenomenon

Neither the national nor international literature recognizes a single definition of business crisis (Staw et al., 1981; Milburn et al., 1993; Shepherd, 2005; Pretorius, 2009). Nevertheless, scholars agree that the phenomenon is both dynamic and degenerative (Giannessi, 1960; Müller, 1985; De Sarno, 1982; D'Aveni, 1989; Chowdhury & Lang, 1993; Sheppard & Chowdhury, 2005; Poddighe & Madonna, 2006). Indeed, a business crisis is a process of progressive deterioration, whether fast or slow, of a company's vitality. Regardless of how this degenerative process unfolds (Turner, 1976; Fink, 1986; Mitroff et al., 1987; Guatri, 1986, 1995; Andrei, 1996; Prosperi, 2003; Cestari, 2009; Poli, 2020), it is generally agreed that it involves a sequence of stages of growing seriousness: the succession of the different phases over time leads to an increase in the complexity of the phenomenon itself. The deterioration trend is not necessarily constant and regular, but can be more or less intense, sudden and discontinuous (Müller, 1985; Slatter & Lovett, 1999; Guatri, 1995; Cestari, 2009). This implies that if not promptly and adequately contained and effectively countered, a crisis can lead to the closure of a company (Janis & Mann, 1977; Staw et al., 1981; Appelbaum et al., 2012).

If the symptoms of the disease are not quickly ascertained through an effective diagnostic process, the complex of causes that gave rise to it are not identified and, ultimately, recovery actions aimed at addressing the dysfunction are not implemented, making it impossible to reverse the company's fall. Once this stage is reached, the crisis becomes irreversible, the operating conditions are irreparably compromised, and any remedial action would be in vain.

It should be pointed out that the forced exit of the company from the market does not lead to consequences only for the ailing company itself but, inevitably, for the

M. Aliano et al., *Sustainable Finance for SMEs*, Sustainable Finance,
https://doi.org/10.1007/978-3-031-74193-7_9

entire economic system in which it operates. In fact, as is unfortunately well known, the economic and social repercussions of corporate crises (Milburn et al., 1993; Mitroff et al., 1987; Clark, 1995–1996) are very often dramatic. This applies to the direct consequences but also and above all to the potential knock-on repercussions (the "domino effect") which not infrequently end up seriously unbalancing entire production sectors or local economic areas due to the financial chain or interdependence of the allied industries. It has been established that the dissolution of a company is an event that has a more or less intense impact on the market to which it belongs, generating losses for banks, shareholders, suppliers, the public administration and for all the businesses connected to it in general (Charalambous et al., 2000; Charitou et al., 2004).

Precisely because of these negative consequences, caused by a crisis that takes on increasingly serious connotations over time, the correct and, above all, timely recognition of the pathological phenomenon becomes ever more relevant and pressing (Kiesler & Sproull, 1982; Dutton & Jackson, 1987; Gephart, 1984).

9.1.2 Anatomy

Before going into the merits of detecting a crisis, it is essential to understand its anatomy. As mentioned, the crisis process may unfold in different ways. Nonetheless, in the international literature (Mitroff & Linstone, 1996; MacKenze, 1994; Fink, 2002; Paraskev, 2006), it generally involves the following stages:

1. incubation phase (Turner, 1976) or pre-crisis phase (Shrivastava, 1987);
2. acute phase (Stein, 2004);
3. chronic phase (Boin et al., 2008).

The *incubation phase* is the period in which the company is apparently operating normally, and no particular hazards or threats to its survival are identified. This is the step in which the diagnostic capacity of company management becomes particularly relevant. It is essential to be able to correctly identify any symptoms of an embryonic crisis which, therefore, has not yet unleashed its full destructive potential. Indeed, it is clear that a crisis identified promptly and correctly in the prodromal stage (Fink, 1986), when it has not yet reached full virulence, is more easily remedied than a crisis identified in the acute phase. Obviously, remediation is only possible if the root causes of the phenomenon are identified, and if effective actions are taken to eliminate them.

The *acute phase* of the crisis, on the other hand, comprises the period in which the "precipitating" (Turner, 1976) or "triggering" (Shrivastava, 1987) event occurs. This event generates a more or less sudden course reversal in business management, which transitions from a healthy to a pathological state. Compared to the pre-crisis phase, there is a significant increase in the seriousness of the phenomenon and, with it, also the difficulty in salvaging the company. Indeed, it is in this phase that the main negative consequences of the crisis emerge, namely the involvement of stakeholders; a rapid and intermittent flow of information; limited time; and the emergency underlying effective remedial interventions; etc. (Santos et al., 2016).

It is easy to understand, therefore, that at this stage there is an urgent need for an adequate reaction and rigorously planned recovery measures: targeted and effective actions would make it possible to control the flow of the crisis, its speed, its direction and its duration. This control, if well exercised, could in turn prevent, or at least mitigate, the loss.

Finally, the *chronic phase* identifies the period in which the critical phenomenon, not adequately identified and counteracted, takes root in the company and brings about its end. At this stage, a moment of reflection is inevitable to assess whether attempting to reverse the crisis is still an opportune strategy, in the knowledge that any recovery action will require the expenditure of considerable resources. This is, therefore, the point at which it must be established whether the company will be able to survive and recover, in its original or a new form (the result, for example, of merger or demerger operations), or whether it will cease to exist, following its final collapse. If recovery is attempted, it is agreed that the crisis cycle just outlined will begin again, and that the company will once again reach the incubation or pre-crisis stage (Chekkar-Mansouri & Onnee, 2013; Elliott, 2009; Fink, 1986) (Fig. 9.1).

Italian researchers have proposed that the process be staged differently (Guatri, 1995; Andrei, 1996; Cestari, 2009), partially diverging from the approach most widely adopted in the international arena. Despite the differences, more or less marked, the well-established principle according to which the passage from one phase to the next involves a significant increase in the degree of severity and complexity of the crisis, also applies in the Italian staging systems.

Guatri (1995) identifies two phases: decline, i.e., the period in which the company's economic value progressively deteriorates, and the actual crisis, the full-blown phase of the degenerative process in which the negative consequences for stakeholders are more serious and evident. A company's decline is, in turn, divided

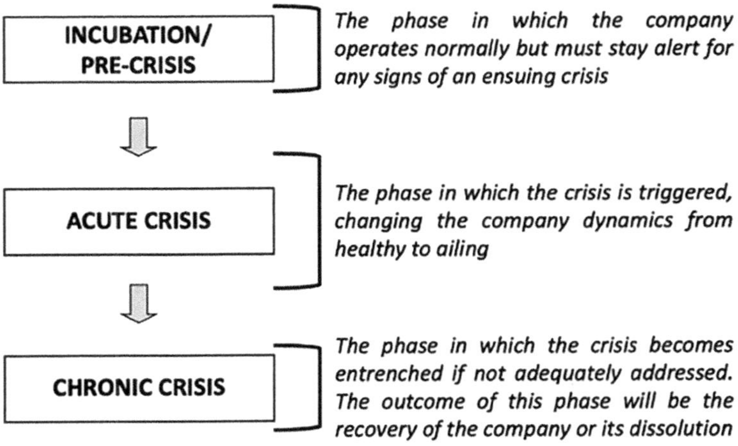

Fig. 9.1 The crisis staging prevailing in the international arena

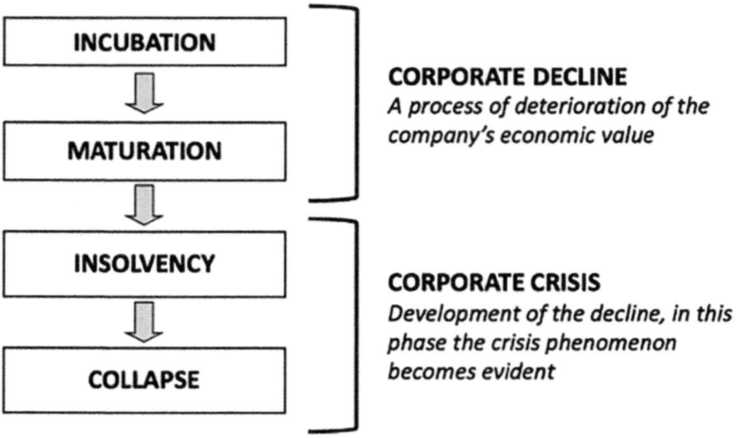

Fig. 9.2 Crisis staging according to Guatri (1995)

into two stages: *incubation*, in which the inefficiencies and imbalances that trigger the decadent trend become manifest, and *maturation*, in which substantial economic losses occur. The crisis proper, on the other hand, involves *insolvency*, i.e., the phase in which the phenomenon impacts financial flows, unbalancing them and taking the company to a state of permanent inability to pay off its debts, and *collapse*, where it is the company's assets that are compromised and there are negative consequences for stakeholders (Fig. 9.2).

Guatri's classification aligns, at least in part, with that proposed by Farooq et al. (2018). This involves a *first phase* characterized by a contraction in income; a *second* in which the company becomes unable to pay, through its profits, the financial debts incurred, and a *third*, characterized by a capital imbalance in which its liabilities outstrip its assets.

Andrei (1996), on the other hand, proposes the staging system closest to that accepted internationally, stating that the crisis develops along a path divided into three stages (Fig. 9.3):

1. *a latent crisis,* in which the alterations behind the crisis manifest themselves but act undisturbed because they are hidden by the company's apparent health. This phase, evidently, is configured as a trend of slow but constant decay;
2. *a manifest crisis*, in which the company's instability becomes clear. This phase, in which both the company and stakeholders become aware of the critical state, is characterized by a significant increase in the speed of propagation of the instability;
3. *an acute crisis*, which, in essence, comprises the Guatri classification's phases of insolvency and collapse, and is externalized by both financial and asset imbalances. This is the final phase of the process, in which the recovery of the critical company is arduous and expensive.

More recently, Cestari (2009) has revisited and revised the crisis classification proposed by Guatri, including stages that, according to the scholar, characterize

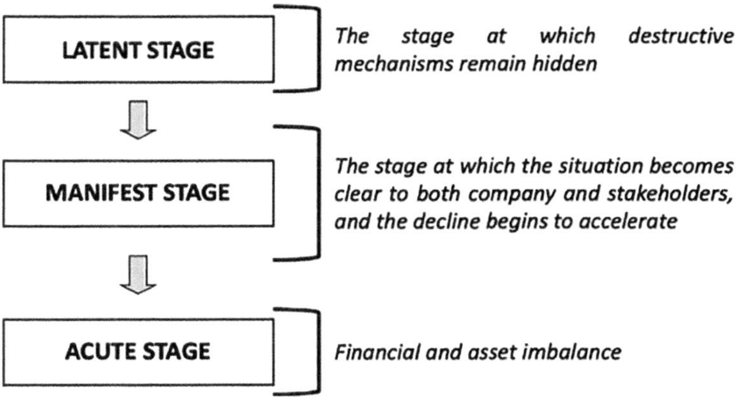

Fig. 9.3 Crisis staging according to Andrei (1996)

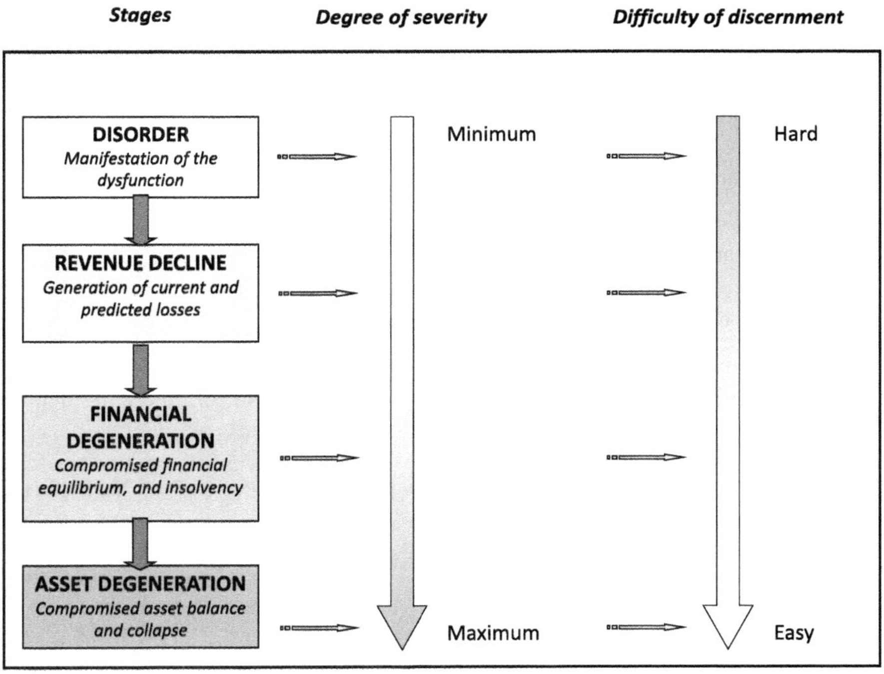

Fig. 9.4 Crisis staging according to Cestari (2009)

the decline (Fig. 9.4). Thus, the crisis is not only traced to the terminal stages of the pathological process in which the disruptive effects could permanently impede the company's operations, and the effectiveness of recovery actions is burdened by uncertainty. According to Cestari in fact, Guatri's approach would induce management to focus too much on the tail end of the process, i.e., when the crisis is acute and easier to discern, and to ignore the initial phases in which the phenomenon could be detected, albeit with more difficulty, and countered with greater success and less expenditure of resources.

9.1.3 The Time Factor

A business crisis is a dynamic phenomenon that can unfold at different speeds and, therefore, the tipping point and consequent closure of the company can materialize more or less rapidly. It is evident, therefore, that the factor time plays an important role in crisis analysis and management (Giannessi, 1960; Boin et al., 2008; Hannah et al., 2009), especially if we reflect on the possibility and effectiveness of actions aimed at interrupting the degenerative process and bringing the company back from the brink.

If we consider the time factor, in fact, we can reasonably maintain that less serious crises that last longer give management sufficient time to detect them, identify the problem (therefore, the "disease"), and potentially remove the cause(s) (Lippitt & Schmidt, 1967; Whetten, 1980). By contrast, more virulent and rapidly spreading crises would not leave sufficient time for intervention, making resolution difficult and potentially ineffective (Hermann, 1963; Billings et al., 1980).

Several factors influence the speed of a company's deterioration, including:

1. the starting point, direction and intensity of the company's trajectory;
2. the causes at the origin of the crisis;
3. the degree of awareness of the crisis;
4. the effectiveness of any corrective actions undertaken.

The degenerative process is ineluctably conditioned by the *position* of equilibrium (healthy) or imbalance (ailing), in which the company finds itself at the moment in which the crisis originates; by the orientation, evolutionary or involutionary, to which the company dynamics tend, as well as by the *strength* (or weakness) of the company's drive (Giannessi, 1960; Caramiello, 1968; Billings et al., 1980). This implies that:

1. the closer the company is to a crisis point, the more sudden the reversal of trajectory and imbalance;
2. the more vigorous the involutionary dynamic, the shorter the dysfunctional path that leads to corporate dissolution will be.

The features of the *causal complex* also contribute to determining the speed of propagation of the crisis. Hwang and Lichtenthal (2000) introduce the distinction between "abrupt crisis" and "cumulative crisis", and state that the former is generated by sudden forces that rapidly shift the company's equilibrium, totally destabilizing it (acute crisis), while the latter gains momentum more slowly but, if left unchecked, leads to the same grave outcome.

Vergara (1988), on the other hand, argues that it is pathological dysfunctions, i.e. alterations that cannot be absorbed by the ordinary reaction forces of the company, that trigger the crisis process, and it is the inherent (*original*) and progressively acquired (*derived*) risk over time that favors its spread. It should be pointed out that this risk, or danger, can be traced back to a single dysfunction or to a complex of existing dysfunctions, observed systematically. The former refers to the intrinsic pathological force of each problem, both underlying and resulting, while the latter incorporates, to the aforementioned specific dysfunctionality, the synergistic scope of the adverse forces that arises from the combination, interrelation and simultaneity of the multiple causes.

Awareness of the crisis, i.e., the concrete and rational cognizance of the phenomenon, inevitably affects its evolution (Weick & Sutcliffe, 2001). Klein (2008) argues that in a tumultuous economy like the present, the only real advantage for an organization is the know-how/experience gained, the profitable use of that know-how/experience, and the speed with which it is able to learn something new. Weick and Sutcliffe (2001) expands upon this consideration, stating that the way in which knowledge is managed within a company positively affects both its resilience, i.e., its ability to withstand adverse forces and/or resolve crises, and the possibility of generating new skills and creating fresh opportunities in the face of adversity.

Crisis awareness undoubtedly forms part of the sphere of business acumen, and is therefore fueled by the know-how of top management and/or executives and by the information and tools available (Jennex & Raman, 2009). In particular, the knowledge gained abstractly or concretely in the field, thanks to previous experience, should favor the understanding of the peculiarities that characterize the conditions of unprofitability, the correct assessment of the predicament, and the implementation of a potentially decisive recovery plan. This, obviously, would defuse the disharmonious force fuelling the corporate decline. The absence of a specific crisis culture (Lizza, 2011), on the other hand, would not only prevent a company from dealing with a crisis promptly and adequately but also, being blind to its distinctive features and therefore unable to implement appropriate recovery actions, would facilitate and speed its degeneration, allowing the pathology to spread unchecked.

Finally, decisions on the fate of the ailing company and the extent of the corrective measures to be taken can affect the trajectory of a crisis, either interrupting the degenerative process or, on the contrary, accelerating it. After identifying, analyzing, interpreting and evaluating the causal complex of the crisis, in fact, it is possible to follow two alternative paths: (1) salvage intervention (i.e., action), which presupposes the definition of the most appropriate treatment to eliminate the causes of the crisis, or (2) the lack of a salvage intervention (i.e., inaction), which will lead the company towards its inevitable collapse. Again, therefore, the crisis can evolve more or less rapidly depending on the choice made. In the event that recovery is opted for, its speed will depend on the effectiveness of the decisive action, i.e., on the timeliness of the intervention (Giannessi, 1960) and on the company's ability to definitively remove the dysfunction(s) at the origin of the crisis. If, on the other hand, the decision is for inaction, the timing will be conditioned by the virulence and speed of the contagious spread of the crisis factors among the company components (static, dynamic and composition of external relations).

9.2 Crisis Recognition

9.2.1 Diagnosis and Forecasting

It has already been mentioned that a business crisis is a dynamic process with growing severity. The escalation of the crisis rarely follows a regular course: it can take place more or less quickly, as can the transition from the reversible to the irreversible stage.

It is clear that this incremental trend highlights the need for timely recognition of the symptoms of the crisis (Mitroff, 2004) before it reaches the most acute phase. This need is felt by both management and external stakeholders who intend to assess the state of company health, with respect to which they have certain expectations and interests. For all these subjects, then, it becomes important to know not only if the company will fail, but also—and above all—*when* it will fail (Sandin & Porporato, 2007).

In order to assess the state of health of the company, it is necessary to conduct a thorough diagnosis. In a generic sense, Darling and Kash (1998) define diagnosis as a process aimed at revealing the nature and causes of a specific phenomenon, while Smith (1995) attributes to this term the meaning of an activity aimed at identifying the symptoms, i.e., the clues, revealing the existence of a problem. In the field of economics, however, the term is further refined and focused: diagnosis is in fact a process that, thanks to the systematic use of different tools and/or models, not necessarily of an economic/financial matrix, allows the appreciation of the health status of a company and, consequently, signals the possible onset of a crisis (Sakalas & Virbickaite, 2011; Garskaite-Milvydiene, 2012; Meiste & Jakstiene, 2015).

The assessment process requires the adoption of an adequate information system (Marchi, 2003; Bastia, 2019) and reliable monitoring tools (Amigoni, 1977; Brunetti, 1989; Bastia, 2019). The former, as is well known, has the aim of providing a general picture, and is directed towards the collection, selection, recording and distribution of information relating to the company system. The latter, on the other hand, have a more targeted function since they focus specifically on assessing the symptoms of critical conditions. Indeed, within the mass of inputs that can be used through information systems, monitoring tools must be able to identify the telltale signs of economic downturns, and to signal the existence of a pathological state. Obviously, in order for these tools to be functional, they must be reliable, and therefore able to formulate an exact appraisal of the state of the company, but also, and above all, timely, i.e., capable of alerting the user correctly and early on.

It follows that the time factor also plays a fundamental role in diagnosis. In fact, the advantage derived from early assessment of the critical state, therefore already in the early stages of the process, is evident: at that point the business malady is still slight and is, therefore, more easily and effectively contained than in a crisis that has reached the later stages, in which the company organism is already seriously compromised.

This opportunity is as true from a theoretical point of view as it is difficult to attain in practice. As has been pointed out, in the early stages of its process, while the crisis is still latent, its assessment presents greater difficulties: the company is relatively far from the terminal stage, in which the "disease" is most manifest, which is why the signs of the malaise are difficult, if not impossible, to detect. This is because, during the incubation phase, the company's weaknesses, barely apparent, are totally or partially offset by its strengths, which contribute to concealing the symptoms of the incipient degenerative process, making them less evident (Zito, 1999). In this state, the company manifests a momentary virtuous position, which is, however, only apparent, and does not ensure the perpetuation of the economic reality, but rather hides the seeds of its disintegration.

Slightly stretching the consensus on the subject, which recognizes the critical phenomenon as a phase of "physiological" latency, it is also possible to hypothesize the existence of an "enforced" latency. While the former is attributable to the congenital specificities of dysfunctions that are not clearly visible and detectable in their minor, embryonic phase, the latter is attributable to the management's desire to keep the critical state from stakeholders inside and/or outside the company. To this end, opportunistic action might be taken to cover and/or conceal key information so as to give a rosy picture of the company's operating conditions. Both cases represent a major obstacle to detecting the crisis, however:

1. physiological latency, having a natural course, is less worrying. Its temporal extension is, however, limited because the dysfunction tends to progressively mature and spread, affecting increasingly large areas of the company system. This propagation helps to trigger the signalling power of the symptoms of the negative dynamic and, consequently, to bring it into the light. Since the crisis, now manifest, is still in its germinal form, it is reasonable to hypothesize that a possible recovery intervention, preceded by a timely recognition of the pathological state, has a good chance of success;
2. enforced latency, on the other hand, takes on decidedly more sinister connotations. Its duration can be particularly extended because it is added to the physiological latency period, and because the management could be determined to prolong the concealment of the ongoing crisis for as long as possible. If, then, the concealment activity proves to be particularly thorough, it could go so far as to hide even the final stages of the degenerative process. If this were the case, the crisis would become manifest too late, when the company's operating conditions were completely compromised, and the foreseeable rebalancing pathways could easily be fruitless.

Returning to the topic of crisis assessment, it should be noted that in some studies the terms "diagnosis" and "forecasting" are used together and/or synonymously. For example, Bagrii et al. (2020) state that '[...] *the diagnosis and forecasting of crisis at the enterprise is a set of economically sound methods and techniques of financial and economic analysis. When they are systematically applied at certain intervals (depending on the size, characteristics, type of activity, etc.) they will allow identifying the crisis on time and evaluating potential functioning and development opportunities.*'

In truth, however, diagnosis and forecasting have profoundly different meanings, operational implications and results. Specifically, *diagnosis* aims to provide a precise identification of the *current* pathology: the diagnostician, therefore, judges a company's state of health at the time of assessment (today for today). *Forecasting*, on the other hand, aims to pinpoint a *future* crisis, to *predict* the health of the organization under investigation (today for tomorrow).

The benefits of accurate forecasting are obvious: information obtained in advance provides internal and external stakeholders sufficient time to be able to formulate well-founded judgments and make informed decisions about the company. Hence, reliable and, above all, timely warnings of a company's economic and financial difficulties would be particularly useful to both:

1. executives and managers, poised to take precautionary measures aimed at mitigating losses (Kou et al., 2021). Indeed, a crisis diagnosed in the early stages of development would allow the company to react quickly and to contain, with a greater degree of effectiveness, the threats of future escalation, and consequently to reduce the risk of insolvency developing;
2. external parties, positioned to fully assess the pros and cons of any relationships with the company subject to diagnosis to be established or already in place.

9.2.2 The Different Forms of Diagnosis and Forecasting

The belief that diagnosis and/or forecasting should follow a single protocol seems to us reductive and excessively simplistic. This is because it would be unable to take into account the different objectives pursued by the various parties interested in knowing the health status of a company. In fact, it is our opinion that timely or predictive crisis action has specific and different characteristics depending on:

1. the particular position of the analyst;
2. the information sources available;
3. the particular aims pursued.

With respect to these parameters, therefore, we believe it is useful to distinguish between diagnosis/forecasting of *state* and diagnosis/forecasting of *function* (Cestari, 2009). The first is conducted by subjects normally outside the company, such as lenders, banks and other financial institutions, as well as suppliers, clients, competitors, ratings firms, public administrations, and others. Although these players have naturally different interests in the company, it is believed that, in the diagnostic and/or forecasting field, there is a sort of convergence of objectives: they, in fact, would aspire to formulate a clear and, above all, synthetic appraisal of the company's state of health.

To conduct this assessment, however, external subjects must make use of techniques and tools fed mainly by official information, with its inherent limitations. The status diagnosis/forecasting process involves the execution of five phases of "data processing" (Fig. 9.5):

1. collection;
2. selection;
3. verification;
4. interpretation;
5. conclusion.

The first four involve processing the available information in order to extrapolate the clues (symptoms) useful for studying the operational conditions of the company; the last phase, on the other hand, aims to reach succinct assessment of its state of health. In a nutshell, the process will end by "simply" establishing whether the company under investigation is healthy or in a critical state.

The outcome of the analysis conducted may stimulate or, on the contrary, discourage external parties from establishing or maintaining new relationships with the company under assessment. Thus, for example, if the company is deemed to be in crisis, banks may decide not to approve a loan requested (inaction). In contrast, the public administrations could establish a new relationship with the ailing firm and provide aid or support (action), as per its nature.

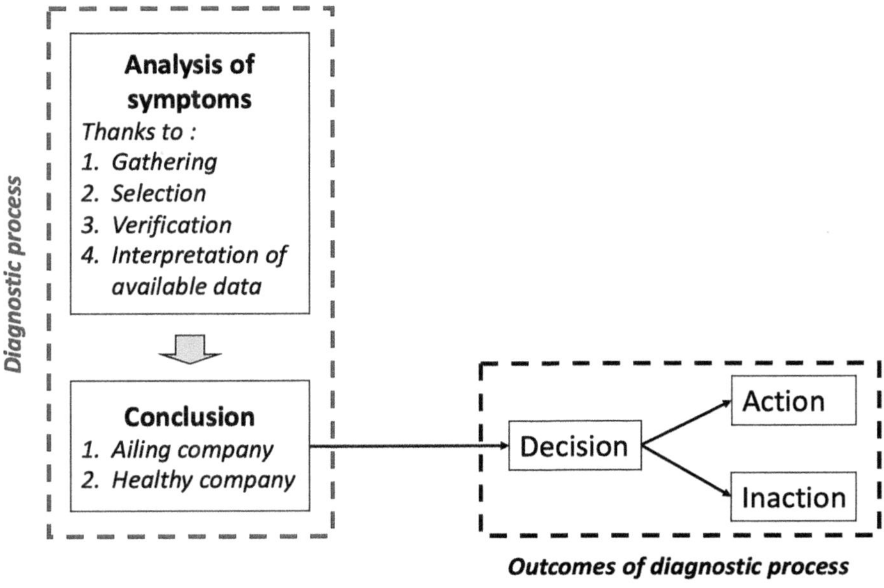

Fig. 9.5 Stages of state diagnosis

Unlike state diagnoses, functional diagnoses are normally made by internal players or—less frequently—by external parties who have, in any event, a deep-rooted involvement in the organization whose health status is under exam. Both figures certainly have a shared interest in ensuring the survival of the company to which they are linked, albeit in different ways, since among other things they derive economic benefits from it, and therefore are invested in the outcome of the diagnostic process.

Functional diagnosis relies on a more in-depth and complex analysis than state diagnosis and is not limited to establishing whether the company is healthy or ailing, but also aims to identify the underlying "disease" that afflicts it. This phase is preparatory to the subsequent study of the causes at the root of the crisis and the possible formulation of an appropriate treatment strategy.

A thorough analysis of the functional diagnosis is naturally possible with the aid of several sources of information, not only official but also non-formalized. In particular, the diagnostic process involves seven stages of data processing (Fig. 9.6):

1. collection;
2. selection;
3. verification;

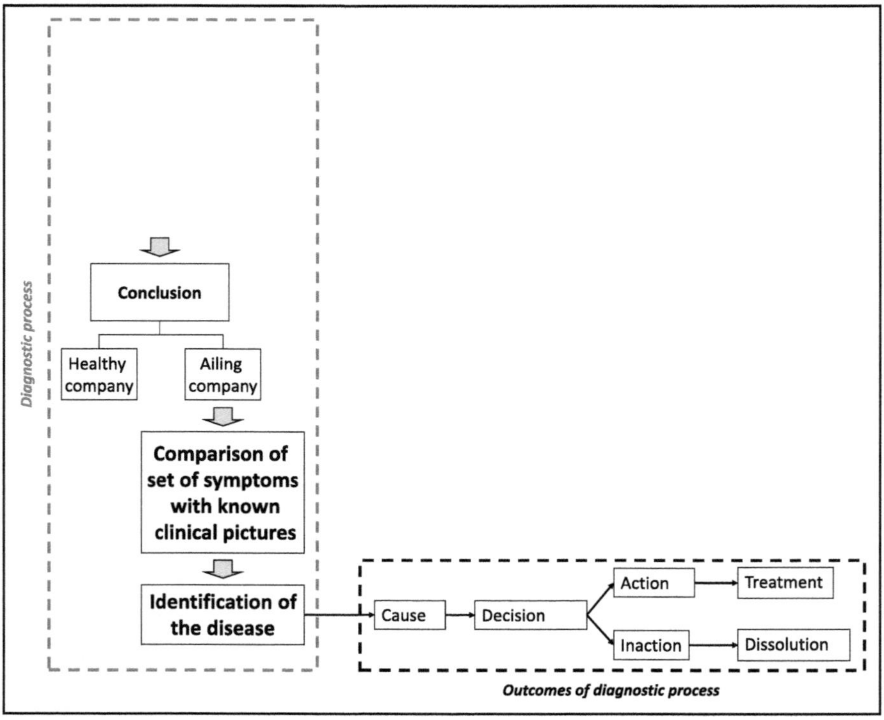

Fig. 9.6 Phases of functional diagnosis

4. interpretation;
5. formulation of a summary judgment on the conditions of the company;
6. comparison of the set of symptoms identified and examined with the known "clinical pictures";

identification of the company's "disease".

On closer inspection, this form of diagnosis is a continuation of that used to diagnose a company's state. In more detail, as in the medical field, the sixth phase involves assessing the specific set of symptoms collected and examined in light of known circumstances, or diseases (Riparbelli, 1950). In this way, the unknown can be made known. The seventh phase, on the other hand, should end with the identification of the disease that has affected and debilitated the company, which may involve inefficiencies, production overcapacity, product decay, poor planning, financial imbalances, etc. (Guatri, 1995).

Once the diagnosis has been made, the next step is to identify and assess the causal complex. Then, a judgment on the seriousness of the company's health status must be formulated and, finally, a decision regarding its future made. At this point the management, for example, may consider it best to opt for:

1. action and, therefore, draw up the most effective treatment plan to resolve the causes of the crisis;
2. inaction, not to take any remediation measures, and therefore consign the company to fail.

The effective assessment of the crisis involves the adoption of adequate diagnostic or predictive tools, foremost among which are models for forecasting insolvency.

9.3 Bankruptcy Prediction Models

9.3.1 Origin, Definition and Operational Advantages

The first embryonic forms of bankruptcy prediction were conceived in the immediate aftermath of the banking crisis which culminated in the collapse of the Wall Street stock exchange in 1929. In those years, banks found themselves granting loans without taking into due consideration the effective ability of the recipient to repay the sums obtained within the agreed deadlines. This rash lending had disastrous consequences, with banks soon being caught in the conflict between the loan recipients, unable to return the capital received, and their savers, who demanded their return.

In this difficult context, the need for intermediaries to have effective, more accurate, and, above all, timely tools for assessing the reliability of borrowers became particularly pressing. And it was precisely the need to obtain reliable information on the future evolution of the *performance* of companies who had already received or requested loans that drove insiders—among others—to the search for investigative tools capable of simplifying and integrating the knowledge acquired with the usual credit risk assessment. To this end, efforts were made to the develop tools able to diagnose the first signs of an ensuing crisis in a timely fashion and with a good degree of reliability. These techniques were designed to provide the analyst with prospective indications, as well-founded as possible, about the possibility that the company under investigation, once given credit, could fall into such a serious critical state as not to allow it to return the loans obtained. Timely information, in fact, would contribute to the increase in quality of credit intermediaries' *screening* and monitoring functions.

The studies conducted in the 1930s in particular had the objective of ascertaining the signalling, discriminatory and predictive capacity of financial indicators (Smith, 1930; Ramser & Foster, 1931; FitzPatrick, 1932; Smith & Winakor, 1935). The positive feedback obtained from this early research then laid the foundations for the development, starting in the 1960s of proper bankruptcy prediction models (BPMs) (Beaver, 1966; Ruozi, 1974; Altman, 1968; Alberici, 1975).

These tools arise from the combination of a more or less large number of independent variables (mainly balance sheet indicators) suitably linked by the application of particular mathematical, statistical or engineering techniques. The disjointed or, rather, joint examination of these parameters makes it possible to obtain a simplified representation of a phenomenon characterized by a high degree of complexity, i.e., the state of health of a company.

A BPM, therefore, focuses the attention of the diagnostician on a limited spectrum of variables considered particularly significant for the representation of the complex crisis phenomenon. Observation of this circumscribed set of parameters makes it possible to formulate a judgment on the company's medium-term *health* status. This feature is doubly advantageous, in both the application phase of the model and in the subsequent assessment of company health. The diagnostician, in fact, must limit themself to calculating and monitoring the few metrics required by the instrument. Interpretation of the result is also constrained: the models, in fact, provide for rigid benchmarks ("threshold parameters") against which to measure the score yielded by the application of the tool. In essence, BPMs establishes assessment "signposts" or guides that define obligatory avenues for interpreting the data obtained. In this way, the judgment cannot be influenced by the analyst's personal considerations. The latter, in fact, will have to limit themself to following the signposted path, dictated by the benchmarks, that automatically yield an assessment of the company examined.

In addition to these operational advantages, BPMs are more reliable than traditional analysis of financial statements. It is believed that this improvement is a consequence of the introduction of statistical techniques which, by limiting the degree of interpretative subjectivity, considerably reduce the possibility of errors of evaluation and/or biased judgments. The adoption of an automated procedure in the evaluation phase of the results, in fact, necessarily constrains the analyst's judgment, depriving them of the possibility of conditioning it based on his own beliefs/feelings.

It is clear, however, that the advantages just mentioned are only effective if the model used:

1. is constructed on the basis of consistent logic that respect the cardinal mathematical and statistical principles;
2. displays adequate predictive accuracy;
3. is applied correctly.

9.3.2 *The State of the Art*

The first models to appear in the literature were developed from univariate (Beaver, 1966) and multivariate (Altman, 1968) discriminant analysis techniques. The main flaw in the univariate approach emerged immediately: since the variables, generally accounting indicators, are considered in isolation, they proved unsuitable for grasping the mutual interdependencies between the elements that make up the company system and, consequently, the correlations between the possible causes of business disruptions (Altman, 1968; Divsalar et al., 2011).

This consideration shifted the interest of scholars towards the multidimensional approach, considered more suitable for representing of the health of a complex reality like a company. In this regard, Altman (1968, p. 592) stated that that technique has 'the advantage of considering an entire profile of characteristics common to the relevant firms, as well as the interaction of these properties.'

In a nutshell, multivariate discriminant models are configured as equations, of the first or second degree, composed of a variable number of independent variables suitably weighted by coefficients. Naturally, the variables are explanatory of the phenomenon to be observed, in this specific case a business crisis, and must be statistically significant. From an operational point of view, the discriminant function aims to separate, committing as few errors as possible, the universe of companies into two mutually distinct groups: (1) healthy companies and (2) ailing companies. This technique, evidently, is based on the principle that ailing companies have characteristics (accounting and otherwise) that are distinct (and therefore recognizable) from physiological ones, differences that the model aims to grasp with reasonable degree of certainty.

Supported by the good reliability progressively demonstrated in the prediction of critical states, multivariate discriminant models have had, and continue to have (Ooghe & Balcaen, 2007; Cox & Wang, 2014; Fernandez et al., 2015; Khemakhem & Boujelbéne, 2015; Altman et al., 2015; Celli, 2015; Prado et al., 2016), ample space in this field of study.

In the international arena, there are many discriminant models. In fact, since Altman's Z Score (1968), there has been a proliferation of studies that, following his approach, have proposed to develop increasingly accurate models (Rossi, 1988; Comuzzi, 1995; Previti, 1996, 1998). A similar line of research has also developed in Italy. The forerunner was Alberici (1975), who tried to replicate Altman's American study in Italy, being followed by Appetiti (1984), Bozzolan (1992), Luerti (1992), Bottani et al. (2004).

From these first formulations, numerous studies have followed in the field of bankruptcy prediction tools, mainly seeking to develop increasingly innovative and high-performance models. Today, in fact, the tools offered by the literature and operational practice are numerous and heterogeneous (Atlman et al., 1981; Zavgren, 1983; Altman, 1984; Poddighe & Madonna, 2006; Bellovary et al., 2007; Pencarelli, 2013). The research in this area has concentrated on refining the technical aspects of such tools, aiming to maximize their predictive accuracy. Some have focused on the composition of the sample to be analysed, both in terms of quality (Taffler, 1982; Gilbert et al., 1990) and quantity (Atlman et al., 1981; Zmijewski, 1984), while others have concentrated on the number (Altman, 1988; Teodori, 1989) and nature (Edmister, 1972; Tennyson et al., 1990; Peel et al., 1985; D'Aveni, 1989; Shumway, 2001a, 2001b) of the indicators to be included in the model, as well as the importance (Eisenbeis, 1977) and degree of correlation (Altman, 1988) of the independent variables.

From the very first models, considerable research effort has been expended to determine which statistical methods to adopt. Early studies focused on the traditional techniques of univariate discriminant analysis (Beaver, 1966; Ruozi, 1974) and multiple discriminant analysis (Altman, 1968; Altman et al., 1977), as well as Bayesian analysis (Forestieri, 1986), principal components analysis (Cascioli & Provasoli, 1986), logit analysis (Martin, 1977; Ohlson, 1980; West, 1985; Platt & Platt, 1991), probit analysis (Zmijewski, 1984), hazard analysis (Shumway, 2001a, 2001b). More recently, attention has been focused on innovative methodologies such as recursive partitioning (Frydman et al., 1985; Pompe & Feelders, 1997), neural networks (Tam & Kiang, 1992; Altman et al., 1994; Wilson & Sharda, 1994; Fletcher & Goss, 1993; Lee et al., 1996; Yang et al., 1999), genetic algorithms (Kingdon & Feldman, 1995; Varetto, 1998; Shin & Lee, 2002) and so on.

Although many models, the result of the different methodological choices just mentioned, have demonstrated a high degree of reliability, even today scholars continue to move towards the development of new tools to achieve what could be defined as "predictive perfection". While believing that this scientific interest should remain alive, it would also be appropriate to direct part of future research towards the examination of the potential use of existing tools and their implications for users (Bellovary et al., 2007). This step now seems to us more necessary than ever to prevent the models from being considered a mere academic exercise and instead finding concrete usefulness in the operational field.

If the observation lens shifts towards the usability of existing tools, it becomes more necessary than ever to formulate reflections on their complexity and sustainability.

9.4 The Complexity and Sustainability of BPMs

As has just been pointed out, over the years more and more refined, reliable, but complex models for forecasting insolvencies have been theorized and applied. At present, we have available BPMs attributed with a satisfactory degree of reliability. However, as just mentioned, this has only been possible at the expense of a more than proportional increase in complexity. The need, increasingly felt by a wide range of scholars, to represent the company as the complex system which it is, has led to the inclusion, in the design of the logical and technical architecture of predictive techniques, an ever-increasing number of variables—both quantitative and qualitative, linked and connected by relationships of mutual interdependence—and to adopt cutting-edge and increasingly refined statistical or engineering techniques.

The phenomenon of complexity is undoubtedly an issue, and not a trivial one. This is even more true when we consider that it is not limited to the technical aspect of the question alone, but also involves important *cultural* and *organizational* matters, which naturally reflect, in a "transversal" way, on the *economic dimension*. The technical issue is obvious: as mentioned, the use of particularly elaborate statistical and mathematical methodologies, but also the number and type of variables involved, inevitably leads to handling technical data that is both sophisticated and complicated. Less evident—but equally important—is the cultural aspect of the issue. There is no doubt, in fact, that the increased level of technical complexity of predictive models is not functional to their diffusion. To put it more clearly, they are not "user friendly". It appears that the sensitivity and attention paid to these investigative tools is in some way related to the ability of the subjects concerned to understand and master them. Therefore, the more abstruse and elusive they prove to be, due to the characteristics of technical complexity we have just mentioned, the less they will find room for use. This is especially true in simpler organizational contexts, where the professional figures involved are often less highly trained. The problem therefore particularly affects Italian companies which, as is well known, are characterized by a lower average size than those in other advanced economies.

The organizational profile is also of great importance. In fact, it has been pointed out that the most refined forecasting systems make use, in addition to more elaborate calculation methodologies, of a very complex system of variables that usually includes both quantitative and qualitative parameters. It is therefore not uncommon for it to be necessary to set up specially designed and dedicated survey systems for the recording of this complex framework of performance indicators. This circumstance clearly leads to a burden, sometimes even significant, on the organizational structures of the companies concerned. Obviously, the growth in complexity, in all the profiles highlighted, will lead to an increase in costs. This economic burden inevitably ends up discouraging the use of such methodologies because of a lack of sustainability and/or cost-effectiveness.

As far as sustainability is concerned, it is clear that the most expensive techniques can only find economic justification for companies that have sufficient turnover (or, in the case of public administrations, endowment of resources). Otherwise, the expense cannot be adequately offset by the revenue generated, and therefore performance monitoring is automatically unsustainable.

However, as mentioned, it is not merely a question of sustainability but also of benefit–cost ratio. Even though investment in know-how (a category which appropriately includes predictive modelling) is particularly important in the context of modern economic institutions, the weighing of risk versus reward typically adopted in the planning of investment in specific production factors applies. In a nutshell, and simply put, whether it is cost-effective. The weighing process is carried out by comparing the benefits that may arise from the specific production factor with the onerous nature of the investment. Only when this assessment indicates that the benefits outweigh the costs will the investment be worthwhile.

In this context, the increased accuracy, precision and reliability of complex models certainly constitutes an added value which, however, can only be gleaned at the expense of a more than proportional increase in costs. As such, the cost-effectiveness deteriorates: a marginal increase in the quality of know-how is very expensive, and only rarely are the (always limited) advantages that arise from it able to compensate for the investment.

In the light of these brief considerations, it is possible to analyze the terms of the issue at hand. While the refinement of theories and techniques has made it possible to have increasingly sophisticated, precise and reliable methodologies, such technical advances led to a significant increase in complexity (which, as we have mentioned, involves several profiles) and inevitably cost. In practice, therefore, the improvement of predictive models has not been matched by an increase in their use; on the contrary, the reliance on these important tools has progressively declined in recent years. As a result, even research and debate on the subject have, for some time now, lost their inspiration and vitality.

In this context, it seems reasonable to reflect on the lines of research development. Although, on the one hand, the value and importance of efforts aimed at improving and refining the predictive capacity of models is undeniable, on the other hand, the choice to focus exclusively on performance could be inappropriate, if not counterproductive. It would therefore be useful to invest at least some research efforts into outlining a different scenario: that is, trying to define a framework for the *sustainability* of BPMs.

According to this different approach, it is assumed that the predictive capacity is not the pre-eminent feature but that this must be reasonably accompanied and weighed against considerations relating to the actual usability of the tool. Hence, the value—operational in this case—of the model is a function of two variables: its accuracy and simplicity. It has not escaped our notice, since the very beginning, how often a sort of trade-off is established between the two parameters: it is undeniable and, at least within certain limits, only natural. However, looking at the problem from a different angle changes perspective: rather than a micro point of view, so to speak, i.e., aimed at maximizing the predictive capacity of the individual model, we could take a systemic view. With this in mind, the research effort should be aimed at identifying, among the models that are characterized by sufficient ease of use, the one that offers the best reliability. In essence, it is necessary to be willing to accept losing part of the precision of the instrument in order to reduce the level of complexity and therefore of overall cost. This should make it possible to create tools that lend themselves to widespread use by overcoming, at least in part, the problems of sustainability and cost-effectiveness examined above.

This approach is functional to meet the knowledge needs of those organizations that, for the most diverse reasons, would not be able to handle the most complex models.

However, it is necessary to verify whether the sustainability conditions of the instruments can be combined with an acceptable reliability condition. Indeed, having a reasonable certainty that the reliability gap between the simplest models and the most refined ones is contained within admissible levels would open up very interesting scenarios.

9.5 The Sustainability of BPM: Generalizability vs. Specialization

As mentioned, BPMs were initially developed to aid decision-making by lending institutions, but over the years further and wider fields of application have been envisaged (Forestieri, 1986; Rossi, 1988; Teodori, 1989). In fact, insolvency forecasting tools have proved their worth in both small and large-scale investigations. Management, for example, can use them to monitor company performance of and/or guide its turnaround process (Altman & La Fleur, 1985). Furthermore, many external parties (investors, insurance analysts, creditors, auditors, bond raters, strategic analysts, public administration, etc.) can make use of predictive models, albeit for different purposes, by applying them to more or less numerous groups of companies.

While on small-scale investigations it can be assumed that any model can be adopted, even those characterized by a high degree of specialization and therefore perfectly adaptable to the company (or to the very few companies) to which it will be applied, in the case of large-scale investigations, therefore on a significant number of often heterogeneous companies, this decision would be counterproductive. In this particular context, in fact, it is essential to reflect on the generalizability of models, i.e., the possibility of their being used effectively for predicting the health of *any* company, whatever its specific characteristics. Surely the choice of an instrument that can be applied indiscriminately would greatly facilitate the diagnostician in mass investigations. This consideration, however, is as reasonable from a theoretical point of view as it is difficult to put into practice.

Indeed, studies have shown that the highest level of reliability is attained by the application of models to companies with characteristics similar to those contemplated in the development phase and are therefore extremely specialized. It follows, therefore, that BPM accuracy decreases significantly if applied to companies with different features (in terms of place, size, sector, purpose, legal status, type, listing etc.) and at different times to those pertaining to the research sample (Grice & Ingram, 2001; Wu et al., 2010). In this regard, Peres and Antão (2017) state that predictive performance is influenced by the different levels of sensitivity inherent to the tools. Going into the merits of the class of discriminant models, then, they specify that they are: territorially sensitive, sectorial sensitive; time sensitive; sensitive to bias in the sample selection; and sensitive to selection assumptions.

Thus emerges the trade-off mentioned above: between sustainability, on the one hand, and model reliability, on the other. This is because generalizability and specialization are not neutral aspects from an economic point of view. In fact, in micro-analysis, the adoption of a specialized model could prove to be the most cost-effective solution and also the most sustainable, especially in continuous monitoring. Indeed, specialization should guarantee very reliable assessment in the diagnoses of one or several companies with homogeneous characteristics. In addition, the investment—even if considerable—incurred in the phase of acquisition of the tool would be adequately compensated for over time. In mass investigations, on the other hand, the adoption of *ad hoc* models to assess the health of a pool of different companies would be difficult to sustain since it would entail an undoubted increase in terms of additional costs.

A "universal" instrument would certainly be more advantageous from an economic point of view, since it could be applied indiscriminately. However, it is a question of assessing whether the loss of reliability due to generalization is acceptable/sustainable for the user. In this context, however, the judgment on the performance of the instrument should not be particularly severe: it is clear that, given the large-scale use, there would naturally be a tendency to favour the simplicity and cost-effectiveness of the instrument. On the other hand, monitoring would enable the identification of a group of companies potentially at risk of crisis. It would then be up to the decision-maker to evaluate, on a case-by-case basis, whether to refine the analysis or settle with the assessment obtained from application of the model. In the former scenario, given that the number of cases to be investigated would be very limited, it would also be possible to think about enhancing the investigation by making use of more refined and, why not, even more complex monitoring techniques.

9.6 The Sustainability of BPMs in Public Administration: Public Policies for the Prevention and Containment of Corporate Crises

The considerations formulated thus far are particularly significant from a perspective of predictive models being used for the handling of corporate crises by the public sector. Public bodies have always wrestled with the issue of supporting companies in crisis, in an attempt to counteract or at least limit the effects of any instability. The policies implemented, however, have always shown considerable limitations. In fact, in most cases public support is provided after the fact, when the disease has already taken root and become evident. In such cases, there are two objectives to consider. The first is to determine whether restructuring the company in crisis—with the aim of safeguarding the integrity of the company, especially as regards the protection of jobs—will be cost-effective or even possible. At the same time, attempts may be made to implement measures and provide the support that, on a case-by-case basis, appear suitable to counteract the spread of the "shock wave" through the allied industries and/or the economic environment in question.

It is clear, however, that with this method the results will hardly be satisfactory. In the first prong of attack, this will be because the damage has already been done and, therefore, it is a matter of interventions for recovery or restoration, which seldom achieve the desired results. The chances of success of the second prong, on the other hand, are higher because, as a rule, the timing of the intervention is better. If prompt action is taken, the harmful knock-on effects have not yet fully materialized. Hence, it might be more appropriate to speak of preventative, rather than corrective, action, with all its relative advantages. Corrective intervention invariably involves numerous players, and therefore, even if concluded with a positive outcome, considerable expenditure in terms of both organizational and (above all) economic resources.

A different and better political line is *prevention*. In this case, the public body prepares a series of dedicated support tools to safeguard the districts, sectors or companies potentially in difficulty. However, it is clear that, not having a suitable filter for selecting interventions, these initiatives naturally tend to be configured according to a dispersive "scatter-shot" scheme. By not identifying a circumscribed target on which to focus the effort, we end up distributing help injudiciously. It follows that this type of policy involves significant investment of resources, now scarcer than ever, with very low efficiency rates. Therefore, even this second perspective, although certainly more appropriate in terms of operational reasoning, usually proves to be unsatisfactory precisely because of the difficulty of correctly selecting the targets of the intervention.

Therefore, tools for predictive identification of company crises that are suitable for the specific use would be needed. The key features are easy to pinpoint:

1. adequate degree of *reliability* of the forecasts;
2. *simplicity* and therefore *sustainability* of the model

It is in fact clear that, if a predictive methodology with such features were available, local public bodies would be in a position—both economic and organizational—to set up good surveillance on the state of health of the companies in the area. In this way, it could effectively select a precise target towards which to efficiently direct resources and support. In other words, by identifying the companies potentially at risk of crisis in a timely fashion, there would be a twofold, and very important advantage: firstly, prevention and containment measures—which, as is well known, are much more effective than corrective or restructuring measures—could be implemented; secondly, at least some of the resources could be dedicated in a targeted way, preventing the well-known dispersion of the uneconomic "scattershot" campaigns.

References

Alberici, A. (1975). *Analisi dei bilanci e previsione delle insolvenze*. Isedi.

Altman, E. I. (1968). Finacial ratios. Discriminant analysis and the prediction of corporate bankruptcy. *The Journal of Finance, 23*(4), 589–609.

Altman, E. I. (1984). A further empirical investigation of the bankruptcy cost question. *The Journal of Finance, 39*(4), 1067–1089.
Altman, E. I. (1988). *The prediction of corporate bankruptcy. A discriminant analysis*. Garland Publishing.
Altman, E. I., Danovi, A., & Falini, A. (2015). Z-score models' application to Italian companies subject to extraordinary administration. *Journal of Applied Finance, 23*(1), 1–11.
Altman, E. I., Haldeman, R. G., & Narayanan, P. (1977). Zeta™ analysis. A new model to identify bankruptcy risk of corporations. *Journal of Banking and Finance, 1*(1), 29–54.
Altman, E. I., & La Fleur, J. K. (1985). I modelli di previsione delle insolvenze: le loro applicazioni alla gestione d'impresa. *Finanza, marketing e produzione, 4*, 77–93.
Altman, E. I., Marco, G., & Varetto, F. (1994). Corporate distress diagnosis: Comparisons using linear discriminant analysis and neural networks (the Italian experience). *Journal of Banking and Finance, 18*(3), 505–529.
Amigoni, F. (1977). Il controllo di gestione e le crisi di impresa, (Aa.Vv.). In *Crisi d'impresa e sistemi di direzione*. Etas.
Andrei, P. (1996). La prevenzione dei dissesti aziendali: alcuni spunti di riflessione, (Aa.Vv.). In *Crisi d'impresa e procedure concorsuali* (pp. 161–210). Giuffrè.
Appelbaum, S. H., Keller, S., Alvarez, H., & Bédard, C. (2012). Organizational crisis: Lessons from Lehman brothers and Paulson & Company. *International Journal of Commerce and Management, 22*(4), 286–305.
Appetiti, S. (1984). *L'utilizzo dell'analisi discriminatoria per la previsione delle insolvenze: ipotesi e test per un'analisi dinamica*. Servizio Studi della Banca d'Italia.
Atlman, E. I., Avery, R. B., Eiseinbeis, R. A., & Sinkey, J. F. (1981). *Application of classification techniques, business, banking and finance*. JAI Press.
Bagrii, K., Romanchuk, A., & Mustetsa, I. (2020). Methods of key problems diagnostics in the system of crisis management. *FBIM Transaction, 8*(1), 1–9.
Bastia, P. (2019). *Crisi aziendali e piani di risanamento*. Giappichelli.
Beaver, H. W. (1966). Financial ratios as predictors of failure. *Journal of Accounting Research, 4*, 71–102.
Bellovary, J. L., Giacomino, D. E., & Akers, M. D. (2007). A review of bankruptcy prediction studies: 1930 to present. *Journal of financial education, 33*, 262–298.
Billings, R. S., Milburn, T. W., & Schaalman, M. L. (1980). A model of crisis perception: A theoretical and empirical analysis. *Administrative Science Quarterly, 25*(3), 300–306.
Boin, A., McConnell, A., & Hart, P. (2008). *Governing after crisis: The politics of investigation, accountability and learning*. Cambridge University Press.
Bottani, P., Cipriani, L., & Serao, F. (2004). Il modello di analisi Z-Score applicato alle PMI. *Amministrazione & Finanza, 1*, 50–53.
Bozzolan, S. (1992). Un modello dinamico per l'analisi e la previsione delle insolvenze aziendali. *Analisi finanziaria, 7*, 71–99.
Brunetti, G. (1989). *Il controllo di gestione in condizioni ambientali perturbate*. Franco Angeli.
Caramiello, C. (1968). *L'azienda nella fase terminale*. Cursi.
Cascioli, E., & Provasoli, A. (1986). La previsione delle insolvenze aziendali, un metodo quantitativo. In M. Cattaneo, F. Cesarini, A. Provasoli, & B. Quatraro (Eds.), *Crisi di Impresa e Amministrazione Controllata*. Giuffrè.
Celli, M. (2015). Can Z-score model predict listed companies' failures in Italy? An empirical test. *International Journal of Business and Management, 10*(3), 57–66.
Cestari, G. (2009). *La diagnosi precoce della crisi aziendale. Analisi del processo patologico e modelli predittivi*. Giuffré.
Charalambous, C., Charitou, A., & Kaourou, F. (2000). Comparative analysis of artificial neural network models: Application in bankruptcy prediction. *Annals of Operations Research, 99*, 403–425.
Charitou, A., Neophytou, E., & Charalambous, C. (2004). Predicting corporate failure: Empirical evidence for the UK. *European Accounting Review, 13*(3), 465–497.

Chekkar-Mansouri, R., & Onnee, S. (2013). Towards a theoretical. Understanding of the recurrence of crises embracing the issue of organizational learning: An illustration with the case of two hostile takeover bids faced by société générale (1988, 1999). *Journal of Contingencies and Crisis Management, 21*(1), 56–68.

Chowdhury, S. D., & Lang, J. R. (1993). Crisis, decline and turnaround: A test of competing hypotheses for shortterm performance improvement in small firms. *Journal of Small Business Management, 31*(4), 8–17.

Clark, J. (1995–1996), Hope for the best, but plan for the worst—The need for disaster planning. *Employment Relations Today*, *22*(4), pp. 41–53.

Comuzzi, E. (1995). *L'analisi degli squilibri finanziari di impresa*. Giappichelli.

Cox, R. A. K., & Wang, G. W. (2014). Predicting the US bank failure: A discriminant analysis. *Economic Analysis and Policy, 44*(2), 202–211.

D'Aveni, R. A. (1989). The aftermath of organisational decline: A longitudinal study of the strategic and managerial characteristics of declining firms. *Academy of Management Journal, 32*(3), 577–608.

Darling, J. R., & Kash, T. (1998). Crisis management: Prevention, diagnosis and intervention. *Leadership & Organization Development Journal, 19*, 179–186.

De Sarno, M. (1982). *Equilibrio e crisi delle imprese*. Cedam.

Divsalar, M., Javid, M. R., Gandomi, A. H., Soofi, J. B., & Mahmood, M. V. (2011). Hybrid genetic programming-based search algorithms for enterprise bankruptcy prediction. *Applied Artificial Intelligence: An International Journal, 25*(8), 669–692.

Dutton, J. E., & Jackson, S. E. (1987). Categorizing strategic issues: Links to organizational action. *Academy of Management Review, 12*, 76–90.

Edmister, R. O. (1972). An empirical test of financial ratios analysis for small business failure prediction. *Journal of Finance and Quantitative Analysis, 7*(2), 1477–1493.

Eisenbeis, R. A. (1977). Pitfalls the application of discriminant analysis in business, finance, and economics. *The Journal of Finance, 32*(3), 875–900.

Elliott, D. (2009). The failure of organizational learning from crisis: A matter of life and death? *Journal of Contingencies and Crisis Management, 17*(3), 157–168.

Farooq, U., Jibran Qamar, M. A., & Haque, A. (2018). A three-stage dynamic model of financial distress. *Managerial Finance, 44*(9), 1101–1116.

Fernandez, G., Prakash, A. J., & Mishra, S. (2015). With one shot, which bullet would you use? Market versus accounting data in bankruptcy prediction—Part II (a strong case of using non-parametric MDA in bankruptcy prediction). *The International Journal of Finance, 26*(3), 275–308.

Fink, S. (1986). *Crisis management: Planning for the inevitable*. American Management Association.

Fink, S. (2002). *Decision making in crisis: The piper alpha disaster, managing crisis: Threats.*

FitzPatrick, P. J. (1932). *Symptoms of industrial failures as revealed by an analysis of the financial statements of failed companies, 1920–1929*. The Catholic University of America.

Fletcher, D., & Goss, E. (1993). Forecasting with neural networks. *Information & Management, 24*(3), 159–167.

Forestieri, G. (1986). *La previsione delle insolvenze aziendali. Profili teorici e analisi empiriche*. Giuffrè.

Frydman, H., Altman, E. I., & Kao, D. (1985). Introducing recursive partitioning for financial classification: The case of financial distress. *The Journal of Finance, 40*(1), 269–291.

Garskaite-Milvydiene, K. (2012). Diagnostics of bankruptcy threat to enterprises. *Journal of Security and Sustainability, 1*(3), 197–203.

Gephart, R. P. (1984). Making sense of organizationally based environmental disasters. *Journal of Management, 10*, 205–225.

Giannessi, E. (1960). *Le aziende di produzione originaria*. Colombo Cursi.

Gilbert, L. R., Menon, K., & Schwartz, K. B. (1990). Predicting bankruptcy for firms in financial distress. *Journal of Business, Finance & Accounting, 17*(1), 161–171.

Grice, J. S., & Ingram, R. W. (2001). Tests of the generalizability of Altman's bankruptcy prediction model. *Journal of Business Research, 54*(1), 53–61.
Guatri, L. (1986). *Crisi e risanamento delle imprese*. Giuffrè.
Guatri, L. (1995). *Turnaround. Declino, crisi e ritorno al valore*. Egea.
Hannah, S. T., Uhl-Bien, M., Avolio, B. J., & Cavaretta, F. L. (2009). A framework for examining leadership in extreme contexts. *Leadership Quarterly, 20*(6), 897–919.
Hermann, C. F. (1963). Some consequences of crisis which limit the viability of organization. *Administrative Science Quarterly, 8*(1), 61–82.
Hwang, P., & Lichtenthal, J. D. (2000). Anatomy of organizational crises. *Journal of Contingencies and Crisis Management, 8*(3), 129–140.
Janis, I. L., & Mann, L. (1977). *Decision making: A psychological analysis of conflict, choice, and commitment*. Free Press.
Jennex, M. E., & Raman, M. (2009). Knowledge Management in Support of crisis response. *Journal of Information Systems for Crisis Response and Management, 1*(3), 69–83.
Khemakhem, S., & Boujelbéne, Y. (2015). Credit risk prediction: A comparative study between discriminant analysis and the neural network approach. *Accounting and Management Information Systems, 14*(1), 60–78.
Kiesler, S., & Sproull, L. (1982). Managerial response to changing environments: Perspectives on problem sensing. *Administrative Science Quarterly, 27*(4), 548–570.
Kingdon, J., & Feldman, K. (1995). Genetic algorithms and applications to finance. *Applied Mathematical Finance, 2*(2), 89–116.
Klein, D. A. (2008). *Strategic management of intellectual capital*. Butterworth-Heinemann.
Kou, G., Xu, Y., Peng, Y., Shen, F., Chen, Y., Chang, K., & Kou, S. (2021). Bankruptcy prediction for SMEs using transactional data and two-stage multiobjective feature selection. *Decision Support Systems, 140*(113429), 1–14.
Lee, K., Han, I., & Kwon, Y. (1996). Hybrid neural network models for bankruptcy predictions. *Decision Support Systems, 18*(1), 63–72.
Lippitt, G. L., & Schmidt, W. H. (1967). Crises in a developing organization. *Harvard Business Review, 45*(6), 102–112.
Lizza, P. (2011). *La cultura aziendale. Profili di analisi e di management*. Giuffrè.
Luerti, A. (1992). La previsione dello stato di insolvenza delle imprese. In *Il Modello Al/93 di Credit Scoring elaborato in base alla IV Direttiva CEE*. Etaslibri.
MacKenze, A. (1994). Dealing with disaster. *Asian Business, 30*(1), 20–24.
Marchi, L. (2003). *I sistemi informativi aziendali*. Giuffrè.
Martin, D. (1977). Early warning of bank failure: A logit regression approach. *Journal of Banking and Finance, 1*(3), 249–276.
Meiste, R., & Jakstiene, S. (2015). Crisis diagnosis in anti-crisis management process in a company. *Institute of Economic Research Working Papers, 9*, 1–12.
Milburn, T. W., Schuler, R. S., & Watman, K. H. (1993). Organizational crisis. Part I. Definition and conceptualization. *Human Relations, 36*(12), 1161–1180.
Mitroff, I. I. (2004). *Crisis leadership: Planning for the unthinkable*. Wiley.
Mitroff, I. I., & Linstone, H. (1996). *The unbounded mind: Breaking the chains of traditional business thinking*. Oxford University Press.
Mitroff, I. I., Shrivastava, P., & Udwadia, F. (1987). Effective crisis management. *The Academy of Management Executive, 1*(4), 283–292.
Müller, R. (1985). Corporate crisis management. *Long Range Planning, 18*(5), 28–48.
Ohlson, J. (1980). Financial ratios and the probabilistic prediction of bankruptcy. *Journal of Accounting Research, 18*, 109–131.
Ooghe, H., & Balcaen, S. (2007). Are failure prediction models widely usable? An empirical study using a Belgian dataset. *Multinational Finance Journal, 11*(1/2), 33–76.
Paraskev, A. (2006). Crisis management or crisis response system? A complexity science approach to organizational crisis. *Management Decision, 44*(7), 892–907.
Peel, M., Peel, D., & Pope, P. (1985). Some evidence on corporate failure and the behaviour of non-financial ratios. *The Investment Analyst, 75*, 3–7.

Pencarelli, T. (2013). *Le crisi d'impresa. Diagnosi, previsione e procedure di risanamento.* Franco Angeli.

Peres, C., & Antão, M. (2017). The use of multivariate discriminant analysis to predict corporate bankruptcy: A review, Aestimatio: The IEB international. *Journal of Finance, 14*, 108–131.

Platt, H. D., & Platt, M. B. (1991). A note on the use of industry-relative ratios in bankruptcy prediction. *Journal of Banking and Finance, 15*(6), 1183–1194.

Poddighe, F., & Madonna, S. (2006). *Modelli di previsione delle crisi aziendali: possibilità e limiti*. Giuffrè.

Poli, S. (2020). *I modelli di previsione della crisi d'impresa. La prospettiva esterna mediante i bilanci in forma abbreviata*. Giappichelli.

Pompe, P., & Feelders, A. (1997). Using machine learning, neural networks, and statistics to predict corporate bankruptcy. *Microcomputers in Civil Engineering, 12*(4), 267–276.

Prado, J. W., Castro, A. V., Melo, C. F., Carvalho, V. K., Cruz Machado, L. K., & Tonelli, D. F. (2016). Multivariate analysis of credit risk and bankruptcy research data: A bibliometric study involving different knowledge fields (1968-2014). *Scientometrics, 106*(3), 1007–1029.

Pretorius, M. (2009). Defining business decline, failure and turnaround: A content analysis. *South African Journal of Entrepreneurship and Small Business Management, 2*(1), 1–16.

Previti, F. G. (1996). Previsione della insolvenza con l'analisi discriminante: modelli proposti in dottrina. *Rivista Italiana di Ragioneria e di Economia Aziendale, 7-8*, 35–46.

Previti, F. G. (1998). Previsione della insolvenza con l'analisi discriminante: criteri di costruzione dei modelli. *Rivista Italiana di Ragioneria e di Economia Aziendale, 1-2*, 16–30.

Prosperi, S. (2003). *Il governo economico della crisi aziendale*. Giuffré.

Ramser J. R., & Foster L. O. (1931). *A demonstration of ratio analysis, Bureau of Business Research, bulletin nr. 40*, University of Illinois.

Riparbelli, A. (1950). *Il contributo della Ragioneria nell'analisi dei dissesti aziendali*. Vallecchi.

Rossi, C. (1988). *Indicatori di bilancio, modelli di classificazione e previsione delle insolvenze aziendali*. Giuffrè.

Ruozi, R. (1974). Sull'attendibilità dei bilanci e sulla loro validità ai fini di previsione delle insolvenze. *Bancaria, 1*, 7–18.

Sakalas, A., & Virbickaite, R. (2011). Construct of the model of crisis situation diagnosis in a company. *Engineering Economics, 22*(3), 255–261.

Sandin, A. R., & Porporato, M. (2007). Corporate bankruptcy prediction models applied to emerging economies: Evidence from Argentina in the years 1991-1998. *International Journal of Commerce and Management, 17*(4), 295–311.

Santos, R., Bandeira de Mello, R., & Cunha, C. (2016). The leadership process during an organizational crisis. *Journal of Operations and Supply Chain Management, 9*(1), 94–109.

Shepherd D. A. (2005, February). The theoretical basis for my plenary speech about our successes and failures at research on business failure, (AaVv) *Proceeding: Regional Frontiers of entrepreneurial research*, pp. 123–134.

Sheppard, J. P., & Chowdhury, S. D. (2005). Riding the wrong wave: Organisational failure as a failed turnaround. *Long Range Planning, 38*(3), 239–260.

Shin, K., & Lee, Y. (2002). A genetic algorithm application in bankruptcy prediction modelling. *Expert Systems with Applications, 23*(3), 321–328.

Shrivastava, P. (1987). *Bhopal: Anatomy of a crisis, Ballinger series in business in a global environment*. Ballinger Pub. Co..

Shumway, T. (2001a). Forecasting bankruptcy more accurately: A simple hazard model. *Journal of Business, 74*(1), 101–124.

Shumway, T. (2001b). Forecasting bankrupty more accurately: A simple hazard model. *Journal of Business, 74*(1), 101–124.

Slatter, S., & Lovett, D. (1999). *Corporate recovery: Managing companies in distress*. Beard Books.

Smith F. R. (1930). *A test analysis of unsuccessful industry companies*, Bureau of Business Research, bulletin nr. 31, University of Illinois.

Smith, R. (1995). Analysis of earth-moving using discrete-event simulation. *Journal of Construction Engineering and Management, ASCE, 121*(4), 388–396.

Smith F. R., & Winakor A. H. (1935). *Changes in financial structure of unsuccessful corporations*, Bureau of Business Research, bulletin nr. 51, University of Illinois.

Staw, B. M., Sandelands, L. E., & Dutton, J. E. (1981). Threat-rigidity effects in organizational behavior. *Administrative Science Quarterly, 26*(4), 501–524.

Stein, M. (2004). The critical period of disasters: Insights from sense-making and psychoanalytic theory. *Human Relations, 57*(10), 1243–1261.

Taffler, R. J. (1982). Forecasting company failure in the U. K. Using discriminant Ana-lysis and Financial ratios data. *Journal of the Royal Statistical Society, 145*(3), 342–358.

Tam, K., & Kiang, M. (1992). Managerial applications of neural networks: The case of Bank failure predictions. *Management Science, 38*(7), 926–947.

Tennyson, M., Ingram, R., & Dugan, M. (1990). Assessing the information content of narrative disclosures in explaining bankruptcy. *Journal of Business Finance & Accounting, 17*(3), 390–410.

Teodori, C. (1989). *Modelli di previsione nell'analisi economico-aziendale*. Giappichelli.

Turner, B. A. (1976). Organizational and interorganizational development of disasters. *Administrative Science Quarterly, 21*(3), 378–397.

Varetto, F. (1998). Genetic algorithms applications in the analysis of insolvency risk. *Journal of Banking and Finance, 22*(10–11), 1421–1439.

Vergara, C. (1988). *Disfunzioni e crisi d'impresa. Introduzione ai processi di diagnosi, risanamento e prevenzione*. Giuffrè.

Weick, K. E., & Sutcliffe, K. M. (2001). *Managing the unexpected: Assuring high performance in an age of complexity, University of Michigan Business School management series* (1st ed.). Jossey-Bass.

West, R. C. (1985). A factor-analytic approach to bank condition. *Journal of Banking and Finance, 9*(2), 253–266.

Whetten, D. A. (1980). Organizational decline: A neglected topic in organizational science. *Academy of Management Review, 5*, 577–588.

Wilson, R., & Sharda, R. (1994). Bankruptcy prediction using neural networks. *Decision Support Systems, 11*(5), 545–557.

Wu, Y., Gaunt, C., & Gray, S. (2010). A comparison of alternative bankruptcy prediction models. *Journal of Contemporary Accounting & Economics, 6*(1), 34–45.

Yang, Z. R., Plat, M. B., & Plat, H. D. (1999). Probabilistic neural networks in bankruptcy prediction. *Journal of Business Research, 44*(2), 67–74.

Zavgren, C. V. (1983). The prediction of corporate failure: The state of the art. *Journal of Accounting Literature, 2*, 1–38.

Zito, M. (1999). *Fisiologia e patologia delle crisi di impresa*. Giuffrè.

Zmijewski, M. E. (1984). Methodological issues related to the estimation of financial distress prediction models. *Journal of Accounting Research, 22*(Suppl), 59–82.

Chapter 10
Bankruptcy Prediction Models: From Predictive Performance to Economic and Organizational Sustainability

10.1 Introduction

In the previous chapter it was pointed out that in recent decades studies on business crisis forecasting models have mainly focused on refining the logical technical system of the instrument in order to enhance its diagnostic capabilities. This trend has been progressively marked by the adoption of increasingly sophisticated statistical techniques and complex input data (independent variables) that is often difficult to capture and handle.

Faced with such a rich and varied panorama, the focus has inevitably shifted from the significant performance now demonstrated to the *usability* of the models in the field of operation. Indeed, it has been shown that the recent adoption of cutting-edge econometric techniques (often of an engineering nature) has contributed to the definition of tools characterized by a declared reliability that, in some ways, borders on perfection. Precisely because accurate tools for predicting critical states are now available, at least from a theoretical point of view, it is appropriate to reflect on their sustainability so as to encourage their diffusion among market players. It is true that, despite the proliferation of academic and professional contributions on the subject of bankruptcy prediction, even today BPMs encounter a kind of resistance from users.

It is no secret that this reluctance depends partly on the user's inability to fully understand and master both the functioning of such tools and, above all, the data interpretation phase. This is all the more true the more sophisticated the methodological framework on which the model relies. We would do well to remember that BPMs objectify and therefore rigidify the company's auditing process, thereby minimizing the discretion of the analyst/diagnostician. On the one hand, this objectivity is considered a strength, given that an assessment that is independent of the analyst's skills or convictions is available; on the other hand, paradoxically, objectivity itself constitutes a barrier to its adoption or, in any event, to its exclusive use.

M. Aliano et al., *Sustainable Finance for SMEs*, Sustainable Finance,
https://doi.org/10.1007/978-3-031-74193-7_10

It is not only this reluctance that disincentivizes the diffusion of models in practice. In fact, the sacrifice that naturally follows the adoption and use of models in the process, whether punctual or prospective, of monitoring the state of health of companies also has a significant influence. This is why contemplation of the burdens imposed constitutes an important stimulus for broader reflection—now more than necessary—on the models' *sustainability*. In economics and business research, reflecting on the sustainability of an information-processing tool like BPM means studying and evaluating its impact, in a broad sense, on the company system. Contrary to what is usually thought, sustainability does not only consider the issue in financial terms, i.e., the burden arising from the application of the tool, but also the constraints, more or less impactful, imposed on the business organization and the management of the related processes.

In the field of bankruptcy prediction, both academic and professional, this topic is still quite new and unexplored. In fact, studies on the subject have so far neglected the organizational and economic implications related to the use of predictive models. In this specific context, the interest of scholars has been limited to estimating the costs deriving from the errors made during BPM application, as well as to the integration of this information into the architecture of the model (Altman, 1984; Gaber, 1986; Johnson et al., 1993; Chen et al., 1997; Barontini, 1997). This burden represents an aspect of undoubted significance for the estimation of the cost of a diagnostic tool but does not allow exhaustive analysis of the issue of its sustainability.

In addition to the financial consequences, of which the cost of error is an important but not exclusive component, it would also be well to dwell on the organizational consequences in terms of management complexity, bureaucratization of the system and logistical superstructures imposed by the adoption of the model. Indeed, the phases of application of some tools, and the interpretation/use of the resulting information can rigidify the organizational chart of the corporate user, due to the need to introduce a new, specifically dedicated figure, and/or a burden on internal management procedures, mostly caused by slowdowns in decision-making processes. These considerations should not be overlooked because they can influence, even decisively, the actual usability of prediction models: some tools, while demonstrating high diagnostic accuracy, are difficult to apply in practice due to the economic and organizational sacrifice that accompanies them during the use phase.

Operators who intend to make use of the information deriving from the application of this instrumentation, therefore, must not limit themselves to observing and appreciating the level of diagnostic performance. The predictive capacity cannot be considered a pre-eminent characteristic but must be reasonably accompanied by and weighed against considerations as to the sustainability of the model. Precisely for these reasons, when choosing a BPM, it should be appropriately deliberated by user, considering, on the one hand, the technical performance that evidences its predictive efficacy, and on the other, the organizational and economic sustainability that represents its efficiency. The following two paragraphs are dedicated to the identification of the criteria considered functional to the evaluation of the performance and sustainability of bankruptcy prediction models.

10.2 Assessment of BPM Performance

Performance evaluation focuses on the appreciation of the purely technical aspects of the model, i.e., its diagnostic performance, demonstrated in correctly forecasting the health status of companies. It follows that the following criteria must be considered for the evaluation of technical performance:

1. the *accuracy/reliability*, that is the capacity to correctly predict the operative status of the investigated firm;
2. the *timeliness*, or rather the speed with which the correct information on the state of health of the studied company is available. As a matter of fact, it is clear that the more precise the evaluation obtained of the real operative status of the firm, and the quicker this correct information is available to the analyst, the more effective the tool. Timeliness, in particular, is a decisive factor in this class of instruments. In fact, forecasting models must not be limited to providing a punctual diagnosis, but they must attempt to formulate a founded hypothesis on the equilibrium or disequilibrium of firms in the mid–long term. Therefore, this information must be acquired as soon as possible: to be notified of the company crisis with congruous advance allows the internal or external analyst to have sufficient margin of time to make more appropriate and more efficient decisions (Giannessi, 1979; Sciarelli, 1995).

10.2.1 The Models' Reliability

The correctness of the forecasts, which, together with timeliness, contributes to defining the reliability of the BPM, can be determined by examining five criteria. These include the performance demonstrated by the tools during processing, measured both by the correct predictions and by the errors made, and also the accuracy checks carried out in subsequent periods. Reliability tests on control samples, in fact, contribute to ascertaining the statistical robustness of the model.

More analytically, reliability is measured through the examination and interpretation of the following criteria:

1. the overall percentage of correct classifications;
2. the percentage of type I errors (when the model classifies an ailing firm as healthy);
3. the percentage of type II errors (when the model classifies a healthy firm as ailing);
4. the possible application of the model to a control sample;
5. the possible application of the model to subsequent samples with respect to the one it was developed on.

The first criterion (the overall percentage of correct classifications) estimates the capability of the model to correctly classify the sample under examination, considered as a whole. In ex-post analyses, which are used in the development of BPMs, the correctness of the results is measured by matching the prediction formulated by the model with the real status of the company being assessed. The prediction is accurate if there is a correspondence between the outcome of the model and the vital conditions (healthy or ailing) of the company known beforehand. If not, a type I or II error is committed. Type I errors occur when the model classifies a company as healthy that is actually not. Type II errors are found in the opposite case, i.e., when a productive company which appears to be operating normally is predicted to become insolvent. Therefore, observation of this percentage allows us to appreciate the *overall reliability* of the diagnostic model.

Meanwhile, the next two parameters (the percentage of the type I and type II errors) highlight the instrument's potential in correctly respectively classifying firms as "healthy" or "ailing". Thus, these measures, unlike the one above, allow us to estimate the *specific reliability* of the model, as the assessment is limited to a subgroup of the sample under examination. As easy as it may be to understand, this is an indirect assessment, because it follows from the examination of errors made in classifying the two classes of companies. Consequently, the analysis of type I errors allows us to appreciate the model's performance in diagnosing the status of ailing companies. Analysis of the type II errors, on the other hand, enables us to draw analogous but diametrically opposed considerations: in this case the potential of the instrument to qualify the companies as healthy can be deduced.

For an accurate evaluation of the forecasting models, the combined appreciation of both overall and specific effectiveness parameters becomes unavoidable. Indeed, the mere total percentage of correct classifications, although a relevant criterion, could bring to the formulation only approximate and, sometimes, even misleading judgments. In particular, this occurs when the specific analysis highlights for one of the company groups, a percentage of correct classifications near to zero. In this case, it is easy to see how the model effectiveness would be neutralized because the discriminant activity between the healthy and ailing companies diminishes. As a matter of fact, the model could similarly qualify almost all the firms.

The fourth and the fifth evaluation criteria (model application to a control sample and to subsequent samples) aim to verify the subsistence of validations of the model's accuracy on different samples relative to the one used for development testing. It is a frequent occurrence that the diagnostic reliability is observed by applying the instrument to the same sample studied during the elaboration process. It is clear that the verification of the instrument potential through the mere re-application to the group of companies that was observed in order for the model to be formulated allows us to obtain undoubtedly positive results, that are generally overestimated. Therefore, in this case, the accuracy could only be ascribed to the capability of the model to represent in detail the managerial features of a few sampled companies. With considerable certainty, the same instrument would be able to guarantee a similar diagnostic performance if extrapolated and applied outside the development context. In fact, the firms' features could be affected, even profoundly, by the contingencies characterized by the development of the surrounding economic environment. Consequently, the spatial and temporal stability of the models could depend on factors such as: structural changes in the economic cycle, variations in the inflation rate, and the conditions of monetary permissiveness. For these reasons, in evaluating the real forecasting abilities of a BPM it is necessary to extend the verification of its specific performances to control samples, derived from the development sample or *ex novo* formation sample, or to groups of firms sampled over different timeframes than that considered during its development (Rossi, 1988).

10.2.2 The Models' Timeliness

In the previous chapter, the decisive role of the time factor in the detection and management of the corporate crisis was introduced. In fact, it has been reiterated several times, how crucial it is to be aware of a looming crisis as soon as possible, so as to allow:

1. internal stakeholders to intervene promptly and implement recovery measures that are as effective and efficient as possible;
2. external stakeholders to establish whether to undertake any economic relationship with the company.

If this is the goal, it is easy to understand how prompt diagnosis, i.e., the recognition of the current state of health of the company, is an undoubtedly indispensable monitoring activity for companies, albeit less advantageous than prospective analysis. In fact, it is forecasting which, if correctly carried out, can have the greatest influence on the degree of success of a company's recovery.

It is easy to see, then, how timeliness with respect to which the correct information on the health of the company is obtained is certainly an important aspect in the evaluation of BPM performance. Pompe & Bilderbeek (2005) say that 'The prediction of failure only 1 year before the moment of failure is too late for undertaking actions such as the extraction of cash by an investor, or the execution of a turnaround plan. In order to take effective measures, the failure needs to be predicted a few years in advance.'

Timeliness assessment involves the evaluation of two parameters:

1. the investigated critical event;
2. the number of reliable years of the model.

It is the crisis definition that requires the appreciation of the first of the two evaluation criteria (investigated critical event). As a matter of fact, the symptoms of a crisis do not present all at once, but in a process of progressive worsening of the positions of business equilibrium (Guatri, 1986, 1995; Ferrero, 1987; Andrei, 1986).

While recognizing the dynamic nature of a corporate crisis, for the elaboration of the model it becomes essential that the degenerative process as a whole can be traced back to a specific event that unmistakably identifies the conditions of corporate distress. This is clearly a simplification from which, however, practical advantages can be derived. Indeed, recognizing the pathological condition in a specific critical event, allows us to qualify unequivocally the firms as ailing or healthy simply by confirming, in each one, the existence or not of the investigated fact. In this way, it is believed that any recognizable event of a pathological phenomenon (Sciarelli, 1995; Andrei, 1986) can be properly diagnosed.

Nevertheless, in practice, moments formalized by legal judgment relating to the final stages of involutional dynamics are preferred. Indeed, beside these events the differences between healthy and ailing firms are definitely accentuated and easy to appreciate. For this reason, researchers usually develop models to predict corporate bankruptcy, an event that usually precedes a company break up (Caramiello, 1968). However, there are numerous models that have been developed with the aim of predicting the corporate disease before the same legal judgment. Therefore, the monitoring of econometric models relative to the moment in question proves profoundly heterogeneous. This aspect must not be overlooked when pronouncing a judgment of the timeliness of such tools: it is clear, indeed, that a model designed to recognize in advance the early moments of the involutional dynamics must be considered more well-timed than an instrument that forecasts its last steps. In fact, in the first case internal or external users would have a greater time interval to make more appropriate decisions on corporate investment.

The second parameter, on the other hand, allows us to verify and evaluate the number of years before the investigated event in which the model proves to be reliable in classifying the operative status of the firms. It is clear that the longer the period of reliability before the critical event that is proposed to be predicted, the better performing the model will be.

10.3 Assessment of BPM Sustainability

Evaluating the sustainability of a BPM means, in a nutshell, appreciating its degree of efficiency from the user's perspective. Since the point of view is that of the individual user of the tool, sustainability cannot be measured in absolute terms: this assessment, in fact, is inevitably influenced by the characteristics (dimensional and sectoral) and conditions (structural, procedural, technological and economic/financial) of the company, and by the repercussions that integration of the BPM entails in both economic and organizational terms. The adoption of any information tool, including predictive models, has strategic, organizational, economic, financial and operational implications that must be carefully examined through evaluation of the costs, benefits and risks involved. So, it is clear, for example, that models that are more onerous from an organizational and economic point of view would be deployed only by the companies that have sufficient turnover. Otherwise, the expense incurred for the acquisition of the tool would not to be adequately offset (Madonna & Cestari, 2012).

In an attempt to simplify and schematize the problem, we believe that the sustainability of a model can be determined by evaluating two main aspects:

1. *organizational sustainability*, which involves implications for the organizational structure of an economic operator following the choice of an econometric model;

2. *financial sustainability*, which measures the cost of the adoption and/or the employment of the diagnostic instrument. Financial sustainability can be assessed by examining two classes of costs:
   - *direct costs*, that is the economic sacrifices made during the acquisition and introduction of the diagnostic model in the users' analysis system;
   - *indirect costs*, that is the gain resulting from future deployment of the model.

The identification of sustainability parameters is a very arduous step. This difficulty mostly arises from the absence in the literature of specific contributions dealing with the economic and organizational sacrifices associated with the use of forecasting models. However, these instruments belong to the wider class of the corporate information systems. Therefore, aiming to identify efficiency parameters, we have examined the studies that have analyzed the costs involved to the general class of corporate information systems (Maggiolini, 1981; Marchi, 1993; Bonmassar, 1996).

10.3.1 Organizational Sustainability

With regard to organizational sustainability, it is interesting to focus on three criteria:

1. The need and the complexity degree of recording systems for the determination of input parameters.
2. The need for a specific qualified figure in the organizational structure.
3. The interpretative complexity of the results of diagnostic modelling.

The first parameter of comparison (need and complexity of recording systems) focuses on analyzing the effects of the introduction of the model into the corporate instrumentation in terms of the intricacy of the information systems to support. This is mainly a result of the greater or lesser complexity of the logical and technical framework of BPMs. The complexity of this architecture could depend on several factors. Among the main elements, the most important are: the number of variables provided, the degree of sophistication of the statistical methodology adopted, the refinement of the data used, and the nature of the information to be acquired (quantitative, qualitative, accounting, non-accounting data).

It is clear that the need for data not provided in the ordinary corporate information systems requires the activation of a process of acquiring and/or *ex novo* processing of this information. This process often requires the adoption of new and more sophisticated recording systems. Moreover, the use of a specific predictive model may also involve the introduction of an appropriate, dedicated staff member in the organizational structure of the user company (second parameter of comparison). As a matter of fact, the mind, the specific professional qualities, the intuition and the experience of the analyst may considerably affect the results of the assessment process of corporate vitality. For this reason, the use of some models requires that the economic operators have a solid background in business economics, mathematics and statistics and, sometimes, engineering and computer studies.

The word "use" has to be understood in its broad sense, or rather not only as mere application of the instrument but also, and especially, as its handling, i.e., updating, remodeling and maintenance over time. Indeed, while some BPMs are characterized by a static logical-technical framework, for which further interventions of adaption and modernization are not needed (e.g., models developed via the multivariate discriminant analysis technique), others have a very dynamic structure and, therefore, require more or less radical correctives in order to maintain the same degree of predictive reliability (think, instead, of neural networks, which require a complex learning process that allows the performance of the model to be maintained or even improved over time).

Finally, our attention must focus on the degree of complexity arising from the interpretation of the results provided by the diagnostic instrument (third parameter of comparison). As everybody knows, BPMs formally define the parameters against which the information obtained may be assessed. Therefore, the application of this instrument allows us to appreciate the status of the company investigated by minimizing (if not even eliminating) the subjectivity of the analyst's evaluation. This determinism may involve a rigidification of the interpretative process, so much as to make it difficult to use. Obviously, this depends on the type of instrument adopted and, in particular, on the statistical methodology used for processing the data input into the analysis process.

10.3.2 Economic Sustainability: Direct Costs

As regards direct costs, i.e., those strictly attributable to the implementation of the model, including integration of IT systems and subsequent handling, it is considered of interest to include the following items:

1. development or acquisition;
2. maintenance;
3. support tools;
4. handling.

The first evaluation criterion examines the economic sacrifice made by the user to internally develop or to externally acquire the econometric model. These costs refer to the complexity involved in the instrument: the high degree of articulation of the model and the employment of highly sophisticated technologies involve a greater monetary investment than simpler support tools developed through traditional methodologies.

Once acquired, the instrument may entail further expense for maintaining, updating, and reshaping the logical-technical framework (second assessment parameter). These costs may be minimal or non-existent for BPMs characterized by a fixed or static structure. Such instruments, as easy as they are to understand, do not require sudden and frequent modifications to adapt to environmental changes over time.

Several observations can be drawn for the most dynamic instruments, or rather for models that:

1. Require the structure to be updated in light of the changes in time and space that have occurred before application.
2. Need a continuous influx of new information in order to maintain a satisfactory degree of diagnostic reliability

The introduction of a predictive instrument usually requires incurring costs for the software and hardware needed to support its functioning (third assessment parameter). Once again, it is easy to understand that the costs influence the complexity of the tool: complex models require more sophisticated and, therefore, more expensive instrumentation; meanwhile opposing considerations can be formulated in the case of more traditional instruments.

Finally, the costs imputable to the handling of the models have to be examined (fourth assessment parameter). This expense mainly arises from the organizational implications deriving from the introduction of a BPM. In more detail, the evaluation parameters examine the increase in the labor costs due to the introduction of a new figure in the business management of the firm or for the periodic training of the analyst already present in the company.

Economic Sustainability: Indirect Costs

The use of predictive models also generates indirect costs that the user must consider when identifying the tool that best suits their needs and possibilities. In particular, we refer to the following cost classes:

1. costs for the information retrieval required by the model;
2. costs associated with the rigidification of the organizational structure;
3. costs associated with the errors made by the model.

As explained before, the elaboration complexity of the models adopted may cause implications in terms of the reduction of organizational flexibility. This decrease in flexibility is due to the adaptation of information systems and/or the changes to the user's organizational chart. On the one hand, this generates an increased rigidification of the procedures used to analyse the health status of the firm. On the other, it has major economic repercussions (first and second assessment parameters). For instance, if one thinks of the investments needed for the research, selection, processing and verification of information required to input the BPM or, again, of the costs resulting from the possible strictures on the user's decision-making processes. This increase in complexity may ensue from the need, felt by the corporate heads, to subordinate decisions on the application of the predictive instrument. The need arises from the purpose of verifying, through the results provided by the model, the effects of these strategic choices on the business performance.

Finally, the costs correlated to the type of errors made by the model must not be underestimated (third assessment parameter). This is easy to understand: to classify a distressed company as healthy (type I error, or false negative) generates different costs to a situation in which the model qualifies a healthy firm as ailing (type II error, or false positive). Simply put, a false negative is more expensive than a false positive. Knowing this superiority, though, it is not possible to univocally estimate the size of the gap between the costs of the error type made. In fact, that is the job of the specific of the analyst.

For lending institutions, the cost of a type I error arises from the loss generated from the missing (or partial) return of the loan granted to the company that has become insolvent. On the other hand, the sacrifice implied by a type I error must be evaluated in terms of opportunity cost, in other words, comparing the sacrifice coming from the renunciation of the proceeds on a loan that has not been granted and the profit obtained by using alternative forms of investment.

For the firm using models for internal monitoring, the cost of type II error can be linked to needless expense arising from the activation of unnecessary recovery processes. Vice versa, the economic consequences of type II errors can sometimes be critical: for instance, if the critical status is not recognized in good time and its causes are not definitively removed the increasing amplification of the annual losses, and the consequential effects on assets and financial status. The functional differences of the users and the concrete difficulties in measurement have practically discouraged research in the field of evaluating costs of classification errors. At present, the major contribution in this field has provided an estimate on the costs of type II errors derived from examining the behavior of 58 American lending institutions in the ordinary activity of granting loans (Altman, 1977). The analysis found an average cost for type II error of 70% of the loans granted. The cost of type I error, on the other hand, was estimated as 2%. Therefore, in comparing these percentages it emerges that the cost of an incorrect classification of an ailing company is 35 times higher than one made for healthy firms.

10.4 Performance and Sustainability of BPMs: A Comparative Analysis

At this point, it is possible to identify some useful parameters for assessing both the performance, and therefore the diagnostic accuracy, and the economic and organizational sustainability of BPMs. As mentioned above, the appraisal of a predictive tool is burdened by a high degree of discretion since, during the evaluation, the judgment expressed by each potential user inevitably takes into account:

1. the specific peculiarities of their own business context;
2. the information demands that the tool must meet, especially if the analysis is developed on a small or large scale;
3. the organizational chart and available skillsets;
4. the economic conditions

It follows that any form of generalization of the result would necessarily entail a loss of significance of the evaluations expressed. Although aware of this limitation, it would nevertheless be interesting, if not even opportune, to give substance to the theoretical reflections formulated thus far, with a view to developing an application on a sample of models. In a nutshell, the analysis described in the rest of this chapter aims to evaluate a small pool of BPMs from Italy and elsewhere, making use of the performance and sustainability criteria illustrated above.

In particular, this analysis was prompted by two questions. The first of these is whether a relationship exists between the performance of the models and their sustainability and, if so, what kind. Comparative investigation can provide information on whether the link between these two factors is direct or indirect, proportional or not, or more than proportional, and so on. Furthermore, on the basis of the results of the comparison, the ambition is to formulate reasonable hypotheses about the future evolution of studies on the subject, with a view to their concrete use in the business and/or professional field.

Research based on a deductive framework derives its hypotheses from the existing literature, integrates them into a conceptual model and verifies the validity of the considerations formulated through empirical applications (Sharma & Mahajan, 1980; Miller & Friesen, 1983; Singh et al., 1986a, 1986b; Cameron et al., 1987a, 1987b; Sheppard & Chowdhury, 2005). In particular, the analysis has been brought about by comparing the data derivable from the examination of the original contributions, in which scholars have outlined the main characteristics and the results of their diagnostic models. Indeed, in our opinion a comparison of the instruments based on a deductive logic, depending on the information reported by several authors, allows us to obtain an initial but significant contribution with a view to developing several founded observations on the sustainability of the models and the relation between the efficiency and the diagnostic effectiveness.

Getting to the heart of the matter of more operational aspects, the research project is divided into five sequential steps:

1. selection of the models to be examined;
2. collection and processing of the data needed for assessing the performance and sustainability of the model;
3. determination of the criteria to be used for the data comparison;
4. development of the comparison of the obtained information;
5. interpretation of the results attained.

10.5 The Sample Analysed

The sample subjected to analysis is made up of the models briefly reported and described in Table 10.1.

The choice of the forecasting models to be examined has been mainly influenced by the importance of the instrument both in national and international investigations in the field of the techniques used to diagnose a corporate crisis (Altman, 1983; Rossi, 1988; Teodori, 1989; Ecchia, 1996; Barontini, 1997; Poddighe & Madonna, 2006; Bellovary et al., 2007; Shi & Li, 2019). Above all,

Table 10.1 The sample of BPMs subjected to evaluation

Altman's Z score (Altman, 1968)	
Identification code	M1
Year of elaboration	1968
Investigated critical moment	Bankruptcy
Sample	The instrument was developed with reference to a sample composed of 66 American firms of medium and large size. All the companies belonged to the manufacturing sector.
Model features	The model was developed adopting linear discriminant analysis. The instrument is represented by a linear equation composed of five accounting ratios, conveniently weighted through specific coefficients.
Model performance	The model correctly classified 83% of the investigated sample two years before bankruptcy, while a year before, this percentage rose to 95%.
Alberici's discriminant function (Alberici, 1975)	
Identification code	M2
Year of elaboration	1975
Investigated critical moment	Bankruptcy
Sample	The instrument was developed with reference to a sample of 42 Italian firms, heterogeneous in size and sector.
Model features	The model was developed using linear discriminant analysis. The instrument is represented by a linear equation composed of seven accounting ratios, conveniently weighted through specific coefficients. Therefore, the author opted to calculate different coefficients for each year before the investigated event. In this way, Alberici essentially developed five distinct instruments.
Model performance	Two years before the critical event, the model correctly classified 85.75% of the sample. A year before, the model performance assessment yielded a similar percentage (85.5%).
The linear zeta of Altman, Haldeman and Narayanan (Altman et al., 1977)	
Identification code	M3
Year of elaboration	1977
Investigated critical moment	Bankruptcy
Sample	The instrument was developed with reference to a sample composed of 111 American firms (53 bankrupt companies and 58 healthy companies) with an investment capital of over 100 million US$. All the companies belonged to the manufacturing and commercial sectors.
Model features	The model was developed adopting linear discriminant analysis. The instrument is represented by a linear equation composed of seven ratios, of both accounting and mathematical/statistical origin, conveniently weighted through specific coefficients.
Model performance	Two years before the bankruptcy, the model correctly classified 80% of the examined sample. A year before, this percentage rose 92.8%.

(continued)

Table 10.1 (continued)

The quadratic zeta of Altman, Haldeman and Narayanan (Altman et al., 1977)	
Identification code	M4
Year of elaboration	1977
Investigated critical moment	Bankruptcy
Sample	The instrument was developed with reference to a sample composed of 111 American firms (53 bankrupt companies and 58 healthy companies) with an investment capital of over 100 million US$. All the companies belonged to the manufacturing and commercial sector.
Model features	The model was developed adopting linear discriminant analysis. The instrument is represented by a quadratic equation composed of: (1) ratios of both accounting and mathematical/statistical origin; (2) variables obtained by squaring the ratios' measures; and (3) combinations obtained by multiplying the ratios by each other.
Model performance	Two years before bankruptcy, the model correctly classified 84.7% of the sample examined. A year before, this percentage rose to 92,8%.
Appetiti's dynamic model (Appetiti, 1984)	
Identification code	M5
Year of elaboration	1984
Investigated critical moment	Insolvency (firms declared "outstanding" or "stranded" by the "Anagrafe Centrale Dei Rischi" of the Bank of Italy).
Sample	The instrument was developed with reference to a sample of 50 Italian manufacturing firms.
Model features	The model was developed using linear discriminant analysis. The instrument is represented by a linear equation composed of two indicators. The independent variables are the main feature of this model: In fact, the author makes use of trend indicators.
Model performance	Three years before the insolvency, the model proved able to correctly classify 88% of the sampled companies.
The reduced decisional tree of Frydman, Altman and Kao (Frydman et al., 1985)	
Identification code	M6
Year of elaboration	1985
Investigated critical moment	Bankruptcy
Sample	The instrument has been elaborated with reference to a sample composed of 200 firms (58 bankrupt companies and 142 healthy companies), working in the manufacturing and commercial sectors.
Model features	The model was developed using the nonparametric recursive partitioning algorithm technique. The instrument, with a classic tree structure, is a subtree of more complex decisional tree. All the variables used by the model have an accounting nature.
Model performance	A year before the bankruptcy, the model correctly classified 95% of the sampled firms.

(continued)

Table 10.1 (continued)

The enlarged decisional tree of Frydman, Altman and Kao (Frydman et al., 1985)	
Identification code	M7
Year of elaboration	1985
Investigated critical moment	Bankruptcy
Sample	The instrument was developed with reference to a sample composed of 200 firms (58 bankrupt companies and 142 healthy companies), working in the manufacturing and commercial sectors.
Model features	The model was developed using the nonparametric recursive partitioning algorithm technique. The instrument is represented by a tree structure with several levels of branches. All the variables used by the model have an accounting nature.
Model performances	A year before the bankruptcy, the model correctly classified 95% of the sampled firms.
Forestieri's bayesian model (Forestieri, 1986)	
Identification code	M8
Year of elaboration	1986
Investigated critical moment	Initiation of a credit-retrieval procedure by a bank.
Sample	The instrument was developed with reference to a sample composed of 223 Italian firms (27 bankrupt companies and 196 healthy companies), heterogeneous in size and sector. The company details were extracted from the funding portfolio of an Italian bank.
Model features	The model has been elaborated using Bayesian methodology. The instrument is represented as a linear equation in which, in addition to the independent variables (accounting ratios) and coefficients, two other parameters are included: (1) the priors, that are the probability of a firm to be qualified as healthy or critical, and (2) the cost of errors made by the model.
Model performance	Two years before the critical event investigated, the model correctly classified 93.3% of the sample examined. A year before, this percentage rose to 93.7%.
The neural network (15, 6, 1) of Altman, Varetto and Marco (Altman et al., 1994)	
Identification code	M9
Year of elaboration	1994
Investigated critical moment	Instability
Sample	The instrument was developed by examining a sample composed of 808 small and medium enterprises.
Model features	The model was developed adopting the methodology of the neural network. This is a technique that emulates, through an artificial instrumentation, human brain function. The instrument is represented by a network of three layers, respectively composed of 15, 1 and 1 individual units. Each unit represents an artificial neuron (or node) and has the task of establishing and processing the network's information output

(continued)

Table 10.1 (continued)

Model performance	3 years before the critical event investigated, the model correctly qualified 97.4% of the examined sample. A year before the crisis, the instrument reliability decreased to 87.3%.
Shah and Murtaza's neural network based on clustering procedure (Shah & Murtaza, 2000)	
Identification code	M10
Year of elaboration	2000
Investigated critical moment	Bankruptcy
Sample	The instrument was developed with reference to a sample of 60 firms (54 companies in stable financial conditions and 6 bankrupt companies) in the computer component manufacturing sector.
Model features	The model was developed using the neural network methodology, based on a clustering procedure. This instrument is represented as a neural network composed of three layers with accounting information (ratios) as input.
Model performance	Four years before the bankruptcy, the model correctly diagnosed the status of 73% of the sampled companies.
Altman and Sabato's model based on logit analysis (Altman & Sabato, 2007)	
Identification code	M11
Year of elaboration	2007
Investigated critical moment	Bankruptcy
Sample	The instrument was developed with reference to a sample composed of 2010 American firms (120 bankrupt companies and 1890 healthy companies), with sales less than 65 million dollars.
Model features	The model was developed using logit analysis, and it is composed of five accounting ratios.
Model performance	The instrument was able to correctly classify 87.22% of the sampled companies.

the selection has also considered the particular mathematical and statistical techniques adopted to elaborate the predictive instrument. The econometric methodology represents an element that provides better characterization of forecasting models. In fact, the employment of one technique over another is due to the need to emphasize the diagnostic capability of the accounting and non-accounting indicators included in the structure of the model (FitzPatrik, 1931; Ramser & Foster, 1931; Merwin, 1942; Hickman, 1957; Ruozi, 1974; Caprara, 1990). Consequentially, they become more explanatory of the thriving or ailing operational position of the companies. In the analysis, the comparison of models elaborated through the application of many different techniques has been considered advisable. This decision allows us to verify any correlation between the statistical methodology used and the organizational and economic sustainability degree of the instrument.

Finally, a comparative analysis of eleven BPMs was carried out from the point of view of their effectiveness and efficiency. The main features of the forecasting models studied are briefly described in the table below.

10.6 Evaluation of Sampled Models' Performance

10.6.1 The Data

In line with the deductive approach mentioned above, the data necessary to carry out the comparison were identified and extrapolated directly from the research that gave rise to the sampled BPMs. In fact, such studies usually take care to describe the architecture of the model, the operating logic, the degree of accuracy and the time period in which the predictions given are statistically significant, as well as any reliability tests carried out.

Through careful, conscious and, above all, critical study of these contributions, in fact, it is possible to obtain the functional elements for appraisal of the technical qualities of predictive tools. In particular, Table 10.2 summarizes, for each model examined, the data representative of the reliability of the sampled instruments, namely: the percentage of correct predictions; the percentage of type I errors; the percentage of type II errors; the test carried out on a control sample; and any application in subsequent contexts.

Table 10.3, on the other hand, contains the data collected for the assessment of the sample BPMs' timeliness, i.e., the crisis investigated and the number of years prior to that moment in which the model proved reliable in diagnosing the state of health of companies.

Table 10.2 Reliability parameters: the data

Model identification Code	Model application to original sample	Model application to a control sample	Model application to subsequent samples		
	Overall correct classifications	First type error (the model classifies as healthy a critical firm)	Second type errors (the model classifies as critical a healthy firm)		
M1	95%	6%	3%	Yes	Yes
M2	85.7%	14.3%	14.3%	No	No
M3	92.95%	4.8%	11%	Yes	No
M4	92.85%	5.7%	8.6%	Yes	No
M5	88%	8%	16%	No	No
M6	91.5%	8.62%	8.45%	Yes	No
M7	91%	15.52%	6.34%	Yes	No
M8	93.7	25.9%	3.6%	Yes	No
M9	87.3%	9.50%	15.90%	Yes	No
M10	73%	17%	28%	No	No
M11	87.22%	11.76%	27.92%	No	No

Table 10.3 Timeliness parameters: the data

Model identification Code	Investigated critical event	Number of reliable years
M1	Bankruptcy	2
M2	Bankruptcy	5
M3	Bankruptcy	5
M4	Bankruptcy	5
M5	Insolvency	1
M6	Bankruptcy	1
M7	Bankruptcy	1
M8	Initiating credit-recovery procedure	2
M9	Insolvency	3
M10	Bankruptcy	1
M11	Bankruptcy	1

10.6.2 The Rating Scale Adopted

Once the data necessary for the comparison had been collected, the need emerged to establish a rating scale to be adopted for comparing the technical performance of the investigated models. In order to enable quick comparisons, at that point we assigned a measurement scale that makes use of symbols: plus (+) or minus (−) signs were assigned to each parameter observed in the original contribution, as illustrated in Table 10.4.

For the measurement of reliability parameters, no particular problems arise because it is a matter of attributing one or more positive signs to figures exceeding certain percentage thresholds. As regards the tests aimed at proving the accuracy of the instrument, on the other hand, it was decided to report the + symbol if existing and the—symbol if not.

Different and more complex, however, is the reasoning underlying the measurement of timeliness parameters which, in fact, is less intuitive. First of all, for the first selected parameter (critical event investigated) to be established, depending on the time used as reference to diagnose the insolvency, if this aspect is to be understood in a positive or negative light. In other words, we questioned the usefulness of forecasting methods that use as a point of reference for the diagnosis of the crisis the time of filing for bankruptcy. It is obvious that at the time of these events, the difference between a healthy and insolvent company is all the more obvious. In our view, a BPM should allow operators to react before the event, with ample time to explore the options and/or prepare a reorganization plan.

For this reason, if the model identifies the conditions for insolvency at the time of declaration of bankruptcy, we evaluated this parameter in the negative with a minus sign (−).

Finally, on the same point, for the second parameter of timeliness (the years of reliability of the model) we put a plus sign (+) for each year preceding the critical event for which the method showed good predictive ability. Indeed, the better and

Table 10.4 The ratings scale for performance parameters

Reliability Parameters			
Parameters	Classification	Assigned rating	
	Overall percentage of correct classifications	50–75%	+
		75–90%	++
		90–100%	+++
	Percentage of type I errors	0–10%	–
		10–20%	– –
		20–30%	–––
	Percentage of type II errors	0–10%	–
		10–20%	– –
		20–30%	–––
	Model application to a control sample	Yes	+
		No	–
	Model application to subsequent samples	Yes	+
		No	–
Timeliness parameters			
Parameters	Classification	Assigned rating	
	Investigated critical event	Bankruptcy	–
		Before bankruptcy	+
	Number of the model's reliable years	For each year before the investigated event	+

earlier the model performs, the greater its accuracy to predict a crisis and, consequently, the higher the score given the models.

10.6.3 The Results

The application of a ratings scale to the data collected for the sampled models allowed us to obtain a synthetic representation of the results in terms of both reliability (Table 10.5) and timeliness (Table 10.6).

Observing Table 10.5 we can do some initial analysis. Taking into consideration the overall correct classifications, almost all models attain positive results. In fact, excluding M10, all models reach correct evaluation percentages of over 85%, and most of them even over 90%.

The examination of the different type of errors, I or II, is useful for formulating considerations that evaluate the gravity of incorrect previsions, as well as the adequacy of the predictive instrument used in the different circumstances. In general, as we have already observed, the type I error occurs when the model classifies a productive company that subsequently experiences a crisis (false negative). In this way, a fact so important to the economic and financial disequilibrium is not identified as

Table 10.5 Reliability comparison

Model identification code	Model application to original sample	Model application to a control sample	Model application to subsequent samples		
	Overall correct classifications	Type I error (the model classifies a critical firm as healthy)	Type II errors (the model classifies a healthy firm as critical)		
M1	+ + +	–	–	+	+
M2	+ +	– –	– –	–	–
M3	+ + +	–	– –	+	–
M4	+ +	–	–	+	–
M5	+ +	–	– –	–	–
M6	+ + +	–	–	+	–
M7	+ + +	– –	–	+	–
M8	+ + +	– – –	–	+	–
M9	+ +	–	– –	+	–
M10	+	– –	– – –	–	–
M11	+ +	– –	– – –	–	–

Table 10.6 Timeliness comparison

Model identification code	Investigated critical event	Number of reliable years
M1	–	+ +
M2	–	+ + + + +
M3	–	+ + + + +
M4	–	+ + + + +
M5	+	+
M6	–	+
M7	–	+
M8	+	+ +
M9	+	+ + +
M10	–	+
M11	–	+

critical by the control network. This fact has to be considered very serious when the aim of the monitoring action is actually to identify the firms potentially at risk. This is the case, for example, of the perspective of a public observatory aimed at the prevention and control of the social and economic effects of a firm's crisis. In this context, the possibility of actuating remedial interventions before the crisis reaches the most acute phase has to be considered the fundamental condition for efficient and effective sustainability policies. In this case the predictive model is used to guide the selection and identify the critical facts necessary for prompt actions of support and assistance. If one of these combinations should be overlooked by the monitoring network, it constitutes a failure of the prevention system. Unfortunately, this an inevitable and very serious phenomenon: from this perspective the phenomenon has to be evaluated in a rigorous way, and different models proven to minimize this type of error has to be chosen.

Type II errors occur in cases in which the model classifies a healthy firm, which is stable and, in any event, not ailing, as critical (false positive). In this case the control net catches a firm that does not have the characteristics of risk. If this error does not have an important significance in the hypothesis of the public observatory for the prevention and control of the effects of the corporate crises (as it can, at the very least, lead to insufficient deployment of resources and, consequently, a less efficiency on the action against it), could instead be very serious in other circumstances. As an example, if BPMs are used as a discriminating filter for financial decisions (financial trust), a false positive error will stigmatize a company as "unreliable". In all probability it will not therefore have access to financial resources, despite being healthy and worthy of financial support. Thus, the firm's investment and development plans would be those of a company capable of generating positive returns to the entire economic context. It is clear that, from this perspective, it is the type II error to be evaluated in harsh terms, creating great repercussions on the single company and, especially, on the entire economic fabric that would have benefited from the positive returns generated by financing the investment and development projects (obviously we would reach different conclusions if we evaluated the situation from the financial subject's point of view).

Therefore, judgment as to the gravity of the different types of errors, and consequently to the importance to be given to this parameter, cannot be given on the basis of an absolute evaluation: as we have argued, it depends on the context and on the purpose of the prediction model. It is, however, important to dispose of a disarticulated and specific data so that it is possible to distinguish and consider the different types of error and their respective consequences.

The fourth and fifth parameters analyzed (application to control sample and samples subsequent to the one used in development) aim to verify whether the prediction models used are versatile, able to guarantee an adequate flexibility of use. It often occurs that the models have been conceived to maximize the predictive reliability of a specific original sample, so it is to be considered normal that they result particularly exact with reference to a specific range. Hence, it is not rare that they lose their predictive efficacy outside the original context and that, to maintain sufficient reliability levels, they have to undergo significant adaptations, creating a loss of the efficiency of use. In this case the accuracy could be exclusively given to the aptitude of the model to promptly represent the management characteristics of the sample firms. Therefore, BPMs, as precise as they be in the reference context, are frequently not capable of guaranteeing adequate diagnostic performance if used elsewhere in time and space, except after major (and burdensome) adaptation interventions. This obviously creates a problem that influences in a significant negative way on the overall performance (and on the judgment) of the predictive instrument. It is clear, in fact, that the spatial and temporal stability of the diagnostic capabilities of the models defines the versatility of use and it is a qualitative parameter much appreciated in the judgment on their efficacy. Therefore, it would be very useful for these predictive instruments to be tested (so to dispose of proof of their reliability degree) on samples different from the original reference one.

With reference to this aspect, we learn that only Altman's Z Score (M1) meets both criteria, while others (M2, M5, M10 and M11) have not been tested outside the development context (on neither control sample nor later samples).

Finally, regarding the judgment on the timeliness of the prediction (Table 10.6), we noted that it essentially depends on two parameters. First, we considered the critical event inspected, which can arise at any point along the developing course of the degenerative process: evidently, all things being equal, the more rapidly the symptom we are trying to predict emerges, the more timely the diagnosis will be. Second, we evaluated the reliability level of the model over time, in other words, its capacity to make correct predictions even long before the critical event investigated. Obviously, from this point of view, the ideal situation would be to use a model that focuses the prediction on an reliable advance warning of an early symptom of the crisis. On this front, the comparative analysis of the models bring us to observe that there are some (M2, M3 and M4) that, despite demonstrating a great diagnostic precocity, do so by referring to a very late symptom in the process of the progressive virulence of the crisis. While there are some models (M5, M8 and M9) that demonstrate the ability to predict an early symptom with a good margin of advance notice, others, on this judgment element, yield contradictory results.

10.7 Sustainability Assessment of the Sampled Models

10.7.1 The Data

The thought process that led us to measure the parameters of sustainability was, in many ways far more insidious, but perhaps because of this it has given us some interesting moments of critical reflection. First it seems necessary to point out that at present there have been no attempts to "quantify" the organizational and economic sustainability of any of the predictive models developed so far. Our contribution will therefore not be exhaustive on the subject concerned, but rather aims to be a stimulus to a deeper analysis. It is, in other words, a timid attempt to measure the parameters that until now have never been emphasized by scholars in the field.

By measuring the sustainability of the forecasting models, we are forced to appreciate and assess the organizational and economic implications of the adoption of an econometric model. As discussed in the previous paragraphs, organizational and economic sustainability parameters are mostly qualitative elements that hardly lend themselves to numerical quantification. For this reason, measuring the efficiency led us to call on a panel of potential users of BPMs. We used a questionnaire and, based on initial results, we began to assign ratings to the parameters selected.

Although this is obviously a study in its commencement phase, it has already produced initial results. Table 10.7 shows the data collected on the organizational sustainability of the models and, therefore, the demands and degree of complexity

Table 10.7 Organizational sustainability parameters data

Model identification code	Need for and complexity of recording systems	Need for a specific qualified figure in the organizational structure	Interpretative complexity of the results
M1	No	No	No
M2	No	No	No
M3	No	No	No
M4	No	No	No
M5	Yes Moderate/low	Yes Moderate/low	No
M6	Yes Moderate	Yes Moderate/high	No
M7	Yes Moderate	Yes Moderate/high	No
M8	Yes Moderate	Yes Moderate	No
M9	Yes Moderate/high	Yes Moderate/high	Yes High
M10	Yes Moderate/high	Yes Moderate/high	Yes High
M11	Yes Moderate	Yes Moderate/high	Yes High

of the data collection systems envisaged by the methodological framework; the need for specially dedicated organizational figures with specific skills to be able to effectively implement and handle the model; and the degree of complexity in the interpretation of the results obtained.

Table 10.8, on the other hand, summarizes the opinions expressed regarding the direct costs strictly attributable to the integration of predictive models into the user's IT system, as well as to their subsequent use. In detail, we refer to the costs of: development from scratch or acquisition from third parties; maintenance; the instrumentation, generally computerized, needed to support the application of the tool; and its subsequent handling.

Finally, the data collected on indirect costs are summarized in Table 10.9. In particular, the costs related to: (i) the retrieval of model input data; (ii) the rigidity of the organizational structure and internal processes; (iii) and the type of error made. As can be observed, however, the survey was not able to highlight significant data regarding the second indirect cost, that attributable to tightening of the organization and procedures.

Regarding the enhancement of the costs associated with misclassifications made by the model, we have been inspired by what emerged from the contribution by Altman in his study aimed at identifying the costs of errors of type I and II by examining the behavior of 58 regional and provincial banks in the U.S. during their ordinary activity of corporate lending (Altman et al., 1977). This study indicated an average cost for type I errors of 70% of the premium paid, and type II errors 2%. The quantification shown in the table above follows, therefore, the application of

Table 10.8 Economic sustainability parameters—the direct costs: data

Model identification code	DIRECT COSTS Elaboration/acquisition costs	Maintenance costs	Support instrumentation costs	Handling costs
M1	No	No	No	No
M2	No	No	No	No
M3	No	No	No	No
M4	No	No	No	No
M5	No	No	Yes moderate	Yes Moderate/low
M6	No	Yes Moderate/high	Yes Moderate/high	Yes Moderate/high
M7	No	Yes Moderate/high	Yes Moderate/high	Yes Moderate/high
M8	No	No	Low	Yes Moderate/low
M9	Yes High	Yes High	Yes Moderate/high	Yes High
M10	Yes High	Yes High	Yes Middle/high	Yes High
M11	Yes Moderate	Yes High	Yes Moderate/high	Yes Moderate/high

these percentages to the percentage type I and II errors declared by the author in his contribution originating. For example:

Cost associated with the errors made by the model Z Score.

Cost of type I errors:	% type I errors (6%)	*	70%	=	4.20
Cost of type II errors:	% type II errors (3%)	*	20%	=	0.06
Total cost					4.26

10.7.2 The Ratings Scale Adopted

In line with the ratings scale of values adopted for evaluating the technical performance of the BPMs, with the aim of increasing the degree of comparability of the results we decided to adopt the + sign to denote a positive sustainability parameter and the—sign those we believe to be negative.

Table 10.10 shows in detail the ratings attributable to the possible readings of each evaluation criterion.

Table 10.9 Economic sustainability parameters—the indirect costs: data

Model identification code	INDIRECT COSTS		
	Costs for the information retrieval required by the model	Costs associated with the rigidification of the organizational structure	Cost associated with the errors made by the model
M1	Low	…	4.26
M2	Low	…	10.30
M3	Low	…	3.58
M4	Low	…	4.16
M5	Moderate	…	5.92
M6	Moderate/high	…	6.203
M7	Moderate/high	…	10.9908
M8	Low	…	18,20
M9	High	…	6.97
M10	High	…	12.46
M11	High	…	8.7904

Table 10.10 Ratings scale for sustainability parameters

Organizational Sustainability Parameters			
Parameters	Classifications	Assigned rating	
	Need and complexity of recording system of model input parameters	No	+
		Moderate/low	–
		Moderate	– –
		High	——
	Need for a specific qualified figure in the organizational structure	No	+
		Moderate/low	–
		Moderate	– –
		High	——
	Interpretative complexity of the results	No	+
		Moderate/low	–
		Moderate	– –
		High	——
Economic sustainability parameters			
Parameters	Classifications	Assigned rating	
Direct costs			
	Development/acquisition costs	No	+
		Moderate/low	–
		Middle	– –
		High	——

(continued)

Table 10.10 (continued)

Organizational Sustainability Parameters			
	Maintenance costs	No	+
		Moderate/low	–
		Middle	– –
		High	——
	Support instrumentation costs	Not	+
		Moderate/low	–
		Moderate	– –
		High	——
	Handling costs	No	+
		Moderate/low	–
		Moderate	– –
		High	——
Indirect costs			
	Cost for retrieval of information required by the model	No	+
		Moderate/low	–
		Moderate	– –
		High	——
	Costs associated with the change in organizational structure	No	+
		Moderate/low	–
		Moderate	– –
		High	——
	Cost associated with the errors made by the model	Not	+
		Moderate/low	–
		Moderate	– –
		High	——
	Cost associated with the errors made by the model	Errors ≤5%	–
		5% < errors ≤10%	– –
		10% < errors ≤15%	– – –
		15% < errors ≤20%	– – – –

10.7.3 *The Results*

As we have pointed out previously, we have structured the judgement on the efficiency of the models examined by referring to two groups of parameters: those pertaining to organizational sustainability and those to the economic sustainability, the direct and indirect costs associated with usage of the models.

Regarding the profile of the organizational sustainability, we based the evaluation on three parameters:

i. The need (or not) to adopt a specific recording system for the determination of input parameters for the model, and the degree of complexity of its recording system.

Table 10.11 Organizational sustainability: comparison

Model identification code	Need for and complexity of recording systems	Need for a specific qualified figure in the organizational structure	Interpretative complexity of the results
M1	+	+	+
M2	+	+	+
M3	+	+	+
M4	+	+	+
M5	+	−	+
M6	− −	− −	+
M7	− −	− −	+
M8	− −	− −	+
M9	− − −	− − −	−
M10	− − −	− − −	−
M11	− −	− −	−

ii. The necessity to equip the firm's organizational structure with a professional figure qualified for the job.
iii. The level of interpretative difficulty—in terms of technical and cultural complexity, and to a greater or smaller degree, the subjectivity—of the results given by the specific predictive tool.

The ratings given for each criterion representative of organizational sustainability are shown in Table 10.11.

With reference to the necessity and complexity of the information systems, in general we need to observe that, strictly theoretically way, we have to limit ourselves to examining the additional needs. So, we must evaluate the systems of recording the data imposed by the adoption of the instrument and the ones already adopted for the specific type of firm. In this regard, we have to consider that this parameter is more onerous with for small companies, which usually are characterized by a simple and less articulated accounting/IT system.

Vice-versa, the more structured firms are normally equipped with more refined control instruments and perform monitoring based on a greater and more refined bank of data. Therefore, all things being equal, we can suppose that the burden on a small company would be more challenging to bear.

With reference to the parameter studied, the results of our analysis reveal that the models developed using multivariate discriminant analysis (linear, M1–M5) are less expensive, while those further down the list (from M6 to M11) are characterized by a higher requirement more effort, especially the ones based on neural networks (M9 and M10).

The need to have a qualified professional figure is the second parameter considered, and this depends on the intrinsic characteristics of the model chosen and on the peculiar qualities of the corporate context in which it is to be used. Technical skill, analysis capabilities, experience and personal sensibility can influence, sometimes in a decisive way, the results of the diagnostic process. Considering this, once again, models based on linear analysis (with the exclusion of Alberici's dynamic model, M5) are characterized by the low effort required. Vice-versa the other models, above all those based on neural networks, necessitate, in addition to complex recording systems, specific professional figures.

Finally, we evaluated the degree of complexity of the interpretation of the results of a diagnostic model from the predictive model. In this case as well, much depends on the peculiar properties of the BPM used: in some cases, the strong determinism of the basic statistical techniques limits the flexibility of the interpretative process, with the consequent practical issues that we are easy imagine. On this matter, we have to recognize that the majority of the models do not create particular difficulties, if we exclude the ones based on neural networks or logit analysis (M9, M10 and M11).

As anticipated, the economical sustainability is analyzed by evaluating the costs, direct and indirect, linked to the adoption of different predictive models. Among the evaluation parameters of the direct costs we considered:

i. development/acquisition costs;
ii. maintenance;
iii. support instrumentation;
iv. management.

The ratings given for each class of direct costs evocative of the economic sustainability of the models are shown in Table 10.12.

The first of these parameters is intimately connected with the complexity of the specific instrument: very refined models, which process a large quantity of data following "personalized" and complex algorithms with stepwise procedures are larger monetary investments than more simple instruments based on traditional methods.

Table 10.12 Economic sustainability—a comparison of direct costs

Model identification code	Direct costs			
	Development/ acquisition costs	Maintenance costs	Support instrumentation costs	Handling costs
M1	+	+	+	+
M2	+	+	+	+
M3	+	+	+	+
M4	+	+	+	+
M5	+	+	–	–
M6	+	– – –	– –	– – –
M7	+	– – –	– –	– – –
M8	+	+	–	–
M9	– – – –	– – – –	– – –	– – – –
M10	– – – –	– – – –	– – –	– – – –
M11	– –	– – – –	– –	– – –

Likewise, what we have observed regarding the interpretative complexity of the results, it must be admitted that the majority of the models analyzed have some problems on this front, except, once again, for the ones based on neural network or logit analysis (M9, M10 and M11), which instead necessitate a greater outlay and maintenance costs.

These are connected to the necessary activities or review and revision, periodical calibration, updates, and re-modulation of the setup. The field of variability is rather broad: maintenance costs would be negligible if the structure has a tendency to be static (essentially the models based on the linear analysis—up to M5—and Forestier's model —M8) becoming quite onerous for the more dynamic diagnostic instruments; these, for their correct functioning, need continuous and major re-development, especially the ones that adopt the neural network (M9 and M10).

Furthermore, we have to consider the support instrumentation costs (essentially hardware and software). Even though usually not extremely onerous investments, we have to underline that the linear analysis-based models (excluding Alberici's M5) have more limited management costs.

The same considerations can be done referring to the last parameter considered, the handling costs, essentially referable to all the acquisition costs and/or the personnel's training needed to manage the predictive instruments: the models are based on the linear analysis (excluding the Alberici's M5) are characterized by a lower cost of use.

Finally, the indirect costs deriving from the adoption of predictive models have been evaluated on the base of the following parameters:

1. Costs for the retrieval of information required by the model.
2. Costs associated with changes in the organizational structure.
3. Costs associated with the errors made by the model.

The ratings given for each class of indirect costs representative of the economic sustainability of the models are shown in Table 10.13.

The need to retrieve the information required by the model can in some cases make it necessary to adopt complex and articulated IT systems that require a lot of time and attention from the different levels of the organizational structure (these are tasks and performances with an unclear utility and often are poorly tolerated by the user, worsening the workplace climate and even creating conflicts among personnel). The models based on linear analysis (excluding Alberici's M5), being fed available data, usually do not create the problems seen with models based on neural network or logit analysis (M9, M10 and M11).

For the second parameter analyzed (rigidification of the organizational structure) we can observe that, as explained before, the complexity of the models adopted may cause implications in terms of the reduction of organizational flexibility. This parameter influences not only the data retrieval and processing phase, but also the consequent decrease in the speed of the decision-making process attributable to the speed reduction needed to run the procedures of the resulting analysis, and the complexity of the processing of directional decision-making. It will have to involve

Table 10.13 Economic sustainability—a comparison of indirect costs

	INDIRECT COSTS		
Model identification code	Costs for retrieval of information required by the model	Costs associated with rigidification of the organizational structure	Cost associated with the errors made by the model
M1	+	...	+
M2	+	...	– –
M3	+	...	–
M4	+	...	–
M5	– –	...	– –
M6	– – –	...	– –
M7	– – –	...	– – –
M8	+	...	– – – –
M9	– – – –	...	– –
M10	– – – –	...	– – –
M11	– – – –	...	– –

evaluating, with careful attention, a greater number of variables that are not always easy to interpret. On this front, it must be said that the investigation has not yielded a satisfactory result: regarding the estimate of the cost associated with the rigidification of the organizational structure, we have been able to appraise, at this early stage, a mechanism that allows us to make a reliable quantification. Therefore, we have preferred not to hazard unsatisfactory estimates at this time but do hope to define this aspect in the future.

Finally, as regards the last parameter, costs associated with the errors made by the different models, as outlined in sect. 10.3, this is a function of the probability of error of each model and the level of cost given to the specific category of error. The table clearly shows that Altman's model Z score is associated with tolerable levels of cost of errors.

10.8 Concluding Remarks

After proposing a method for measuring the parameters used to assess the performance and sustainability of predictive models, we move on to the stage of comparing the results obtained. The comparison, as stated in the previous paragraph, was based on the critical reading of the original research articles, and the initial results of the outcome of a survey.

First, we should discuss the comparison of the performance declared. From Table 10.5 it emerges that all the models considered in this study display a good and, in some cases, excellent reliability in forecasting the sample studied during the development process. Specifically, the Z Score, linear and quadratic Zeta, reduced and enlarged decisional trees and Bayesian model display the best diagnostic performance, with more than 90% of classifications being correct.

However, the overall reliability must be examined in light of the type of errors resulting by the models. Indeed, this analysis can provide a qualitative estimation of the gravity of the different types of error, so that we can judge more precisely the performance of the models. For instance, considering the percentage of type I errors, the most burdensome for users, allow us to put the positive judgment that we have previously given to the enlarged decisional tree and the Bayesian model in the right perspective. These instruments are characterized by a percentage of type I errors higher than 15% and 25% respectively.

The parameters examined so far permit us to evaluate only the reliability of the models to classify the sample analyzed during the development process which, in general, is overestimated. The evaluation of the two other criteria (model application to a control sample and to subsequent samples) allows us to formulate an initial judgment as to the real forecasting capability of the models. The tables show that only seven out of the eleven models have been effectively applied to control samples, and only the Altman Z Score has been applied to other samples that the one relied on for its development.

With reference to timeliness (Table 10.6), it is evident that the models studied are aimed at predicting the corporate bankruptcy, with the exception of Appetiti's dynamic function, the Bayesian model and Altman, Frydman and Kao's neural network.

With respect to years of reliability, on the other hand, few models are effective from the fifth year before the critical event investigated (Alberici's model, linear and quadratic Zeta).

From a sustainability point of view, however, Tables 10.11, 10.12 and 10.13 show that the models developed using the most advanced statistical techniques cause bigger organizational and economic onerous. In particular, neural networks, decisional trees and the model based on the logit analysis have the harshest implications on the organizational structure of the users. These implications are mainly associated with the complexity of the systems for recording model input parameters and the need for a specific qualified figure in the corporate organizational structure.

Analogous considerations can be made from observing the economic criteria. In this case too, the most expensive models are those involving more advanced statistical methods. This is true for both direct and indirect costs.

Based on this, in order to answer our first research question, we proposed a cross-comparison. To simplify this, we constructed a summary table (Table 10.14) obtained by counting the positive and negative aspects of each model (marked with + and –, respectively).

The strengths outweighed the weaknesses we have assigned a + sign to the method studied, otherwise the summary analysis has been marked with a minus sign.

In particular, at the beginning of the comparative analysis, we wondered whether there is a relationship between the BPM performance, on the one hand, and their sustainability, on the other, and if so, what kind. Comparison between the summary analysis of the performance and sustainability of each model we propose becomes extremely simple looking at Table 10.14. In particular, it is easy to note that with four of the eleven models studied, there was discrepancy between effectiveness and

Table 10.14 The comparison: negative and positive aspects of each BPM

Model identification code	PERFORMANCE ASSESSMENT	SUSTAINABILITY ASSESSMENT				
	Positive aspects	Negative aspects	Performance: summary judgement	Positive aspects	Negative aspects	Sustainability: summary judgement
M1	+ + + + + + +	–	+	+ + + + + + + +	–	+
M2	+ + + + + + +	– – – – – –	+	+ + + + + + + +	– –	+
M3	+ + + + + + + + +	– – – –	+	+ + + + + + + +	–	+
M4	+ + + + + + + + +	– – –	+	+ + + + + + + +	–	+
M5	+ + + +	– – – – –	–	+ + +	———	–
M6	+ + + + +	– – – –	+	+ +	———	–
M7	+ + + + +	– – – – –	=	+ +	———	–
M8	+ + + + + + +	– – – – –	+	+ + + +	———	–
M9	+ + + + + + +	– –	+	0	———	–
M10	+ + +	– – – – – – – –	–	0	———	–
M11	+ + +	– – – – – – – –	–	0	———	–

efficiency scores. More specifically, this applied to the decision trees (reduced and extended) model, Forestieri's Bayesian model and Altman, Marco and Varetto's neural network. All these models belong to the family of those that in literature are referred to as advanced models (Coronella, 2006; Cestari, 2009). In other words, these are methods in which the attempt has been made to increase the effectiveness of the predictive tool by using increasingly sophisticated techniques.

The only exception is the study conducted by Forestieri, which falls somewhere among the traditional techniques. However, the use of Bayesian methods requires more sophisticated knowledge than applying conventional discriminant analysis. These models, in fact, are based on a probabilistic approach supplemented by additional information: the prior probability (or prior probabilities) and the costs of misclassification (Altman, 1977; Cifarelli, 1986).

The use of innovative methods has undoubtedly improved the diagnostic performance of BPMs, but from the point of view of introduction of these techniques, this has led to unavoidable complications in terms of costs of installation and maintenance of the tools. For these reasons, the comparison carried out has revealed a discrepancy between the good results achieved in terms of reliability, against what emerged from the study on their usability.

In this first phase, therefore, the answer to the first research question can only highlight the existence of an almost inverse relationship between the effectiveness and efficiency of predictive models. In other words, researchers who have so far developed diagnostic models to improve the reliability of the instruments have generally set aside the issue of their usability. The very fact that using increasingly sophisticated techniques had not yet been accompanied by a cost/benefit analysis would have revealed the discrepancy highlighted above.

We will now consider the second research question of the study. As stated, the question was asked whether it is possible to estimate a sort of future trend for research in this field from the perspective of real-world use of models in the business and/or professional field. According to the answer to the first question of the research study, we agree that future studies should try to assess efficiency rather than effectiveness, with a view to an actual use in the professional end business context. This aspect has reached quite a good level of trustworthiness. However, the instrument hasn't been used due to organizational and financial difficulties. We truly wish that researchers would, from now on, pay greater attention to the efficiency of these models, which is not to be considered a minor aspect.

For the future we aim, firstly, to complete the empirical investigation started and achieve more concrete and useful results. Below is our intention to "test", again with the help of questionnaires administered to users of models, the actual effectiveness of these methods. In other words, we will try to answer this research question: *does what emerged from the critical study of original contributions in the field of reliability correspond to what is really practical use of these techniques, or are there differences?*

In brief, we propose to assess whether the effectiveness declared by the authors corresponds to that derived from the effective involvement of users.

References

Alberici, A. (1975). *Analisi dei bilanci e previsione delle insolvenze*. Isedi.

Altman, E. I. (1968). Finacial ratios. Discriminant analysis and the prediction of corporate bankruptcy. *The Journal of Finance, 23*(4), 589–609.

Altman, E. I. (1977). Some estimates of cost of lending errors for commercial banks. *The Journal of Commercial Bank Lending, 60*, 51–58.

Altman, E. I. (1983). *Corporate financial distress: A complete guide to predicting, avoiding and dealing with bankruptcy*. John Wiley.

Altman, E. I. (1984). A further empirical investigation of the bankruptcy cost question. *Journal of Finance, 39*(4), 1067–1089.

Altman, E. I., Haldeman, R. G., & Narayanan, P. (1977). Zeta™ Analysis. A new model to identify bankruptcy risk of corporations. *Journal of Banking and Finance, 1*(1), 29–54.

Altman, E. I., Marco, G., & Varetto, F. (1994). Corporate distress diagnosis: Comparisons using linear discriminant analysis and neural networks (the Italian experience). *Journal of Banking and Finance, 18*(3), 505–529.

Altman, E. I., & Sabato, G. (2007). Modeling credit risk for SMEs: Evidence from the US market. *Abacus, 43*(3), 332–357.

Andrei, P. (1986). *La prevenzione dei dissesti aziendali: alcuni spunti di riflessione, in Crisi di impresa e procedure concorsuali. Spunti critici emergenti da un'indagine empirica*. Giuffrè.

Appetiti, S. (1984). *L'utilizzo dell'analisi discriminatoria per la previsione delle insolvenze: ipotesi e test per un'analisi dinamica*. Servizio Studi della Banca d'Italia.

Barontini, R. (1997). *Costi del fallimento e gestione delle crisi nelle procedure concorsuali*, (AA. VV.) Gli strumenti per la gestione delle crisi finanziarie in Italia, Mediocredito Lombardo.

Bellovary, J. L., Giacomino, D. E., & Akers, M. D. (2007). A review of bankruptcy prediction studies: 1930 to present. *Journal of financial education, 33*, 262–298.

Bonmassar, M. (1996). Riflessioni sul costo dei sistemi informativi nelle imprese. *Economia e diritto del terziario, 8*(2).

Cameron, K. S., Kim, M. U., & Whetten, D. A. (1987a). Organizational effects of decline and turbulence. *Administrative Science Quarterly, 32*(2), 222–240.

Cameron, K. S., Whetten, D. A., & Kim, M. U. (1987b). Organizational dysfunctions of decline. *Academy of Management Journal, 30*(1), 126–138.

Caprara, U. (1990). Ancora a proposito di indicatori per la valutazione dell'affidabilità creditizia. *Rivista dei Dottori Commercialisti, 2*, 177–196.

Caramiello, C. (1968). *L'azienda nella fase terminale*. Cursi.

Cestari, G. (2009). *La diagnosi precoce della crisi aziendale. Analisi del processo patologico e modelli predittivi*. Giuffrè.

Chen, G., Cheung, J., & Merville, L. (1997). Indirect cost of financial distress and sales performance. *Research in Finance, 15*, 35–54.

Cifarelli, D. M. (1986). Analisi discriminante: un'impostazione bayesiana. In G. Forestieri (Ed.), *La previsione delle insolvenze aziendali. Profili teorici e analisi empiriche*. Giuffrè.

Coronella, S. (2006). Le diverse metodologie di indagine in merito alla misurazione dell'affidabilità della clientela: uno schema di sintesi. In F. Poddighe & S. Madonna (Eds.), *I modelli di previsione delle crisi aziendali: possibilità e limiti*. Giuffrè.

Ecchia, S. (Ed.). (1996). *Il rischio di credito. Metodologie avanzate di previsione delle insolvenze*. Giappichelli.

Ferrero, G. (1987). *Impresa e Management*. Giuffrè.

FitzPatrik, P. (1931). *A comparison of the ratios of successful industrial enterprises with those of failed company*. Washington.

Forestieri, G. (Ed.). (1986). *La previsione delle insolvenze aziendali. Profili teorici e analisi empiriche*. Giuffrè.

Frydman, H., Altman, E. I., & Kao, D. (1985). Introducing recursive partitioning for financial classification: The case of financial distress. *The Journal of Finance, 40*(1), 269–291.

Gaber J. (1986, January/February). *Une évaluation des coûts de défaillance d'entreprise*. Revue Française de Gestion.

Giannessi, E. (1979). *Appunti di economia aziendale, con particolare riferimento alle aziende agricole*. Pacini.

Guatri, L. (1986). *Crisi e risanamento delle imprese*. Giuffrè.

Guatri, L. (1995). *Turnaround. Declino, crisi e ritorno al valore*. Egea.

Hickman, W. B. (1957). *Corporate bond quality and investment performance, Ed.* National Bureau of Economic Research.

Johnson, D., Wolfe, G., & Lynch, L. (1993). A market assessment of bankruptcy cost and liquidation costs. In E. I. Altman (Ed.), *Bankruptcy & distressed restructuring*. R. Irwin.

Madonna, S., & Cestari, G. (2012). Affidabilità ed efficienza dei modelli di previsione delle insolvenze nel contesto economico ferrarese. *Riflessioni nella prospettiva dell'intervento pubblico a supporto della crisi aziendale*. RIREA Aziende.

Maggiolini, P. (1981). *Costi e benefici di un sistema informativo. La valutazione economica dei sistemi informativi aziendali*. Etas Libri.

Marchi, L. (1993). *I sistemi informativi aziendali*. Giuffrè.

Merwin, C. L. (1942). *Financing small corporations in five manufacturing industries 1926–1936*. National Bureau of Economic Research.

Miller, D., & Friesen, P. H. (1983). Successful and unsuccessful phases of corporate life cycle. *Organization Studies, 4*(4), 339–356.

Poddighe, F., & Madonna, S. (Eds.). (2006). *Modelli di previsione delle crisi aziendali: possibilità e limiti*. Giuffrè.

Pompe, P. P. M., & Bilderbeek, J. (2005). Bankruptcy prediction: The influence of the year prior to failure selected for model building and the effects in a period of economic decline. *Intelligent Systems in Accounting, Finance and Management, 13*(2), 95–112.

Ramser J. R., & Foster L. O. (1931). *A demonstration of ratio analysis*, Bureau of Business Research, bulletin nr. 40, University of Illinois.

Rossi, C. (1988). *Indicatori di bilancio, modelli di classificazione e previsione delle insolvenze aziendali*. Giuffrè.

Ruozi, R. (1974). Sull'attendibilità dei bilanci e sulla loro validità ai fini di previsione delle insolvenze. *Bancaria, 1*, 7–18.

Sciarelli, S. (1995). *La crisi d'impresa. Il percorso economico della crisi aziendale*. Cedam.

Shah, J. R., & Murtaza, M. B. (2000). A neural network based clustering procedure for bankruptcy prediction. *American Business Review, 18*(2), 80–86.

Sharma, S., & Mahajan, V. (1980). Early warning indicators of business failure. *Journal of Marketing, 44*(4), 80–89.

Sheppard, J. P., & Chowdhury, S. (2005). Riding the wrong wave: Organizational failure as a failed turnaround. *Long Range Planning, 38*(3), 239–260.

Shi, Y., & Li, X. (2019). An overview of bankruptcy prediction models for corporate firms: A systematic literature review. *Intangible Capital, 15*(2), 114–127.

Singh, J. V., House, R. J., & Tucker, D. J. (1986a). Organizational change and organizational mortality. *Administrative Science Quarterly, 31*(4), 587–561.

Singh, J. V., Tucker, D. J., & House, R. J. (1986b). Organizational legitimacy and the liability of newness. *Administrative Science Quarterly, 31*(2), 171–193.

Teodori, C. (1989). *Modelli di previsione nell'analisi economico-aziendale*. Giappichelli.

Printed by Printforce, the Netherlands